4-5-14

To Betty —
a real warrior
for the needs of
people.
Thanks for
the great memories!
Sincerely
Glenn

ForeWord Reviews
Clarion Review

Five Stars (out of Five)

Warner's prose is both lyrical and clear, revealing the spiritual beauty he sees in nature.

Glen W. Warner's *Meeting the WORD in the World* asks people to take a step back to admire the workmanship of God, asserting that those who notice the glory of nature fully accept their place in God's kingdom.

Warner discusses the sacred spaces in everyday life and how they offer the opportunity for rich discovery. For example, he explains how a typical day working on a dairy farm forever inspires him. All it took was hearing a song by Les Paul and Mary Ford for him to wake up to the world around him. In a moment, everything seemed possible. *Meeting the WORD in the World* is about finding such special moments and making the most of them.

To explore how science and history can peacefully coexist with scripture, Warner describes everything from maple syrup season in Northeast Ohio to the tragedy of the Titanic sinking. These facts are a concrete way to explain people's amazing accomplishments. For example, the author explains how more than two hundred astronauts have worked on the International Space Station and traveled 1.5 billion miles. Warner's point is clear: God makes us greater than we could ever imagine.

Language is both accessible and lyrical in this book. Warner's awe of nature is clear in his specific and creative descriptions. For examples, he makes something simple like blue flowers seem magical. In "Down to Earth," Warner explains how "brave little blue flowers . . . are trembling in the chilly breeze" and that they "are the world's laughter." Personification helps people see the true meaning of God's projects.

Though the book has an optimistic tone, Warner does not avoid tough subject matter. For example, the "Perspective" chapter discusses a horrific school shooting. Warner deftly explains not just the horror of the experience but also the silver lining of the community coming together. As the author writes, "real spiritual maturity is the ability to live successfully without all the answers."

While each chapter is only a few pages long, Warner amends the text with short anecdotes, facts, and scripture. This hodgepodge structure keeps the content fresh and engaging. By using creative acronyms like GPS to describe "God's Plan in Scripture," Warner further explains how to find inspiration.

Meeting the WORD in the World provides coordinates for sacred spaces full of wonder, and shows how we can find peace and focus in a chaotic world.

Lisa Bower

Meeting the
WORD
in the World

Meeting the
WORD
in the World

Enjoying our place in God's Creation and discovering that we are a part of "God's workmanship, created in Christ Jesus to do good works, which God prepared in advance for us to do." (Ephesians 2:10)

GLEN W. WARNER

authorHOUSE®

AuthorHouse™ LLC
1663 Liberty Drive
Bloomington, IN 47403
www.authorhouse.com
Phone: 1-800-839-8640

Published by AuthorHouse   03/18/2014

ISBN: 978-1-4918-3201-1 (sc)
ISBN: 978-1-4918-3200-4 (hc)
ISBN: 978-1-4918-3202-8 (e)

Library of Congress Control Number: 2013920386

Biblical Citations

Dedication

To my parents, Stanley and Elmina Warner, and to my four older brothers, Alva, Garth, Maurice and Richard, I gratefully dedicate this work. Through them has come to me the love of God and the eyes to see the WORD in the world.

A more complete expression of my gratitude to them may be found in the back of this book.

Foreword

Christian Gospel artist *SANDI PATTY* sings **Were it not for Grace,** strengthening the faith of thousands. She sent us this message for this page about God's grace in the beautiful world He created.

> *"It's when I am alone in nature that I often find myself thinking about the wonder of our great God. I sometimes find myself thinking, how could this God love someone like me? We all know that life can be filled with high highs and low lows. For me, God's grace keeps my head high and mind focused on what is important. Were it not for grace, I don't know where I would be. This song speaks about that and reminds me that the God who created oceans, mountains and deserts is the same God who knows and extends grace to me."*

Sandi

WERE IT NOT FOR GRACE

"Time measured out my days. Life carried me along. In my soul I yearned to follow God but I knew I'd never be so strong. I looked hard at this world to learn how heaven could be gained, just to end where I began, where human effort is all in vain.

"Were it not for grace, I can tell you where I'd be, wandering down some pointless road to nowhere, with my salvation up to me. I know how that would go. The battles I would face, forever running but losing this race, were it not for grace.

"So here is all my praise, expressed with all my heart; offered to the Friend who took my place, and ran a course I could not start. And when He saw in full, just how much His love would cost, He still went the final mile between me and heaven, so I would not be lost.

"Were it not for grace, I can tell you where I'd be; wandering down some pointless road to nowhere, with my salvation up to me. I know how that would go, the battles I would face, forever running but losing this race. Were it not for grace."

SONGS FOR THE JOURNEY –Sandi Patty
1997 Dayspring Music, LLC and Sony ATV SongsLLC
All rights reserved. Used By Permission

For more about Sandi's prayer breakfast concert in Ashtabula, read "Green Flash" in this book.

"For ever since the world was created, people have seen the earth and sky. Through everything God made, they can clearly see his invisible qualities – his eternal power and divine nature. So they have no excuse for not knowing God." Romans 1:20

<u>New Living Translation of the Holy Bible</u>

Contents

The WORD In The Country

List of Photographs

All photographs are the property of Kurt Fink Photography and are used with permission.

List of Figures

Acknowledgements

The desire to express the enthusiasm for life and learning might be called the **passion of the mind.** Describing it and noting every aspect by discussing it with trusted others keeps one grounded. There have been so many to thank over the years that it is impossible to list them all here.

First of course is my beloved wife, Nancy, who believes and teaches ways that our family can all be more instrumental and fulfilled in our own futures. I also thank our children Garth and Bethany, their spouses Heather and Andre, and their children who all encouraged me to write down some things for reflection.

I acknowledge Christian friends in business, especially Joan Riffe and Kurt Fink for their wonderful attitudes, skills and support. Our very good friend, Virginia Matrisciano, provided many hours of invaluable proofreading and excellent editorial suggestions.

The love and encouragement of the members of Second Congregational Church in Ashtabula over 40 years, corporately and individually, have served me far more than I could serve them. It is a caring congregation of special friends and shared lives.

In even deeper history I am eternally grateful to my Verona, N.Y., Seventh Day Baptist Church Pastors and congregation, for their devotion to our youth fellowship in the great era of the 1950's. What a wonderful time and place it was. Such relationships are irreplaceable.

Composer Ken Medema (www.kenmedema.com), Dave and Beverly VanderMolen are creative geniuses who have been caring, guiding lights and friends to us throughout this writing process.

I want to acknowledge the powerful influence of mentors Lois Wells and my Pastors over years gone by. Pastors Alton Wheeler, Sam Wells, Fran Saunders, Elmo Randolph, Rex Burdick, Vic Skaggs, Dr. Ken Smith and Dr. Wayne Rood have all touched my life in profound and indelible ways. I thank God for them and their teachings. I am also grateful to Patricia Inman who has used my writings for her church's study group. Her comments are found in the Reader's Guide on the last pages of this book.

Then there is the strong influence of Christian music by many fine artists, too numerous to name. Their healing touch on the soul works because they sing of our God who sets us free from a past we cannot change.

Sarah Smith, my advisor and coordinator at Authorhouse patiently and skillfully guided the submission of the manuscript. I greatly appreciate her help. DeShawn Easley was also most helpful as Design Consultant.

Advisor and friend, Mike Parziale of MSSB Investments continues to provide reliable wisdom and encouragement for our goals, including this book, in these retirement years.

Finally, I am grateful to Tauk Tours for the most **outstanding** trip through the National Parks. It was simply excellent. I also express appreciation to the Grand Canyon National Park's courteous staff and also to the Zion Natural History Association for their stewardship of God's earth and observations about the treasures of our planet. As their literature states, it is a **place drawn by God's own hand.** Everyone should visit these parks, with Bible in hand, somehow in their lifetimes.

Preface

This book has been in process, at least in my mind for most of my life. We all want to have experiences that affirm our reason for living and remind us of the hope that the best is yet to be. These are **sacred spaces,** times of discovery when we realize great new thoughts and opportunities. For the Christian, this is "Kingdom Country" within us, wherever we may be when it happens.

When I was about 13, I was working in our dairy barn early one summer morning. I was sweeping up to the cows, brooming their grain closer to them in their manger so they could lick up the last bites. Those 40 Holsteins stretched their necks to reach it all and were munching away before being let out to pasture for the day. My dad and two brothers were doing the morning milking, starting at the eastern end of the barn, working westward toward the new milkhouse. The two DeLaval milking machines were pulsating rhythmically and the morning sun was streaming through the windows. It was a timeless, contented time and place. We sold milk in 10 gallon cans, marked with our red #13, to the milk station. It was our living.

The morning farm show was playing on the old barn Bendix with its wire antennae bent like a Z to pick up the best signal, linking us up with other early workers in other places. The weather, news, music and a little humor expanded our small world as we worked among our cattle. I began to shake out a little alfalfa to our girls. I remember clearly that I was smiling at some happy thought.

Then something very new and surprising happened. A song on that old radio stopped me in my barn shoe tracks.

Dear one, the world is waiting for the sunrise. Every rose is covered with dew.

And while the world is waiting for the sunrise, then my heart is calling you!

A strange new passion swept over me, suffusing my mind and heart with light. I felt strange but thrilled as a big new world opened before me. Great possibilities were out there for me! The music that stirred me so, was by the famous Les Paul and Mary Ford and their amazing new electric guitar. The song was a hopeful oldie written in 1919 in the orchestral style of that era, by Lockhart and Seitz. Les Paul kicked it up 30 years later for the new generation. It sold a million records. (You can still hear it on the internet – Library of Congress National Jukebox). I can only describe it as a religious experience for me that morning so long ago.

Looking into the faces of those black and white cows for answers that morning I wondered how I could ever repeat that experience and feel that way again? Time marches relentlessly on, and we cannot ever go back to the very same combination of facts and moments. I wanted to, but while such a return was impossible, a new sensitivity was begun. No one ever really knows the future, but we can learn to watch for such illuminating moments as time goes by. The intention in these pages is to learn more about watching for, and meeting, the WORD in the world.

How can we find these sacred spaces in our daily lives? Watch for this symbol.

Introduction

Are you normal?

It is a beautiful sunny morning and there is a feeding frenzy going on a couple of hundred yards offshore in Lake Erie. Hundreds of gulls have discovered a huge hatch of tiny fish. Their wheeling flight, diving and screaming is nature in the raw, awesome to behold.

As I try to fulfill my hunger to express the totality of my spiritual awareness, it seems like those aggressive gulls. It is impossible to capture everything, all the times of God's grace in our lives. Can we ever get enough? It is a long look back, a reverse and then a fast forward of years of impressions of beloved people, amazing opportunities, great desires, hard challenges, and wonderful experiences.

In all humility, it is about trying to put God first in your life, over and over as time goes by. To do so is to reach a sense of timelessness, to be overwhelmed with **eternity** and the infinite grace of God which is as boundless as the universe he created . . .

> *"O the depth of the riches both of wisdom and knowledge of God! How unsearchable are his judgments, and his ways past finding out!"* Romans 11:33 <u>KJV</u>

It is all about tuning in to the abundance and permanence of God's grace. It is about knowing, really knowing that God loves us. We accept this not just in solitary prayer, but in our actual life's walk through the world. As the years pass and the experiences pile up, we have the certainty that, *"With God all things are possible."* Mark 10:27 <u>KJV</u>

At times, this is certainly not easy to believe. Our world, with all its beauty, can be stark and terrible in its anguish. We may, in all human honesty, wonder how such sadness can be possible if God loves us? The answer to that has long been made plain. God is at work for peace and justice, for health and harmony, working to clean up the messes we make, bringing in a new day. We believe this deeply and so ask ourselves, what are we doing about it ? **Are we a part of God's Plan or a part of the problem?**

When it seems to us that life is headed in the wrong direction, we can remember that God's eternal grace can guide our own thoughts and actions if we truly desire that. It takes your breath away to know that God depends on the likes of us, we who can make such big mistakes, do the right thing for the wrong reason or the wrong thing for the right reason; we who are so perfectly imperfect, so exquisitely flawed. It's a real wonder, a staggering mystery. So this book is about the glorious but seeming **impossibilities** of our lives.

Out in Illinois there's a town named **Normal**. It is the site of Illinois State University which formerly was a teacher's college. Teacher's colleges were called "normal schools," which explains the name of the town. Near Normal, there's a small rural community called **Oblong**. One day the local newspaper printed an article with this headline: "Normal Boy Marries Oblong Girl."

That's just a frivolous metaphor for our faith about our Perfect Savior living here with very imperfect people. It's a partnership now, unequal of course, but mutually dependent. *"We love him because he first loved us."* I John 4:19 <u>KJV</u> It is the right and satisfying way to live. Believing this deep down does help keep you realistic and humble, about your own need for God's living presence in your life.

I dreamed death came the other night and Heaven's gates swung wide,

An angel with a halo bright ushered me inside.

And there to my astonishment the folks I'd judged and labeled,

As quite unfit, of little worth and spiritually disabled.

Indignant words rose to my lips and never were set free,

For every face showed stunned surprise, for no one had expected me!

Anonymous

GPS has become a familiar tool for travelers worldwide. The GLOBAL POSITIONING SYSTEM includes 24 satellites flying precise routes 12,000 miles above the earth. Traveling at 7,000 miles per hour, they each circle the globe twice every 24 hours. They are solar powered and have small booster rockets to keep them on their assigned pathways in the heavens. Each weighs 2,000 pounds and is 17 feet in width. They constantly process information about location and by communicating with established towers on earth can pinpoint where your vehicle is at any time.

It is amazing technology for someone driving a car who wants to know the best way to get to a certain destination. The driver simply types in the desired address and within minutes can see the written directions and map on his mobile screen in the car. Also, a firm, friendly voice gives updated instructions, such as 'In 1 mile, bear left on Hwy 290'.

Considering the helpful nature of this modern technology, wouldn't it be great if such direction could be given for our life choices too? God always greatly desires to help direct us to his purpose for our lives.

"I know the plans I have for you declares the LORD, plans to prosper you and not to harm you, plans to give you hope and a future." Jeremiah 29:11

GPS – **G**od's **P**lan in **S**cripture. Enjoy his perfect guidance for your life!

Prologue

One evening recently a large owl glided in, flaring his four- foot wing span to land on the flat tip of the flag pole overlooking the Lake Erie shore. Since no flag happened to be flying on the fifty foot staff, he had found a perfect lookout perspective. Rotating his head 270 degrees, he silently observed hundreds of yards of the lake, beach, riparian and the commons. His eyesight, which is roughly one hundred times greater than humans, swept this wide vista several times, watching, ready and expectant. What a bird, and what a place to see his world!

It was a very beautiful evening. The sunset suffused the western skies. The colors were spectacular; pink, salmon, crimson, cerise, deep purple and tangerine against a robin's egg blue sky. As the brilliant sun was slipping down into the horizon, a path of liquid gold shone across the water to our shore. As the colors began to fade, the lacy higher clouds above were backlit by rich and brilliant gold leaf, the edges being sharply trimmed with glory. The owl suddenly left, heading east into the growing darkness as though it was time to punch in and report for his third shift work.

I have always liked heights. To be able to see things from an airplane or a mountaintop provides a much broader understanding with fewer distracting details. Is it possible to see our human condition totally from above, from God's point of view? Of course not, but we can find a greater spiritual perspective from the **scripture of nature**. There is wisdom there, and strength if we will do more than just quickly glance.

We can realize deeply that nothing in all of nature is just secular, that everything has been made sacred in its origin by God.

 "Do you not know? Have you not heard? The LORD is the everlasting God; the Creator of the ends of the earth . . . those who hope *in the LORD will renew their strength. They will soar on wings like eagles; they will run and not grow weary, they will walk and not be faint."* Isaiah 40:28, 31

The WORD In The Desert

Descending Light

JOHN 3:16-21

My wife Nancy gave me a wonderful gift this summer. I had always wanted to see some National Parks and was musing through a tour catalog which included a 10 day journey through six parks in the southwest USA. "Why don't you go?" she asked. I said it was lengthy and not cheap. In her usual wisdom she pointed out that seeing six parks in one journey was cheaper than separate trips. So with her encouragement, I went and it was wonderful. I didn't want it to end.

Our group was congenial, only 18 of us on a new 40 passenger tour bus. The tour director was knowledgeable and courteous. We visited Arches, Bryce Canyon, Canyonlands, Capitol Reef, Zion and the north rim of the Grand Canyon. Some travel was by small planes and hiking was available at all stops. Each day exceeded the impressions of the previous one. The incredible beauty, age and size of these places are indescribable. To be immersed in these experiences is truly to sense that we are a miniscule part of eternal, ongoing creation.

When looking into an ancient canyon which reveals millions of years of geologic history, each colored layer of rock like a very long chapter, one cannot really grasp, in ordinary human terms, how it came to be. One of our speakers, Marty Ott, quoted geologist Clarence Dutton (1889): "These dimensions have no meaning to our senses. What we are left with is a troubling sense of immensity."

The sunrises were one of the best parts of the trip. We were blessed with clear, cool September days and the early morning dawns opened the day, as John Muir said, "Shouting Hallelujah!"

It was one morning like that in my favorite stop, Zion National Park. I was up early. Pine scent was in the air, fresh and cool. No one else was around. Zion is a place where you look up at the sandstone cliffs from the canyon floor rather than looking down from a rim. As I watched, the sun was rising, lighting the skies high above the canyon walls. Then, concurrently, slowly, silently, the light descended down the copper colored monoliths, down, down to the place where I was sitting. It was a timeless experience, a revelation of eternity.

In awe, I tried to identify some reference point in my little life – some memory or past human meaning of such an experience. It was beyond any such effort.

And then the great words of I John 1:5 somehow came out of my mouth, *"God is light, and in him is no darkness at all."*

For many people of faith, linking the awesomeness of nature with our belief in God as creator is just natural. For others who are more skeptical, there is an uncrossable chasm of disbelief in such thoughts. Theirs is a dilemma that if unsolved perhaps leads only to some form of humanism as their faith.

Later in the day I thought about that wonderful dawn experience. I do not think it was a coincidence that I happened to be reading some thoughts by Rabbi Jonathon Sacks on the meaning of life. He quotes Ludwig Wittgenstein: "The meaning of a system must lie outside it. Football, for instance, is governed by a system of rules. If you want to learn how the game is played, you would be well advised to study that system. But if you want to understand what the game means to its players and fans, you would have to consider things like honor, camaraderie, local pride or the desire for heroes – things not in the rule book ... Science takes things apart to see how they work. Religion puts things together to see what they mean." The Great Partnership

I really like that. It is possible to have both – knowledge of how things work, and what they mean. As long as I live, I will always remember that dawning of descending light in Zion.

"But whoever lives by the truth comes into the light, so that it may be seen plainly that what he has done has been done through God." John 3:21

Conversation at the edge

I PETER 3: 15-16

The walking trail along the edge of Bryce Canyon National Park has a few rustic benches for restful viewing. So it was on a clear and breezy September day, there was a sense of just 'swimming in the invisible air' of the graciousness of God. It was close to perfect, the weather and the view at 8,000 feet elevation were outstanding.

This park has several natural amphitheaters etched by erosion into the sides of the Navaho sandstone cliffs. They house thousands of bizarre humanoid shapes, colored rich red and orange known as **hoodoos**.(They are especially spooky in the moonlight.) People enjoy talking about what or whom the shapes look like to them. It is also a place of life-giving thunderstorms with stupendous lightning displays. Wind, rain, snow and ice are constantly, gradually sculpting Bryce National Park.

Trying to take this all in, I was suddenly aware of another person coming along, also deep in thought. It was a retired heart doctor and we immediately fell into a lengthy, very interesting conversation. We sat on one of those benches watching the changing light on the **hoodoos** and talked of faith and religion. He had studied both for many years in connection with his surgical practice. He was now enjoying the learning and stimulation of travel to interesting places.

I cannot fully recapture the vitality of our discussion so these thoughts are partial. His knowledge was more extensive than mine but his questions paralleled many of my own. We **hit it off** as people say, an example I think of the translation that **the kingdom of God is between you.** I asked him if I could make some notes on his thoughts. He grinned and agreed.

He had practiced and lived medicine for over 32 years and had watched so many people suffer and die, even with good medical care, that he started to ask, "What is faith? What is real?" Facing the deep questions of the brevity and uncertainty of life in that setting was awesome.

He said that life seems totally random and chaotic, that scientific research tries to make sense of it all, but it seldom really succeeds. Therefore, we can learn to make use of chaos, harnessing some of it but never able to fully change the nature of it. He believes in our consciousness, our awareness of all of life, but that we have not even come close to being aware of who we are or what we can do. His viewpoint reinforced the belief of some that we use less than 1 % of the billions of brain cells we each have. We do have symptoms of greatness, he said, such as spiritual reverie when visions of possibilities occur. Medically this means that blood is moving to a different part of the brain. So what can we discover, really?

What then, is life itself? Does religion give us any really good knowledge of it? What can Christianity really bring to the world? I mean REALLY. What should be taught to the younger generations who are moving into a future in which they have no experience?

I ventured to ask the Doctor if he is an atheist and found out that at this point he did not know, but did not like the implication. He liked the term **secular religion**, living out a Christian philosophy in word and deed. He is still an active church member and donates heavily to a certain charity, but smiling, added that maybe that just bribes his conscience. He noted that he wondered where the truly hungry people were, since many who came to the mission meals he supported were quite overweight.

The great statement made by Jesus, "*I am the resurrection and the life,* "he thought to be quite meaningless to most people, because we

7

are so spiritually illiterate. More and more he believed that Christianity should be able to bring good things to the less privileged in the world. He noted the prevailing attitude in America, and maybe the whole world, that people will not help themselves as long as someone else is taking care of them.

He was really rolling along and the give and take of the conversation was exciting. In a pause, I looked out at those strange **hoodoos** and thanked him for the interesting conversation, one of the best in my memory. "What do you think?" the Doctor asked. "What real use can we make of the chaos we meet every day in the world? What purpose is there to life?"

Pop Quiz!

After the honest mental calisthenics of the past hour, I could see this was not just a polite casual question. He was sincerely searching. There was no wimpy, sentimental answer for this one! It was one of those times when answers come forth that you didn't know you were thinking.

After a few moments I responded something like this: "We are standing on the edge of a fantastic canyon, and we also are standing at the edge of the potential of our brains. I will probably never know all that my brain can do, but I will make use of the wonder that I feel. It matters most how I respond to the unknown and this is not new to us in our generation. I believe there is a purpose that must be worked out in each of us whenever, wherever we have lived. I don't fully understand it, so it is enough for me to believe and live by faith."

He was closely listening, so looking out again at the amazing beauty of Bryce and feeling so invigorated by the good discussion with him I remembered these words, and said:

"Even before he made the world, God loved us and chose us in Christ to be holy and without fault in his eyes." Ephesians 1:4 Then we just sat in silence at the wonder of it all.

Foundation of the world

PSALM 8

Seen from its perimeter rim of 2,750 miles or from an airplane, the multicolored beauty and hundreds of square miles of the Grand Canyon are an overwhelming spectacle. It is like seeing the very foundation of the world.

Some see it as a **stone city** resembling "an ancient ruined metropolis dense with elegant public buildings, skyscrapers, cathedrals, theaters, apartment buildings, aqueducts and highways . . . as if every nuance of line and hue of every stone palace and temple were planned by a master architect." Views beyond the Beauty by Gary Ladd

It is interesting to simply listen to the comments made by people as they stand at the rim for the first time. Some remark about the length of time and the geologic forces that produced such a natural wonder. Others simply worship God who created it all. Is this about Geology or Theology ? Can it be both?

Science and Religion both wonder in their own ways at the miracle of our earth and life upon it. Each approach is deeply significant. Science seeks to know and explain our origins and HOW we got here. Religion seeks to explain WHY we are here and what it means so we can understand human behavior.

At least 12 different colored layers of geologic history are definable to the eye, and represent unimaginable time spans which some experts say total 350 million years. Each layer is uniquely different from the others. At the very base of the Canyon, the oldest visible rock is called "Vishnu" and is said to be 1.6 billion years old igneous. The total earth is estimated by some to be 4 billion years old. These observations bear little relation to the time we see on our wristwatches, calendars or even the passing of the sun each 24 hours.

Trying to see this in human perspective, our tour guide spoke of it this interesting way. Imagine a seven-volume set of average size books, each with 200 pages. Each single letter in each book represents 1500 years. At the start of Volume I, earth was formed but modern humans do not appear until the beginning of the last line of the last page of the last book. Finally, all of recorded human history is contained in the **last three letters of the very last sentence.**

In our Judeo-Christian tradition, we quote Genesis 1:1, *"In the beginning God created the heaven and the earth."* The first chapter of the first book continues through a six day creation cycle of everything that exists and then chapter 2 tells us that, *"God rested on the seventh day from all his work which he had made. And he blessed the seventh day and sanctified it; because that in it he had rested from all his work, which God created and made."*

Do we have to choose which is the right, factual way this old world came to be?

I once posed that question to a respected and highly educated elder in church. He smiled and replied, "I believe creation happened in seven evenings and mornings." I have always found that to be a satisfying answer, bridging the scientific and the religious approaches to our beginnings.

Now shift focus with me for a moment all the way down from the rim of the Grand Canyon into our daily lives and routines. Standing in line at the market recently, I noticed the trash tabloids with the latest scandals and troubles of celebrities. The garish pictures and headlines all reflected the self absorption and confusion of **celebrities** trying, like very confused adolescents, to find happiness only within themselves.

Then, the young cashier zipped my items through the barcode reader, humming an old hymn from church. I was amazed and walking out to the car remembered myself as a 17- year -old at a youth retreat trying to **find myself,** as they say. The speaker for that day was, and still is, one good answer to my questions. Not just what he said, but he, himself, was an answer. He had found his passion in life and loved what he was doing. He had found meaning and knew that we young people in that crowd that day on those hard benches were all trying to figure out our lives and what we should do. His own life was an excellent example.

He read Ephesians 1:4 to us, *"According as he has chosen us in him before the **foundation of the world**, that we should be holy and without blame before him in love."*

Then he closed the Bible and with strong conviction said to us, "There is no greater knowledge than to believe that you were called to your purpose before the foundation of the earth." It was a new, powerful thought that meant every person can have a destiny of divine origin. Without that knowledge, he said, life is just fate. Destiny, or fate - which shall it be?

The modern way of expressing this is **God has a plan for your life.** I began to believe it that day, and I believe it even more today after many years of living by trial and error.

Four billion years ago, before the foundation of the world and the Grand Canyon had not even begun to exist, you and I were being chosen to live the life that God planned for us.

"For you created my inmost being; you knit me together in my mother's womb. I praise you because I am fearfully and wonderfully made; your works are wonderful, I know that full well. My frame was not hidden from you when I was made in the secret place. When I was woven together in the depths of the earth, your eyes saw my unformed body. All the days ordained for me were written in your book before one of them came to be." Psalm 139:13-16

11

Coffee on the rim

PSALM 1

It is dawn on the north rim of the Grand Canyon. There is a rocking chair not far from my cabin overlooking the eastern horizon from an altitude of 8200 feet above sea level. There is a fresh pot of steaming coffee by my door. I take my cup and walk to my box seat to watch and wonder at the sunrise of another new day. The morning air is cool and full of pine fragrance. A Kaibab squirrel breaks the silence, chattering at me – asking where **his** coffee is, I guess. It is a timeless experience of perfect wonder.

Speechless, I watch the light of the rising sun flowing its life- giving rays over the countless colors of the canyon. The anonymous folk poem of our ancestors comes to mind:

> *The clock of life is wound but once, and no man has the power,*
> *To tell just where the hands will stop, at late or early hour.*
> *The present only is our own, to seek to do God's Will.*
> *Tomorrow holds no promise, for the clock may then be still.*

These moments are so still, overwhelming and surreal that I wonder if I am really here. Somewhere from deep within, a favorite, old memory verse emerges: *"Do you want more and more of God's kindness and peace? Then learn to know him better and better. For as you know him better, he will give you, through his great power, everything you need for living a*

12

truly good life; he even shares his own glory and goodness with us." II Peter 1:2-3 <u>LB</u>

Somehow these words fit perfectly with that sunrise experience as I watched the glory of the new day beginning and sensing the glory of God at the same time. It was enthralling, an awareness of the WORD in the amazing country before me. It was beyond time and our modern overscheduled lives with all the texting, tweeting, twittering, facebooking, flickering, messaging and e-mailing.

A much better signal than any of those was coming in loud and clear. It was wordless, but the message was undeniable: **Surely the presence of the WORD is in this place.**

I remained there as long as possible – then other people began coming by. My coffee cup was empty, the quiet half hour was complete, and I thought the sense of visitation was rich in depth, if not in length. Realistically I knew that I cannot sit in a rocking chair on the north rim of the Grand Canyon every day, but since the WORD is with us wherever we are in the country, we can connect anytime, anywhere.

I recently overheard the remark, "Multitasking while you pray can cause you to lose the signal." You know what multitasking is, don't you? It's the modern term for the old ranching expression; "too many irons in the fire." It has become something of a modern badge of achievement, this doing many things at one time. We are squeezing more and more activities into our lives and doubling up on the things we somehow feel compelled to do.

Witness people driving cars and talking or texting on their phones, for example. People of Christian faith are certainly not exempt from these excesses. Some speak of the Proverbs 31 woman. Read it and you'll be exhausted at the long list of commitments that some homemakers routinely carry out. We may have come to think that the more things we do, the richer our lives will be.

Are we giving God a chance to speak to us alone? Or is that just another option to be added somewhere on a long list of tasks?

Giving time back to God in solitude is a very rewarding and liberating experience. It goes even further than that actually. We start out thinking that solitude with God will help us recharge our batteries in order to win the rat race. Eventually we discover that this special time with God allows us to ignore the rat race completely. We discover that we are rich enough, young enough, healthy enough and even important enough. We can just drop those compulsions that have taken over as we realize that life has been doing us instead of the other way around. We find that it is really true that we are never **less alone than when we are alone with the WORD.**

"Pray without ceasing," we read in I Thessalonians 5:17. Is that really possible? It is when you maintain an open line with the WORD, always ready to listen to him during your busy days. It is when you love God in your subconscious thought life so that the impulse to communicate with him is just always there.

It is a skill to be learned through practice. Do you think your life is too confusing and busy for this? I remember my father-in-law's comment; **you are never stronger than when you are being tested.**

Yes, let us *"Pray without ceasing"* and if necessary, use words.

Geology and Theology

PSALM 19

Most geologists believe that the Grand Canyon is six million years old and at the very bottom of it at least 1.7 billion years old. It is about 275 miles long, 10 miles across at its widest and a mile deep. It defies complete description. When President Teddy Roosevelt saw it he said, **Leave it alone. The ages have been working on it.**

It is truly majestic and you can really only see a fraction of it, no matter how long you look. Film maker Ken Burns remarked, **"We still are at the morning of creation."** That surprising comment reflects that the Colorado River, seeking sea level, continues like endless liquid sandpaper to cut its way down through the rock about an inch each 100 years. It is sourced in the Rocky Mountains, falling 11,000 feet to the entrance of the canyon, and another 2,000 feet as it flows through the canyon. The river's force and speed are influenced by the amount of snowfall in the Colorado, Wyoming and Utah mountains.

The South Rim is most accessible for travelers, with plenty of accommodations. The North Rim is 1,000 ft. higher and is more remote and much less traveled. Its uniqueness includes more trees and vegetation due to more precipitation. It is a forested island standing above the surrounding area. The lodgings are much simpler and less crowded than the South. Among its wildlife is the black and white Kaibab squirrel with tasseled ears. It is not known anywhere else, perhaps because it has always been cut off from other environments. It is sometimes mistaken for a skunk that can climb trees.

The Lodge at the North Rim has a magnificent stone deck with comfortable chairs. Sitting there for a few hours one is able to see the constantly changing light, colors and shadows of the canyon as the earth continues its daily revolving journey around the sun. It is not a place to be in a hurry. The longer you stay there, the slower your body rhythms seem to be moving. It is as though time stops. It is a touch of eternity.

The overwhelming power of this geology brings theology to mind. It is a great place to read once again Psalm 19 – a creation psalm about the threefold revelation of God: A. The handiwork of God's Creation; B. The same eternal nature of his guiding laws; C. Our acceptance and response to his creation and guidance. Revelation, after all, isn't revelation if we don't **get it**.

Perhaps you are not reading this psalm while sitting by the Grand Canyon, but it can inspire you in any natural setting of God's creation. It is a good, easy psalm to memorize, especially in the classic King James Version.

A. *"The heavens declare the glory of God; and the firmament sheweth his handywork. Day unto day uttereth speech and night unto night sheweth knowledge. There is no speech nor language, where their voice is not heard. Their line is gone out through all the earth and their words to the end of the world. In them hath he set a tabernacle for the sun. Which is as a bridegroom coming out of his chamber, and rejoiceth as a strong man to run a race. His going forth is from the end of the heaven, and his circuit unto the ends of it: there is nothing hid from the heat thereof.*

B. *"The law of the LORD is perfect, converting the soul: the testimony of the LORD is sure, making wise the simple. The statutes of the LORD are right, rejoicing the heart; the commandment of the LORD is pure, enlightening the eyes. The fear of the LORD is* clean, enduring forever; the judgments of the LORD are true and righteous altogether. More to be desired are they than gold, yea, than much fine gold; sweeter also than honey and the honeycomb. Moreover by them is thy servant warned; and in keeping them there is great reward.

C. "Who can understand his errors? Cleanse thou me from secret faults. Keep back thy servant also from presumptuous sins; let them not have dominion over me; then shall I be upright, and I shall be innocent from the great transgressions.

"Let the words of my mouth and the meditations of my heart be acceptable in thy sight, O LORD, my strength and my redeemer."

Sacrifice or Blessing?

II SAMUEL 24:18-25

Millions of people visit the National Parks every year, each person witnessing beauty and majesty in individual ways. The sounds, the colors, even the air leave deep and lasting impressions in the mind and heart.

Some are content to just stay in one place and take their fill of it all. Others can't get enough that way, so they hike the trails at all times of day to experience personally more and more wonder.

At the Grand Canyon, for example, starting the day right might mean rising from sleep at 5 a.m. and going out to the rim to watch the sunrise. Leaving the warm comfort of bed for the dark and chilly hike to a good vantage point requires a strong desire to see something unusual – perhaps for the only time in your life. When I got out there, congratulating myself on my effort, I was surprised to find several who had been there all night, just waiting for what naturalist John Muir described as," The dawn . . . is beautiful; and when the first level sunbeams sting the domes and spires with what burst of power the big, wild days begin."

Truly, it was beautiful beyond description, both in natural beauty and what it does within your own heart and soul to have made the effort.

As a wise friend says, "Sacrifice is usually irksome, only love can make it enjoyable." Yes, if you want to know the highest and best of life, it's going to take some real effort, and strong desire.

As the morning light strengthened and the wilderness silence lengthened, the words of King David illumined my little life," **I will not offer unto God that which cost me nothing."** If you have not read that fascinating Bible story, I invite you to do so. It is a key to a new experience of knowing God.

We often hear the common wisdom, "You only get out of life what you put into it." I would agree when it comes to our average efforts and responsibilities on routine day–to–day matters.

However, a more significant and powerful energy takes place when the WORD himself is included in our relationships with others. Will you make the extra effort there?

 Paul, writing to the Christians in Colossae said: **"Whatever you do, work at it with all your heart, as working for the Lord, not for men. It is the Lord Christ you are serving."** 3:23

Do you work with all your heart? If you learn to love the WORD, as he loves you, sacrifice is not irksome, but a blessing. Living this way, thoughtfully and wisely, will multiply your happiness, many, many times over.

Albert Schweitzer said it so eloquently: "But kindness works simply and perseveringly. It puts to flight mistrust and misunderstanding, and it strengthens itself by calling forth answering kindness. Hence it is the furthest-reaching and the most effective of all forces." Memoirs of Childhood and Youth.

If you want real blessings in your life, do not offer God that which costs you nothing – either from the pocketbook or personal plans.

Hanging out with the stars

PSALM 33

Yes we can, every night, but in a much better place than Hollywood or Broadway! Being in the high Utah desert on a crystal clear night many miles from any artificial lighting, creates boundless awe of the "glorious scene that is ours" as it says in the old western song. Someday I hope to visit the first **International Dark Sky Park** located in Natural Bridges National Monument, Utah. Its million acres at 9,000 ft. elevation is a long way from anywhere. Bluffs and plateaus separate it from the little town of Blanding which is 40 miles away. Viewing the night sky there is totally different than viewing from our highly illuminated cities.

Preparing to tour the southwest, I did much reading about all the National Parks and the beauty of thousands of geologic formations. I was, however, unprepared for the night sky. Late one night I just happened to look up there and was startled to see how thickly populated it was with brilliant stars beyond number. A shining full moon was riding high, reminding me of Emerson's comment that if the stars were only visible on one night in our lifetimes, the whole world would be out there in fear and total amazement.

Many people have tried to find the words to express how looking at the stars makes us feel. President Abraham Lincoln is said to have noted: "I can see how it might be possible for a man to look down upon the earth and be an atheist, but I cannot conceive how he could look up into the heavens and say there is no God."

As I looked and looked up into the endless night sky, the words of Edwin Way Teale came to life: "As the sky grew velvet and the last of the daylight ebbed away in the darkness, the stars seemed hanging low all across the heavens. They spread in all directions. They clustered together. They glittered in constellations. They ran across the firmaments in the heaven-wide galaxy of the Milky Way – that great silver river of the sky." Autumn across America

Such an experience brings endless, awesome wonder, both scientific and spiritual. The scientist can look back in time with giant telescopes and see things as they were when light was first sent forth to us. They conclude that the universe is infinitely expanding and that there is no **middle, edge, or center** to it all.

Nobel laureate John C. Mather recently said, "We did not see an explosion (Big Bang). We only see the expansion. There doesn't have to be a beginning. This is something that's a little surprising to a lot of people because we are very intuitively sure that time runs along at a certain rate, and therefore there has to be a beginning. But I don't know that that's true." (Clemson University speech – 11/28/12) In 2018 a new telescope will be sent out a million miles into space, seeking to observe every stage of the universe's creation.

I am grateful for this scientific information and admit to being really curious about how we got here. I do know that looking up into those stars can bring us to our knees and strong emotion in praise to the WORD, who is continuing to create it all.

"To whom will you compare me? Or who is my equal? says the Holy One. Lift your eyes and look to the heavens; Who created all these? He who brings out the starry host one by one, and calls them each by name. Because of his great power and mighty strength, not one of them is missing . . . Do you not know? Have you not heard? The LORD is the everlasting God, the Creator of the ends of the earth. He will not grow tired or

weary, and his understanding no one can fathom. He gives
strength to the weary, and increases the power of the weak."
Isaiah 40:25-29

We belong here, it is true. The secrets of the universe are endlessly fascinating and so is the fact that we are a part of it – **a tiny speck to be sure, but still a part of God's creation.**

Believing and accepting this brings new courage to our living. If all those stars are possible, then courage, hope, strength and creativity are possible in my life too. It is an act of faith. As living beings we have the same spark of creation in us that brought it all into being. We may not be able to fully reason our way to that fact, but our disbelief is suspended when we worship God.

When this fact hits home, our thoughts become clear, confusion slinks away and we discover, **with either a microscope or a telescope** the pattern that God has planned for us. *"I will show wonders in the heaven above and signs on the earth below. Everyone who calls on the name of the Lord will be saved."* Acts 2:19

When life becomes overwhelming, just step outside and gaze at the heavens. It is mysterious and totally fascinating to realize that our God, who holds all that in place, certainly can hold us in the palm of his hand. Isaiah 49:16

If you, like me, can't find words to express this wonder, just enjoy it anyway. Let it wash over and through you again and again. Make it part of your daily life. What matters most when we behold the wondrous night sky is the response of our hearts and the enrichment of our faith.

If the night sky is clouded over and you cannot see the stars, they are still there, aren't they? You can believe they exist even if you don't see them, and you can also believe in God, even in those times when he is silent.

Proposal Point

PSALM 84

Well, actually the real name is Bright Angel Point. It is said to be the place on the North Rim of the Grand Canyon with the most panoramic view. It is also known as a place where marriage proposals are frequently . . . well, proposed. Dropping to one knee to make the offer, however, is discouraged because of the 2,000 foot drop- off on three sides of the narrow lookout! Enthusiastic responses are advised to be exercised elsewhere!

It is a unique place to watch the sunrise, but to do so requires a half-mile hike in the predawn darkness. It is an experience unlike anything else as you hike out there on the paved trail in the desert stillness. Your own footsteps may suddenly pause if you hear some other unknown sound in the black night all around you. You think seriously about the statistic of 1 or 2 deaths yearly from falls over different edges of the Canyon, most of them men. (Children seem to have the common sense not to risk that danger.)

Fortunately the tour director provided a handy, stubby flashlight about 4 x 1 inches. It shone a brilliant circle of light on the path before you, which descends and ascends enroute to your destination. It is a very sensible tool and helps to avoid missteps or falls. Remember that you have it and remember to turn it on! However, that life saving circle of light does temporarily isolate you from the enormous canyon experience. You feel quite alone while surrounded by the total unseen magnificence of creation. You just want to get safely out there to the point for the glory of the new morning. Watch your step!

Hiking along carefully in this dark solitude, I kept thinking,"*Your word is a lamp to guide my feet and a light to my path.*" Psalm 119:105

That stubby little flashlight removed the fear of tripping over some obstacle or getting off the path, in pursuit of the beauty of the sunrise. The scriptures can do the same for our spiritual lives. We sometimes walk through risky or dangerous circumstances in this life, but the Bible really can be our light to show us the way ahead. It is the inspired Word of God, "*All scripture is inspired by God and profitable for teaching, for reproof, for correction, for training in righteousness.*" II Timothy 3:16

"*The LORD is my light and my salvation, whom then shall I fear? The LORD is the strength of my life, of whom shall I be afraid?*" Psalm 27:1

Goliath

PSALM 147

Somewhere back in the 40's, The Grand Canyon Suite, composed by Ferde Grofe in the 20's, was frequent radio music in the evening. Its five sections were a very 'visual' depiction, of the Grand Canyon, to the ear. Especially interesting was **On the Trail,** the rocking, clip clop of mule hooves descending into the depths. It even became the theme song for Philip Morris cigarettes. Can you hear it now?

I loved it and dreamed that one day I could ride a mule down into the Grand Canyon. I heard that a ride cost only $1.00 in those days. This desire was reinforced more and more as I read a lot of western novels by Zane Grey and others. I visualized what it might be like, and being familiar with saddle horses and equipment, I wondered what sort of mount I would have.

As life worked out, 60 years later I got my ride at the North Rim of the Canyon. I did not have a reservation but to my surprise and delight they had a saddle open. The wrangler, who was **western wise,** looked at me and asked my weight. Hearing what it was, he matched me up with Goliath, his largest, dapple gray mule. Hmmm. "He is smarter than we are," he said. "Just let him do the work," as we all started down the trail.

How can I describe this experience? The gentle rocking motion and creaking leather were really happening at last! **On the Trail** was going through my head. I just dropped the lines on Goliath's neck and tuned in to the rugged beauty all around. We descended into the mile deep incision in the earth I had only dreamt about.

The trail narrowed, more and more, and became steeper as we plodded along, down and down. We passed a small hand carved wooden sign:

> *"All the earth worships Thee. They sing praises to Thee, sing praises to Thy name."*
>
> Psalm 66:4

This was totally awesome! I loved it! We passed by a natural arch, a tunnel carved in a rocky overhang and then the curves started, some of them quite sharp switchbacks . . . At one of them, I could not see the drop- off edge to my left, and Goliath did his **zero turning radius** moves. I couldn't even see his sure footed hooves but we were a team! He did the work and I, as a sort of co-pilot, did the praying!

I laugh now at the exciting pleasure of that day and my freedom to appreciate God's creation, thanks to Goliath's reliability. When we reached our destination, we all dismounted and rested a while, then remounted for the return ascent. All I had to do was look at the changing light on the immense, ancient walls all around and be safely carried by the strength, patience and knowledge of Goliath.

Thinking of those times when I started to pick up those lines and try to tell Goliath what to do, I wondered, how often in our lives do we really let God be in control?

It is not easy to surrender our fondest hopes and dreams to the WORD – in the desert or anywhere. We can take it from St. Paul, who knew everything about depending on God whether in prosperity or poverty: *". . . I have learned to be content in any and every situation, whether well fed or hungry, whether living in plenty or in want. I can do everything through him who gives me strength."* Philippians 4:11-12

26

Who's in charge? There are those who sentimentally claim that God is their co-pilot in life. Isn't it true, however, that we ourselves are the co-pilots, relying on God to direct our paths?

I continue to relive and learn from that day with Goliath and I can't wait to go again.

Roy G. Biv

GENESIS 9:8-17

Recently, a huge rainbow formed over the western horizon of the lake. It was like a gigantic picture frame over a glorious scene that was clearing into sunshine after a summer rainstorm. Many neighbors came out to see it, trying to take pictures (hard to do). It faded, then returned even more brilliantly, then doubling its arc, bringing awe and deep thoughts. One visitor was weeping, out of sadness in the personal life, and with the hope that only rainbows can bring to us. Another didn't see it at all until he turned around and saw it behind him. Sometimes hope can be found behind us, in the past.

> *My heart leaps up when I behold*
> *A rainbow in the sky*
> *So was it when my life began*
> *So is it now when I am a man.*
> William Wordsworth

Imagine Noah and his family stepping out of the ark into a world where there were no other human beings. How incredibly lonely! The account of the great flood is crowned with the sign of God's promise to be with them, *"I do set my bow in the cloud, and it shall be for a token of a covenant between me and the earth."* Genesis 9:13 KJV

It is the will of God that human beings should get into moral relationship with him, and his covenants are for this purpose. The reality of our relationship with God is based on what He has really done, not just on our changeable feelings about it.

Keeping Covenant with God is a call to personal maturity, a challenge to grow up and beyond our naturally selfish nature and to realize our responsibilities to him, others and to ourselves. It is a call to **joyful service**, gladly doing our part if we are to be God's people in the world. So often it seems that good ideas do not get beyond the **intention** stage. "I always meant to do that," we may say when it is too late.

Professor Leo Buscaglia often assigned his students to write a paper on, "If you had only five days to live, how would spend them? And with whom?" Some students wrote that they would tell someone, "I'm sorry," or "I love you," or that they would take the long deferred walk on the beach and watch the sunset. They turned in their papers and when they got them back, Buscaglia had written a note: "Why don't you do these things **now?**"

Whenever you see a rainbow, you may see Red, Orange, Yellow, Green, Blue, Indigo, Violet (ROY G BIV) and it fades fast away. Or perhaps it would be a good time to think - **R**eally **O**utdo **Y**ourself **G**iving **B**ack **I**ntensely **V**oluntarily.

You may have heard that, "Once upon a time there were four people named: Everybody, Somebody, Nobody and Anybody. When there was an important job to be done, Everybody was sure that Somebody would do it. Anybody could have done it, but Nobody did it.

When Nobody did it, Everybody got angry because it was Everybody's job. Everybody thought that Somebody would do it, but Nobody realized that Nobody would do it.

So it ended up that Everybody blamed Somebody when Nobody did what Anybody could have done in the first place."

God has made his promise to us. *"What shall we say about such wonderful things as these? If God is for us, who can ever be against us?"*

Romans 8:31 <u>NLT</u>

Dangerous Beauty

PSALM 40

The eastern entrance to Zion National Park is a paved two lane road through a mile- long tunnel, with a few large window openings looking out at many towering colorful cliffs. Our tour director played some beautiful instrumental music as we drove in, since no words can describe this place. As we emerged from the tunnel the first view of the park was simply awesome.

Many consider it the most intimate and impressive National Park, partly because it is viewed mainly from the canyon floor, rather than from the heights. It is a glorious place of steep cliffs, narrow canyons, varied wildlife and unpredictable weather. Hikers are advised to be extremely careful. It is also frequently noted that cell phones often do not work well here if you should get in trouble.

The copper colored monoliths rise many hundreds of feet and have names, such as The Sentinel, The Altar of Sacrifice, The Great White Throne and The Three Patriarchs. Perhaps this testifies to the desire to humanize ceremoniously these unimaginable formations, as the early Mormon settlers did when they named the park Zion (Promised Land). For thousands of years before that, the Native American tribe of Paiutes lived here. Many of their artifacts have been found and are on display.

Much of Zion was created by the North Fork Virgin River which flows through the main canyon. There are several hiking trails of varying difficulty. It is a wild, beautiful and somewhat dangerous place.

If you want to hike to Angel's Landing, for example, be aware that the brochure states: "It is a destination only for those of strong body and nerve and – some might even say – faith. To get there, you must hike a route with steep drop-offs on both sides. People who have a fear of heights should not try it." Further warnings are posted: "Be Prepared, Plan Well, Live Long. Falls cause most injuries and deaths at Zion. Avoid high places when lightning threatens. If you hike, carry a gallon of water." Don't let the thrill turn into a kill!

As the evening shadows fell, they rose from the floor of the canyon, growing up, up toward the peaks of the monoliths. I was looking at the **Three Patriarchs** and wondered what it would be like to climb them? How dangerous could it be? In naïve thought and having Rangers nearby for safety, scaling the Navaho sandstone monolith seemed to be a tempting possibility. I dreamed of doing it, and perhaps seeing a cascading waterfall up close, and also some shy wildlife.

Then In vesper thought I remembered the WORD in the desert with Peter, James and John when they climbed a mountain to be alone. There, we are told in Mark 9, they were joined by two patriarchs, Moses and Elijah, who represented the Law and the Prophets. The WORD was transfigured with dazzling white robes and not surprisingly the three disciples were terrified. Peter, who always seemed to have something to say, proposed building three memorials right then and there to honor the occasion. **Sometimes we rush to DO something when impressed, but God may have yet deeper truth to teach us.**

This was impulsive, not a good idea, and perhaps a dangerous one. His hasty response to this unexpected event, like our own sometimes, was very mistaken. This occurrence was to be kept secret until after the resurrection. *"Tell no man,"* was the instruction, in order to keep life on God's schedule. Don't be too hasty and run ahead of his plan.

Climbing mountains, physical or spiritual, can be a very rewarding experience partly because of the unknowns. It is a learning experience, a thrilling education about new things that can draw out the new and best in us.

"Exercise daily in God — no spiritual flabbiness please! Workouts in the gymnasium are useful, but a disciplined life in God is far more so, making you fit both today and forever. You can count on this. Take it to heart."
I Timothy 4:7-9

Ravens at Dawn

PSALM 148

Very crisp fresh air and the early sunrise at Arches National Park in Southwestern Utah are a totally awesome way to start a new day. In complete silence, the burning disc rises from the pitch black eastern horizon, ever so gradually flooding the huge Arches with transcendent light.

The Arches are magnificent and there are thousands of them across the Southwest USA in various stages of creation. The millennia it takes for nature to carve them, dwarfs human history, and their rugged beauty really is indescribable.

Over this ancient salt ocean bed, which geologists think is over 300 million years old, two ravens are flying, and then land on the very summit of the largest arch before us. It's an amazing juxtaposition – the ancient formations, and a living being, whose own ancestry is also thought to be millions of years old.

Ravens are the largest songbirds in the world. They are capable of 64 different sounds and are smart, always working in pairs. Two feet tall, they are dominant and territorial, adapted fully to life in the desert. Playful and energetic, their nests often contain shiny items like coins or tinfoil, as well as jewelry. They are said to play with wolf pups in their dens, befriending them so that in adulthood they will help each other find food in the wilderness.

In these morning moments of wonder and worship, the WORD who created and is eternally in the country resounds in the silence: *"He provides food for the cattle and for the young ravens when they call. His pleasure is not in the strength of the horse, nor his delight in the legs of a man; the LORD delights in those who fear him, who put their hope in his unfailing love."* Psalm 146:9-11

If there is uncertainty or fear in your life, it is best to just sincerely worship the LORD, for this is pleasing to him . . . If there are times when we do not understand ourselves or the situations we are in, it is right and good to really get our minds off ourselves and turn our thoughts toward him. We can learn that happiness does not depend on circumstances. The more that we do this, the more we will become what he has created us to be. As the old camp song says:

> *Turn your eyes upon Jesus; look full in his wonderful face*
> *And the things of earth will grow strangely dim,*
> *In the light of his glory and grace.*

Those ravens at dawn apparently had no fears about survival or purpose on that, or any other day. They also reminded me of something else the WORD said: *"Look at the birds, free and unfettered, not tied down to a job description, careless in the care of God. And you count far more to him than birds."* Matthew 6:26 <u>TM</u>

This is a much discussed teaching of the WORD. Aren't we supposed to work and make money? Of course we must think about the basic needs of food and clothing, thrift and savings. No one works harder than those ravens at making a living, even in the barren desert. However, they do not worry and become immobilized about the future. They just live.

The WORD continued his teaching to that crowd on the mountain, *"Seek first his kingdom and his righteousness, and all these things will be given to you as well."* Matthew 6:33

Our style of living is not just a style that we put on. Our way of life in the WORD is the natural outflow of simply staying focused on God, living and learning in that trusting relationship with him. Our minds have both a focal and a marginal function. What is truly central for us? Someone has pointed out that birds are not amphibious like frogs, living half under water and half on land. Let us not be halfway people either!

We may be genuinely concerned about important things, but we do not become consumed with **worry disease.** Consider the people who influence and help us the most. They live their lives simply; balanced and unaffectedly. Those are the lives that mold us.

May every bird you see remind you of the WORD's care and provision for all of his creation.

"You will keep in perfect peace all who trust in you, all whose thoughts are fixed on you! Trust in the LORD always, for the LORD GOD is the eternal Rock." Isaiah 26:3-4

Ask –Seek-Knock

MATTHEW 7: 7-12

Watching six rock climbers, with their equipment, on the vertical face of the red sandstone cliffs of Zion National Park, I thought about their detailed preparations for the challenge of the climb. From the floor of the canyon, they appeared as small as bugs, several hundred feet up there, with a web of red climbing ropes. What did they do to get ready for this? Just pray?

Regarding our sincere prayers for desired results, a preacher on national television recently made an excellent point. He said that the time comes when we should stop incessantly praying the same prayers, and begin thanking God for the answer that is already on the way. It is similar, he said, to a child constantly begging a parent for something instead of trusting in the parent's love and judgment to respond to the request. It means that we can stop pounding on heaven's doors and begin to live in faith, knowing that God will do what is best.

I liked that thought, but what then did Jesus mean, when teaching about prayer, about the **importunity** or persistence of one who sought a desired answer at night from his neighbor ? The Message translation expresses it this way, *"If you stand your ground, knocking and waking all the neighbors, he'll finally get up and get you whatever you need."* Luke 11:8

We all know that our prayers are not all answered in the way we want them to be. As we begin to look to God for help with specific challenges, there are a few things we need to check out about ourselves first. **1.** Does God want this done? **2.** Can I surrender my own idea of what he should do? **3.** Am I really in the right relationship with God?

When we clearly and honestly answer these questions, then we are more ready and flexible to learn what God's will is for the matters at hand. It is then that God can mold us into the vessel which can receive his answer. He can help us when we are not trying to tell him what to do.

Regarding the persistence issue, it means not pounding on God's door, but diligently asking ourselves those personal questions. As we think through the matter we are concerned about, new insights emerge about it, and also about ourselves. In a way, prayer is its own answer. It affects us and the kind of person we are becoming, as we humbly ask what God's will is, for us, and for the bigger concern.

So first, we **ASK**. This means finding the words or thoughts to define what we want to happen. It may be only a groan! So often, being able to express the need well clears our head, and provides at least part of the answer. It is like focusing sunlight through a magnifying glass to a hot pinpoint that is capable of starting a flame on tinder. *"ASK"*, Jesus said, "**and it shall be given you.**" He does not say how or in what form it is given. Very often we may be looking for the answer in one direction, but it arrives from a very different one. Be open to fresh, surprising ideas.

He also said: **"Seek and you shall find."** We are to look or watch for the answer, expectantly. It is not always just delivered the next day like the newspaper, for nothing is said here about when it will come. We live in an impatient and fast paced world. We think stop lights stay red too long and we complain when we end up in the longer line at the toll booth. Sometimes we must seek and watch for a long time – at least it seems long to us. God's time is not our time, **but it is the best time.** One reason why it may take longer than we want is maybe we aren't ready for the consequences that go far beyond the answer.

"Knock and it shall be opened unto you," is the final word. Are you ready for the answer? It is an act of faith, perhaps brand new faith, to knock, taking action that the WORD wants you to take. The disciples asked the WORD to teach them to pray. Perhaps they did not expect to learn that prayer means we must be ready to participate in the answer; that God does not just drop the whole solution into our laps, but in fact wants us to be an active part of it.

Are you really ready to pray and to be a part of the answer? God knows what you need, before you ask, and is always waiting to give you **good things.**

"And it shall come to pass that before they call, I will answer, and while they are yet speaking, I will hear." Isaiah 65:24

Lassiter

PSALM 86

Does that name mean anything to you? It does if you have read <u>Riders of the Purple Sage</u> by Zane Grey, published in 1912. It was the definitive western novel of that era and a blockbuster hit. It still is a great read.

Zane Grey, who may be considered the greatest writer of western novels, said that he desired to chronicle the historic events of the West, but that the full truth could not be told without including the idealism and dreams in our hearts that motivate us all. "Life without ideals is not worth living," he said. He was writing in the years leading up to and including the First World War – the 'Great War,' a time of hard materialism and bitter realism. The aftermath of the war was horrible, seemingly with no place for romance, which he called **another name for idealism**. That perception, however, proved to be the perfect place for the hope he could express.

His core belief about the times he lived in was expressed in Wordsworth's poem, "The world is too much with us." He was aware that much of life seems to be like the parallel rails of railroad tracks. One rail could be the physical events around us; the other deeper, more abstract meaning which is harder to understand.

Such was my thought as I stood next to a very likable scientist on our tour of the Arches National Park. Looking at the incredible scenery, he commented, "Just a bunch of rocks." That's how he saw it.

Zane Grey wrote about his love of the West, with its vastness, contrasts, violence, color, wildness, struggle and beauty. He found in his characters the strengths to really live their ideals, and so become great individuals overcoming major obstacles. He believed that his characters and their actions were secondary to the rugged and beautiful physical settings of the West. He could express in very picturesque language the relationship between man and nature and the wonderful experience of living in the open.

One such scene in the book was of a huge balanced rock standing over the narrow mouth of a box canyon which ascended into a magnificent upper valley. The culmination of this novel includes the hero, a former gunman named Lassiter, laying his guns down on the trail and managing to push the great stone over so that it crashed down, killing the pursuing villain and totally sealing the canyon shut forever.

This is all going through my mind as my scientist friend and I are looking at a huge balanced rock on the Windows road in Arches National Park. There it stands and I like to think that Zane Grey saw it too, all 3500 tons of seamless Entrada sandstone perched on a pillar pedestal rising 100 feet in the air. The supporting pillar is a much softer rock which is gradually being eaten away by the wind driven sand and the infrequent rain. Someday it will surely fall, but who knows when? This year? Next year ? 5 years ? 10 ? 20 ? 100 ? 1,000?

In <u>Riders of the Purple Sage</u>, a balanced rock brought justice and judgment to the evil one, settling the human conflicts and making all things right again. I stood watching this balanced rock, wondering when it would fall and also which way would I run if it fell right now? After a few moments, since it did not fall, I thought about the unpopular subject of judgment. How will my life be judged? How will yours?

I turned away, and walking down the trail in this somewhat uncomfortable frame of mind, found real hope in Hebrews 9:27: *"As just as each person is destined to die once and after that comes the judgment, so also Christ died once for all time as a sacrifice to take away the sins of many people. He will come again, not to deal with our sins, but to bring salvation to all who are eagerly waiting for him."*

What a great difference this fact makes when we consider the finality of our lives and what we are told will happen on the **Great Day**. There need not be fear of punishment or harsh judgment for those who have understood and accepted the life and sacrifice of the WORD. **Judgment Day is already in the past for those who believe.**

It would be quite an event to see that big old rock fall in my lifetime. It seems unlikely but it could happen, and perhaps no one will see it at all when it does.

Our faith tells us that there is to be a much greater event than that. It will be the greatest event of all time when the WORD returns, and judgment will fall upon the nations.

 "Even so come quickly Lord Jesus."
Revelation 22:20

At the foot of the trail I turned and looked back one more time just in case it was time for balanced rock to lie down. It wasn't.

Just a bunch of rocks indeed!

Thirst

II SAMUEL 23:13-15

When were you the thirstiest in your life? What was the best tasting water you ever had?

Pipe Springs National Monument, Utah, is a fascinating place. It proves once again how important good water is in human affairs. The spring is on the 'Arizona Strip,' a vast isolated landscape that lies between the Grand Canyon and the Vermilion Cliffs of Northern Arizona. It is so arid that it seems uninhabitable and lies about 200 miles south of the high plateaus of central Utah. Up there, plenty of rain and snow percolates down to a hard shale underground pan and flows southward to the base of the Vermilion Cliffs. There, after flowing that long distance, the water is forced to the surface of the land in a few places like Pipe Springs.

It is said that for 12,000 years ancestral Native Americans were sustained by this life giving spring of water in the midst of this demanding high desert. Then Mormons arrived and established a tithing ranch there. Its purpose was to supply food for the large construction crews who were building the Mormon Temple and other building projects in St. George. Their arrival and plans created necessary adaptations by previous users, not always friendly.

Nothing was more valuable there than the water. In 1870, two 2 story sandstone buildings facing each other were built. They were complete with gun slits, built as a protective fort facing a small paved courtyard with large wooden gates to allow entry of horses and wagons. The main spring was covered by these buildings and a sluice trough controlled and carried the precious water into a working creamery. The water then poured out of the building into holding ponds for watering livestock and irrigation of gardens. As many as 2,000 head of range cattle were herded nearby. The creamery was fresh and cool enough to preserve milk and produce cheese and butter.

Every two weeks butter, cheese and cattle were taken north to feed the laboring crews. In 1870 the first telegraph office in the area was opened and run by Eliza Luella Stewart, connecting them **electronically** with other Mormon outposts. The entire enterprise became a very successful business venture, all because of the good quality water that came underground from so far away. We need water. We cannot live and thrive without it.

Watching that cool, clear water flowing through the sluice in that old fort's creamery, I thought about its power to unite or to divide people. If used in the right way, it can create tremendously good things and relationships.

A great story that is unfamiliar to some is found in the Old Testament. It is about water and the best kind of loyalty in relationships. King David and his best mighty men were awaiting battle with their enemies, the Philistines, who were encamped in a valley near Bethlehem, David's home area. *"David longed for water and said, 'Oh that someone would get me a drink of water from the well near the gate of Bethlehem !' So the three mighty men broke through the Philistine lines, drew water from that well and carried it back to David. But he refused to drink it. Instead he poured it out before the LORD. 'Far be it from me, O LORD, to do this!' he said. 'Is it not the blood of men who went at the risk of their lives ?' And David would not drink it."* II Samuel 23:13-15

At first this might seem insulting that a much desired gift gained at such risk would be poured out on the ground, but it really reveals the quality of great relationships and great leadership.

It was **Spiritual**. Perhaps you can remember the wonderful taste of certain water from your past lifetime and you know that it takes you back to the very roots of your being. The taste of home is in your brain cells, in your indelible memory connected to the time, place and people of your life then. It may be indefinable, but it is a part of you, of your very soul. It is something that can never be taken away from you and is of great value to you alone, spiritually. You can hardly describe how wonderful it tastes.

It was *Sacrificial*. He would not drink this gift, for it was too holy, and could only be given to the LORD. It was not just the desired water, but the efforts of those who loved him so much that they went through enemy lines to get it. *"He poured it out before the LORD,"* considering it as holy as the blood of sacrificial lambs given in the temple. He would not break the solidarity with his men to his own physical satisfaction. The memorable taste of the water and the dangerous efforts of his men were enough to satisfy his longing.

It was **Sacramental.** The solidarity and equality with his men was sacred. It is easy for charismatic leaders to forget where they came from and the many contributions that have been made for them by others who may not receive any recognition. He avoided the common pitfall of failed leaders who develop a cult of their own personality, losing touch with the very people who helped to make their success and rise to power.

Real leadership, the best leadership, never becomes detached from the people, the community and the faith that eventually brought their devoted efforts into contact with the opportunities that God had prepared for them.

Such is the nature of this Spiritual, Sacrificial, and Sacramental act. It is so completely satisfying that David's descendant, the Messiah, the WORD, spoke of his desired relationship with us. *"Whoever drinks of this water will be thirsty again but whoever drinks the water I give him will never thirst. Indeed, the water I give him will become in him a spring of water welling up to eternal life."* John 4:13

Living Water

READ JOHN 4: 1-26

Dead Horse Point State Park in southeastern Utah, towers 2,000 feet above the Colorado River. In the 1800s, the Point was a good natural corral where wild horses rounded up by cowboys could be safely held, since there is only a 30 foot wide access point. Horses would be herded there and a brush fence could be built to contain them. The sheer cliffs were an effective barrier to escaping. But there was no water.

Now, tourists can stand on those cliffs and see spectacular panoramic views that dwarf human history. There are hundreds of miles of colorful mesas, canyons and standing volcanic plugs, created by natural forces over millions of years. It is awesome and incredibly beautiful to the observer. It is silent there too, with no sounds of civilization. But there is still no water up there, so dehydration, illness and death can result quickly.

Karl, an octogenarian cowboy who 'cowboy'd' there before it became a state park, spoke about his love for "The Big Country" as he called it. He was full of interesting stories, talking for hours on end about what it was like before the government got involved in trying to manage the whole thing. He was fascinating.

He "run cattle" out there on the free range in the old days, both for himself and also for a large cattle outfit. Sometimes he barged the cattle down the Colorado River to greener pastures in the watered box canyons. Then along came Hollywood with its many movies and commercials made out there for 20 years. Karl was often the head wrangler for the horses and could advise on all questions about the dangers and settings.

That was interesting, of course, but his real life was a cowpuncher with real opinions and knowledge about how humans and animals could survive in such a dry place that received very little rainfall each year.

He reminisced about the importance of water management and the building of pothole cisterns to hold water for the stock. These had limited effectiveness because of heat and evaporation. Better than that, best of all actually, was what he called **living water**. Flowing streams or natural springs were of greatest value if they could be found. **Living water** produced the best life conditions in these rocky, dry pastures of scrub, where the juniper trees were hundreds of years old but only 15 feet tall.

Karl said he was not a religious man, and he never quoted the Bible, but his words reflected the truth spoken by the WORD to that thirsty woman in Samarian country: *"If you knew the gift of God and who it is that asks you for a drink, you would have asked him and he would have given you living water . . . Everyone who drinks of this water will be thirsty* *again, but whoever drinks the water I give him will never thirst. Indeed the water I give him will become in him a spring of water welling up to eternal life."* John 4:10-13

The woman knew about our physical need for water, but met and heard from the WORD about our equally important spiritual thirst. She had met the Living Water, the answer to our soul's dehydration. It is one of the greatest meetings in the entire Bible. It was the true situation of her life and of ours also.

There is a thirst within us that only the WORD can satisfy completely and eternally. He can become an artesian well within us, welling up reliably, for as long as we live. It is far more than a simple change of attitude by our own efforts, as good as that may be. It is the life-giving reality of Christ in us, turning us from the dusty, dry internal search for meaning, to an outward flowing of life, love and laughter. And, you don't need to hoard or save this **Living Water** in a stagnant pothole pool. He is there to refresh you constantly.

Like the woman at the well going about her daily chores, we may think only of literal things, facts and events. These occupy our thoughts and energies much of the time. These may obscure the surprises given by the **WORD** who wants to meet us wherever we are and teach us about the Kingdom Country within. It is the bottomless well of **Living Water** of higher things that he makes possible when he lives within us. Drink deeply and live!

Genesis

PSALM 86

Where did we really come from? Deep questions like that are stirred to new personal inquiry when traveling in Castle Valley, Utah. You may stand on a high mesa with sheer cliffs dropping away for hundreds of feet, and walk in dinosaur tracks said to be 150 million years old.

A native Navaho teacher described their view of history as a people to our group. He believes in the land bridge migration from Asia. His living sense of their ancient spiritual life and the sacredness of the desert are new ideas to me. Their religion is entirely rooted in nature, so he began his lesson by asking the earth and sky for permission to speak.

Their four holy colors are black, blue, yellow and white, which all appear frequently in their artwork with symbolic designs which he compared to American quilts. The belief in these colors is very ancient, indicating their migration from the dark north to the blue northwest, then to the yellow of sunny California and finally to the white of the desert. They maintain their language and still practice in the ceremonies of healing and blessing.

His message revealed the very long history of the Navaho, which contains some very sad chapters. The Spanish arrived in the southwest in the 1500s, searching for the cities of gold. They brought Christianity and took over most of the Colorado Plateau. Then the Europeans arrived, trapping beaver for the pelts so much desired in England.

In 1863 the Navaho nation was decimated by these business ventures and the survivors were relocated to Ft. Sumter, New Mexico. There, in the mining fields, they learned metal working, and became highly skilled craftsmen with silver and turquoise.

They maintained their faith through these changes and in 1868 were allowed to return to their homelands. They were free but were kept on a reservation. The children were forced to learn the English language but the Navaho language is still spoken today. It was made famous by its use as a military unbroken true code, used by wartime American troops as shown in the film Windwalkers.

As I listened to his presentation, some of the perceived romance of the old west faded away. In our modern world, diversity is a respectable and frequently used word, but it was not known that way in the 1860's when the West was being won. Hearing this version of our history, being expressed out of a culture that was uprooted by the westward expansion, raised new questions in my mind. Looking at the splendor of a sunset on the Vermillion Cliffs with sunlight reflecting the diverse shades of coral, rose, amber and copper, I wondered; "How do we relate to those of a different culture, especially when they have something that we want?" In an election year this always raises big discussions, sometimes heated, about values, rights, prior claims and especially property or money.

Diversity among people is an undeniable fact of life, and we find many new challenging chasms to cross when learning what others believe and practice. It is not always easy to find **common ground**, those areas of genuine agreement. How tolerant should we really be of other viewpoints? Am I willing to change mine? If so, how much, when and why?

And what of our faith in God, our loyalty to Jesus Christ? How do we execute what the WORD told his followers to do: *"Therefore go and make disciples of all nations, baptizing them in the name of the Father and of the Son and of the Holy Spirit, and teaching them to obey everything I have commanded you."* Matthew 28:19 As we read further, we see that they did go out, very aggressively, and ran into all kinds of different situations. Leaving everything that was familiar to them, they encountered totally new people, religions, customs and countless risks. Strange cities, unknown territories, different languages and deeply rooted political systems confronted them at every turn. The book of Acts is a rich tutorial about living your faith in a complex and diverse world.

They, like us today, sometimes saw a door slam shut violently with a resounding crash. This, however, is common ground to everyone, happening to all of us in some way. We all have disappointments in our lives, religious or otherwise, and that is a point of contact among us.

From our Judeo-Christian heritage, Rabbi Marc Jaglinzer eloquently wrote: "The first stage of life is to accept the fact that time inevitably closes some important doors. We have to realize that we cannot go back; we cannot break these doors, we can only brace ourselves against them. Closed doors, whether a person has closed a door or a door has been closed, involve a redefinition of everything we are comfortable with. We must be willing to redefine our roles and our relationship with others so that we may create brightness in life that will enable us to enter the next room. The courage to move forward in spite of closing doors, to explore new options and open new doors, enables us to enter a new stage of life." Newsletter –Temple Shalom, Middletown, Rhode Island

These well spoken words reflect the complementary colors of diversity, and how it can be not just tolerated, but celebrated. There is wisdom to be learned from other's informed viewpoints. We may all learn to listen to them with interest. We can do this, you know, without compromising our own beliefs, and our lives are much richer for it.

Let us return to the accounts of those first century Christians going out with courage, empowered by the Holy Spirit, into new places strange to them. As those early missionaries grew in experience, they learned that when they were weak before God, they would be strong in the world. A patient and quiet reading of Acts 5:12-42 reveals one of those head-on collisions between diverse cultures, but with emerging wisdom from the differences. The resolution came through the efforts of Gamaliel, a rabbi and highly respected teacher of the law. He was also one of Saul's (later St. Paul) teachers. He knew history and had seen confrontations and slammed doors before. He was a man of faith, a faith born of experience with the same God that the apostles were preaching about, along with their new message of Jesus Christ.

Change sometimes is difficult, isn't it? Gamaliel was of a different conviction but he found common ground with the new messengers. It served both his purpose of keeping his own group together and the apostles' purpose as well, of being free to go forward. Apparently he did not fully accept their teaching, but his words were strong and influential on those who would have killed the new teachers. Here is what he said:

 "Therefore, in the present case I advise you: Leave these men alone! Let them go! **For if their purpose or activity is of human origin, it will fail. But if it is from God, you will not be able to stop these men; you will only find yourselves fighting against God."** Acts 5:38-39

In that wise statement, we find a lot of encouragement for our own personal lives and witness in the fast changing world. If our cause is only by human effort, it cannot succeed. But if it is of God, it cannot fail, regardless of what happens to us.

What is the takeaway point here? It is this. Own your well thought-out faith in God and the WORD. Own it deeply in your soul, and always be willing to share it with others – remembering that sharing is a two-way street. Truly – if the bridge between diverse viewpoints is of God, it cannot fail.

Jars of Clay

JOHN 13:2-5

There is constant evidence of the past winter throughout the high desert. The effects of erosion cause the beauty to change each year as new shapes and colors are exposed. Artwork on the National Park lodge walls shows Native Americans thousands of years ago learning how to live when the summer heat turned to winter's cold.

Included in the display are the precious artifacts of their life and times. Among the most interesting are their spear points, baskets, storage pots and primitive cooking tools. Split-twig figurines date back about 10,000 years. What were those people like? What did they believe?

One replica pot can be picked up and carefully held. It was serviceable and quite heavy.

Then the words about the potter in Jeremiah come to mind: *"But the pot he was shaping from the clay was marred in his hands; so the potter formed it into another pot, shaping it as seemed best to him . . . Like clay in the hand of the potter, so are you in my hand. (says the Lord)"* Jeremiah 18:4-5

Pots and vessels are mentioned throughout the Bible as very necessary tools for living, such as the water pots at the wedding at Cana. We also can find great meaning in seeing ourselves as clay in the hands of the LORD. A little serious thought can reveal to us how we are marred and need to be reshaped. I once watched a potter at his wheel, shaping the clay with his wet hands into an attractive vessel. As he nearly finished it, a small stone was found in the lower side, and to my dismay, he crushed the creation down and started all over.

It was customary in Jesus' times to conceal treasure in clay jars which had little value or beauty and did not attract attention to themselves and their precious contents. Likewise, our bodies may be plain and fragile, but the inner treasure of God's Spirit and power is of supreme value, giving us his strength and endurance.

For what purpose is the vessel of your life shaped? Is the treasure of the WORD within? Are you half full or half empty?

There are contrasting examples of vessels and their purposes in the scriptures. One is found in John 13:2-5. *"After that, he (Jesus) poured water into a basin and began to wash his disciple's feet, drying them with the towel that was wrapped around him."*

The disciples had seen the LORD do many amazing miracles and use his huge popularity to teach enormous crowds about the Kingdom of God. This humble action of foot washing had to be truly surprising to them. It strikes right to our hearts to read his words; *"I have set you an example that you should do as I have done for you." John 13:15* **This is the vessel of joyful service, being willing to do menial tasks for others, after his example to his closest friends.**

A second vessel is a very different kind. We read in Matthew 27:22;24 about Pilate trying to resolve the question, *"What shall I do, then with Jesus who is called Christ?"*... *"When he saw that he was getting nowhere but that instead an uproar was starting, he took water and washed his hands in front of the crowd. 'I am innocent of this man's blood.' He was saying, 'It is your responsibility.'"* **This is the vessel of denial and refusal to stand up for the Lord. The phrase 'washing my hands of it' comes from this verse.**

That day after seeing the ancient pot, I purchased a small replica that sits on my window sill now, a reminder that regardless of our age or situation God wants to shape us. If we will let him, there will be caring service and great music in our hearts, *"In thy presence God, is fullness of joy; at thy right hand there are pleasures for evermore."*

A wise man once commented, "If you want to know where you can grow in experiencing Christ, just ask yourself, 'Is there one service thing I said I would never do? Am I willing to do it for Christ's sake, or is that a mar on the vessel of my life?'"

GPS A person I highly respect has lost much in her life. She once handed me a handwritten card with these words: *"But we have this treasure in jars of clay to show that this all-surpassing power is from God and not from us. We are hard pressed on every side, but not crushed; perplexed, but not in despair; persecuted, but not abandoned; struck down but not destroyed. We always carry around in our body the death of Jesus, so that the life of Jesus may also be revealed in our body."* II Corinthians 4:7-10

Stairs

2 GENESIS 28:10-22

The view from Dead Horse Point State Park in Utah is astounding. In every direction you can see magnificent vistas of mountain ranges, deep canyons and flat top mesas. There is a wide stone stairway that descends several dozen steps to a vista point that looks down 2,000 feet to the Colorado River. It is all well named **The Big Country.** Everywhere you look is a new world of color, beauty and spectacular landscapes. Those steps take you away from your little neighborhood and into a new expanding world. Any worries you have, become as pebbles on the pathway.

The Genesis scripture above records a life changing vision by a man in distress. *"He had a dream in which he saw a stairway resting on the earth, with its top reaching to heaven, and the angels of God were ascending and descending on it."* Genesis 28:12 Jacob encountered the LORD who offered him a covenant agreement, a new life and great future. Jacob's response was, *"Surely the LORD is in this place and I was not aware of it."* v.16 It was clear, two way communication between the man in great need and our God who answers. Listen up!

The stairways of our lives can be sacred spaces, where new faith and good changes become realities. In fact, changes for the better usually require movement and seldom happen in sedentary situations. The inspired decisions that move us forward have an exciting energy that empowers us to go from one level to another. Of course, stairways are useful for both ascending and descending. We usually think of **reaching up** to God, but as many know, the way to God sometimes may be **down**, descending way down. He may be found in the cellar of our lives sometimes instead of up on the highest observation deck.

In either case, up or down, one thing is sure; we are talking stairways here, not escalators! Not the convenience and ease of just riding along, but the satisfying effort and growth from taking it step by step. There is a powerful verse found in I Peter 2:21; *"To this you were called, because Christ suffered for you, leaving you an example, which you should follow in his steps."* This is the origin of the popular question, **WWJD**?

It is true that we are saved by God's grace because of what Christ has done for us. On the next page is one illustration of a stairway process we can use to build the muscle and health of maturity in Christ. It is based on II Peter 1:2-10. Jot your own notes along those steps. Enjoy, and don't worry if you have to go back down a few steps sometimes to remember how God is working in your life!

"Do you want more and more of God's kindness and peace? Then learn to know him better. For as you know him better, he will give you, through his great power, everything you need for living a truly good life, he even shares his own glory and his own goodness with us ! And by that same mighty power he has given us all the other rich and wonderful blessings he promised, for example, the promise to save us from the lust and rottenness all around us, and to give us his own character. But to obtain these gifts you need more than faith. You must work hard to be good and even that is not enough. For then you must learn to know God better and discover what he wants you to do. Next learn to put aside your own desires so that you will become patient and godly, gladly letting God have his way with you. This will make possible the next step, which is for you to enjoy other people and to like them, and finally you will grow to love them deeply. The more you go on in this way, the more you will grow strong spiritually and become fruitful and useful to our Lord Jesus Christ. But anyone who fails to go after these additions to faith is blind indeed or at least very shortsighted

and has forgotten that God delivered him from the old life of sin so that now he can live a strong, good life for the Lord. So, dear brothers, work hard to prove that you really are among those God has called and chosen, and then you will never stumble or fall away. And God will open wide the gates of heaven for you to enter into the eternal kingdom of our Lord and Savior Jesus Christ." LB

Desert Anthem

PSALM 90

Standing on the sheer cliff at 6,000 feet overlooking Castle Valley, Utah, there was utter silence except for the occasional raven's "caw – caw." The valley stretches before you, several miles in width and length. The rising early morning sun slowly warmed the rocky cliff and in sundial fashion, gradually moves the shadows eastward. The aspens on the highest peaks all around us were turning that magical gold. It was an awesome time and place of eternity. The dinosaur tracks in the rock before us were said to be 120 million years old. They called to mind the pessimistic words of Stephen Vincent Benet. "Life is not lost by dying! Life is lost minute by minute, day by dragging day, in all the thousand, small, uncaring ways."

In complete contrast to that viewpoint, the intense value of that day's experience rose in praise to God.

Karl was with us. He is in his eighth decade as a genuine, old west cow puncher. He tells us that in the early 1900's, 50,000 cattle and 250,000 sheep roamed this valley. He talked for six hours, telling legendary stories, fascinating in detail and color. He spoke of cattlemen/sheep men disputes, rustlers, posses, gold miners, and taking cattle to rich bottomland grass down by the Colorado River. He looks like his history, with hat, boots, and cowboy gear. He laughs with the richness and joy of life. "There," I thought, "is who I wanted to be when I was a kid." Sometimes I think I still do.

The natural beauty of this place was beyond description. The remote immensity and sense of eternity seem overwhelming, bringing tears of breathless wonder. It was a taste of infinity. I did not want to leave and knew that if my life ended that day, I would have seen the old West of my dreams. Added to the scenery, was the human side of Karl's commentary on how people hoped, worked, lived and died here.

Is it any wonder that we need and believe in the Eternal God, the Ancient of Days? "Where *were you when I laid the earth's foundations? Tell me if you understand. Who marked off its dimensions ? Surely you know! Who stretched a measuring line across it? On what were its footings set, or who laid its cornerstone – while the morning stars sang together and all the angels shouted for joy?"* Job 38:4-7

Even now as I relive that day and write these words, the delight of just being alive each and every moment of our lives is a **natural high** bringing praise from our deepest souls into the present instant. We give thanks because we can so live that we are pierced to the heart with the sheer blessedness of everyday existence.

This "Desert Anthem" was written by Paul Hummel, a cattle rancher that we knew in Colorado. He was a Christian cowboy who lived daily in the wild beauty of the high desert and the Rocky Mountains.

> *When the Master of the mountains*
> *Rides the round-up of life,*
> *And cuts out all who wear his brand*
> *In dust and dirt and strife;*
> *I don't want to be a maverick,*
> *Or wear the brand of sin,*
> *But I want the marking of the Cross*
> *And so be counted in.*
> *To be herded to the Home Ranch,*
> *Where pastures are all green*
> *And the water comes a'gurgling*
> *The flowery banks between.*

So may I live, so may I do
Wherever I may be,
That all the promises so sure
May always be for me.

 "Only in returning to me and resting in me will you be saved. In quietness and confidence is your strength." Isaiah 30:15 <u>NLT</u>

Natural or Artificial?

PSALM 101

 "After this conversation, Jesus went on with his disciples into the Judean countryside and relaxed with them there." John 3:22

Walking with the WORD in the world can be a wonderful, life-changing experience. It is far more than seeing new scenery, even as enjoyable as that is. It is an important internal journey as new insights from him bring freedom and power into your mind and heart.

A vast expanse of the southwest is known as the Colorado Plateau. The peaks, plateaus, canyons and volcanic peaks cover 150,000 square miles over Utah, Colorado, New Mexico and Arizona. Someone has called it, "Godly architecture where water, ice and wind become Michelangelo."

It is huge. One circle tour of 5 National Parks is 900 miles and that doesn't even cover the Grand Canyon. Even after an inspiring week of driving and looking at this beautiful desertscape, only a fraction of it all has been seen. It is remote and stupendous. "When in the absence of everything you know, or thought you knew, you find the real essence of our very soul." The National Parks, America's Best Idea by Ken Burns

All this beauty has been there for thousands of years, a very important part of our nation's natural resources – not to be dug out of the ground, but to be cherished. A speaker on the subject noted the lack of young people who visit the National Parks because, he thought, "They seem to prefer the virtual, make-believe world of their electronics instead of the real thing. They like to be able to manipulate their games rather than be awed by the majesty of Creation."

How sad.

To adore the majesty of the Parks a bit more and to see the scientific value of them is to return to our deepest roots as humans. "The exposed geology, the changing colors, the proof of the origin of our planet (300 million years), the ancientness, the light in the desert – these are the spiritual signs of our very beginnings, our birth as a world. It is mysterious and we must deal with our real factual history. Mystics go to the desert so that they can **hit on all eight cylinders**." Spirit of the Desert narrative by Ken Burns

Stay in that wondrous place for a while and you will meet your own soul, whom you may not have seen for a while. When you consider the pioneers who first settled and lived in these places, you find modern comforts to be quite unnecessary. Long before I was able to travel and see it for myself, I read the Zane Grey novels over and over. He loved the West and found the vastness, contrasts, wildness, violence, color, struggle and beauty of it to reflect various aspects of our human existence. Grey believed that even the most hard-shell realist needed ideals and dreams to live for. He believed that life without ideals is hardly worth living.

After a great trip through the Colorado Plateau and its ageless enormity, a lot of new awareness enters your thinking. It is a new sense of **smallness** but there is also a growing sense of being a part of it all. Then a new sense of **bigness** about life's possibilities emerges. Every day exceeds the one before and you look forward to tomorrow. There is a new power to live into the future. The American pioneering spirit becomes real.

The scale of this contrast is sharp and clear. At the Fredonia, Utah, visitor's center is a recreated, very small domed pioneer hut. It is just a single room made of earth and rocks. It contains a small woodstove, bed of corn husks, simple table and one chair. The dirt floor is paved with flat rocks. Everything is homemade, including the rough board door with leather hinges and latch.

The next day after that visit, we flew the length of the Grand Canyon into Nevada. The trip ended at the Mandalay Bay Hotel and Conference Center in Las Vegas. Walking through that hotel and staying in a luxurious room after spending ten days out there in God's architecture was surreal. Las Vegas appeared as a giant pinball machine of crowds, noise, traffic, opulence, circus acts and excesses of all kinds.

The desert and canyons offered the silent, eternal beginning and meaning of life. They recalled the primitive vision in our hearts that we are a part of God's eternal purpose, plain and simple.

The city, however, seemed to live only for the present instant with **no** sense of eternity. The artificial stimulation of the five senses eliminated the possibility of awakening the sixth sense. It was a shocking contrast that stretched the mind trying to make the distinctions between **natural or artificial, eternal or temporary.**

Well, not to be too abstract, is it easier to hear, know and follow the WORD in the desert or in a city like Las Vegas? Of course the truth is that whether we are in the desert or the city or anywhere else, the WORD is with us.

Even at his brutal crucifixtion, the criminal on the cross nearby said *"Jesus, remember me when you come into your kingdom".* The WORD replied, *"I tell you the truth, today you will be with me in paradise."* Luke 23:42-43

Hoodoos

PSALM 121

As our tour bus entered Zion National Park, the director said, "No words can describe what you are about to see, so we will just play some music as we continue into the canyon." He was right.

The music that was composed for the Ken Burns's book and film, The National Parks-America's Best Idea, is genuinely American and hauntingly beautiful. The melodies are the **emotional metronome** of the early American West, reminiscent of the majestic wilderness and the timeless eternity of it all. To be free from daily routines and the perceived limits of our lives is a good time to find once again the essence of our soul.

Words can never fully describe this Godly architecture set to music, but here is one effort : "The exposed geology, the changing colors, the proof of the origin of our planet (300 million years), the ancientness, the light in the desert, these are the spiritual signs of our very beginnings, our birth as a world. It is mysterious and we must deal with our factual history. Mystics go to the desert so that they can hit on all 8 cylinders." Tauk Tour Literature

When you are beyond all familiar surroundings, the mind tries to organize and make sense of all the new information and experience. Walking along the rim of Bryce Canyon, one can see a vast expanse of **Hoodoos**, the ghostly shapes of sandstone cliffs now eroded by the geologic jackhammers of wind, water and ice into thousands of standing shapes. Seeing them calls the playful imagination into action. What do they resemble? The mind is tempted to find familiar shapes there – animals, statues, pirates, saints, pioneers, cathedrals, or as one laughing person said, "My boss at my last job."

The 18 mile drive along the rim stirs the imagination again and again. In addition to all the strange, unfamiliar shapes, new thoughts about the future arise from the soul, awakening creative impulses about your life's destiny. The ancient cliffs recalled ancient scriptures, *"Be ye transformed by the renewing of your mind."* Romans 12:2

So often we experience losses of great importance, such as beloved people, events and situations. Old securities are replaced by new challenges. Changes come throughout our lives, some are desirable and some are not. Some of them strengthen our faith, others test it severely.

Seeing the marvel of the **Hoodoos** and contemplating the many changes in life, recalled another long forgotten verse of scripture, *"For God's gifts and his call are irrevocable"* Romans 11:29 More ancient and eternal than these magnificent cliffs and canyons is the open generosity of God who calls us to accept his gifts and grace. He has always called us and will continue to call us. It is an **irrevocable invitation.** He has not changed his mind about this.

A certain man was excellent in retail business and his small store prospered for several years. He was located between two much larger buildings in a connected block with no alleys between. Times changed. One of the larger buildings opened up with great fanfare and competitive products. The large building on the other side followed suit. Soon the small business was caught in the pincer grip of the two giants. His old successes were history. It appeared his business future was going to be very short. He began to wonder if his business life was over. Had he lost his competetive spirit ?

He had not survived for so long and well because he was easily discouraged. He had faced challenges before. He thought new thoughts, returning to the original calling, creativity and passion of his beginnings. He decided to rename his store and soon a new attractive sign went up over his simple door between the two big box neighbors.

His new name? **MAIN ENTRANCE**

Our circumstances and certainties can change, sometimes very quickly and radically, but the gifts and calling of God are irrevocable. Let us use the brains that God gave us to find the future he has in store. After all, he is already out there, waiting.

If God intends

PSALM 103

Two small towns exist on a long, remote stretch of highway near the border of Arizona and Utah. The scenic backdrop is beautiful cliffs and mesas but the towns are cluttered looking places of nondescript buildings, stockyards, construction equipment and unkempt yards. It is an eerie place, with prominent biblical names. We had no desire to stop there, and would likely be unwelcome if we did. It is a closed society where polygamy is practiced even though it is illegal. The reality of this place is far, far different from any romantic image seen on stage or screen. Our tour director said that the older men marry all the younger women, leaving the younger men without a good social future. The houses we can see from the distant highway are large, indicating multiple rooms. Our bus zoomed by and we did not look back at this sad situation.

Our speaker continued with excellent thoughts. He said that these people are known as Fundamentalists, similar to the group in Texas a few years ago that was in the news over aberrant behavior. That group, by the way, appears to have moved away and disappeared. They are not related to any other church organization, but try to continue to practice very old customs. "This is what can happen," our speaker says, "When people refuse to change, clinging too much to certain old ways of the past. They do not grow and adapt to more advanced and healthier customs."

God intends for us to become new creatures, over and over again as our lives mature. If we are in the WORD, "**. . . old things are passed away, behold all things are become new.**" II Corinthians 5:17 Life is meant to be an unfolding adventure of discovery, learning and growth. We may think of this as **progressive revelation**, the way God can reveal the new chapter in our lives as we become open and ready to move forward. It is amazing, isn't it, how a person can grow from infancy into a strong life of faith and accomplishment? A writer once interviewed the mayor of a small town and asked, "Were any famous people born here?" "No," was the reply, "only babies".

While life may sometimes seem to be random in its daily unfolding, the WORD helps us live it as God intends. We do not need to be discouraged about ourselves. Perhaps we have been unsuccessful in overcoming our weaknesses and are not making progress. If so, we may find the greatest support in Christ. If we say to him simply, "Lord, I do not want to be this way anymore!" and truly mean it, he will do for us what we cannot do for ourselves.

Sincere prayer is very important, as it will be the scaffolding around your concerns, making the big difference as Christ changes you, bringing the healthy growth you need. His presence brings courage, strength and good ideas.

Each stage of growth does not diminish or eliminate the one just previous. It is more like building a sequence of successive and rewarding fulfillments. Each one embraces the previous ones, building strength and reliability. We can always go back and remember the ways the WORD has helped us grow through past challenges. In fact, we should do that often. He can and will do it, if we just ask, and of course, respond sincerely to his perfect plan.

Perhaps that does not seem dramatic enough for your highest hopes, but it works.

 "For we are taking pains to do what is right, not only in the eyes of the Lord, but also in the eyes of men." Romans 8:21

The WORD At The Shore

Singaways

NUMBERS 6:24-26

In the early rugged days of the western National Parks, adventurous people could take the Union Pacific railroad to wild canyon vistas for sightseeing trips. In the 30's and 40's, young people, many of them college students, found summer work, staffing the hotels and cabins, and driving the touring cars and busses on the primitive roads. This is said to have been quite scary as the modern safety features such as guard rails and seat belts, that we have today, were not required.

Historic pictures of those days also show those young people entertaining guests in the evenings with music, skits, plays and games, all a part of the way people vacationed then. They also prepared and served the meals and performed other camp duties such as laundry, janitorial and outdoor maintenance. What a great summer job for those young people – full of adventure, new experiences and meeting new people in such beautiful country.

One of their customs was known as the **Singaway**. When the guests were aboard the busses or touring cars ready to depart for the train depot, all the staff would gather outside and sing them on their way. It was a genuinely happy conclusion to living in the wilds for a brief time. Wonderful old photographs show smiling, happy young people standing by the departing vehicles, voices raised in song.

It seems like an unforgettable farewell blessing, a benediction among new friends. I wonder what songs they sang? Perhaps it was :

God be with you 'til we meet again!
By his counsels guide, uphold you;
With his sheep securely fold you;
God be with you 'til we meet again!

Does such simple, sincere pleasure in our relationships exist today? Can we still simply enjoy life like this? Where does such joy come from? What kind of people or organization can do this so naturally?

Some people just seem to have the personality and fun outlook that cheers others up, and helps them with their challenges, (such as realizing that vacation is over). Others have to work at it. Which is YOUR viewpoint?

Each of us can use a real lift from time to time. It is good proven wisdom that when we lift someone else's spirits, we are also helping ourselves. A friend is fond of saying that **Positivity** is infinitely more powerful than **Negativity.**

Our place in the world is much better when we really remember these words by the WORD, *"Come unto me, all ye that labor and are heavy laden and I will give you rest."* Matthew 11:28 Allow those words to dissolve slowly, like a lozenge, in your thoughts. They will ease your burdens and bring good mental rest. If you memorize them, you will carry with you a **five minute vacation** for your busiest days. The WORD continues, *"Take my yoke upon you and learn of me, for I am meek and lowly and you will find rest to your souls."*

Easy does it! Do it his way, and sure enough, music will come forth as you go about your way. *"And the peace of God, which transcends all understanding will guard your hearts (emotions) and minds (thoughts) in Christ Jesus."* Philippians 4:7

 "Don't fret or worry. Instead of worrying, pray. Let petitions and praises shape your worries into prayers, letting God know your concerns. Before you know it, a sense of

God's wholeness, everything coming together for good, will come and settle you down. It's wonderful what happens when Christ displaces worry at the center of your life." <u>TM</u>

What a great philosophy of life!

Enough

 Wherever you may go in this wide world and whatever challenges you may face, God says *"My grace is sufficient for you, for my power is made perfect in weakness."* II Corinthians 12:9

No one has ever said or sung it better in music than composer/performer Ken Medema.

Lord of the Troubled Sea

Lord of the troubled sea, when I'm walking through deep waters you alone can be dry ground beneath my feet.

Lord of the flames, when I'm walking through the fire you alone can shield me from the heat.

And Lord of the desert, when I walk across the burning sand my mouth with living water you can fill.

And Lord of the storms, when the wind would tear my moorings you alone are my word "Peace be still."

That's why I say, you are my all in all. You are the air I breath, the song I sing, the help I call. And when I know I just can't cope, you alone are all my hope, for your grace is enough for me.

Lord of the night, when I walk through the darkness, you are my pillar of fire to lead me on my way.

And Lord of the light, when the burning sun would scorch me you are my Jonah's vine to shield me from the day.

And Lord of the body, when I just can't stand the hurting, you are my healing and relief from pain.

Lord of the mind, when legion brings insanity; you are the Word that restores me once again.

That's why I say, you are my all in all. You're the air I breathe, the song I sing, the help I call. And when I know I just can't cope, you alone are all my hope, for your grace is enough for me.

A Great Lake

*"Many waters cannot quench love; rivers cannot wash it away.
If one wre to give all the wealth of his house for love, it would
be utterly scorned."* Song of Solomn 8:7

The five Great Lakes combined are the largest freshwater resource in the world. They provide clean drinking water to over 30 million Americans and provide 1.5 million jobs, generating $62 billion in wages. Every school child should learn about them, including the HOMES acronym for their names. It is an invaluable resource to our nation.

A visitor to just one of them, Lake Erie, was so impressed with its size and beauty; he took a small bottle of its water home and put it on his mantle. **That's Lake Erie!** he would tell his friends. Truly, a person standing on its shore can see that it is a big lake, but just HOW big is far beyond that tourist's viewpoint.

It is 241 miles long, 57 miles wide at widest point, and over 200 feet deep at its deepest. It is fed by 7 rivers, including the Grand River. Its total surface covers 9,940 square miles. It drains east through the Niagara River and spins huge hydroelectric turbines at Niagara Falls. Canadians call the lake their "thunderstorm capital" where they can watch dramatic lightning displays. The Toledo Blade described it as "Big, flat, beautiful and subject to unpredictable rages." It is a powerful engine of weather, commerce and thoughtful observations. It really is a **Great** lake.

Great is not a word that should be overused. It should be reserved for the exceptional things we are privileged to experience and know in our own lives. The word appears hundreds of times in the Bible describing the immensity of God's love for us. In Mark 5 we read the miraculous story of the man healed of "an evil spirit." After Jesus healed him it says: *"As Jesus was getting into the boat, the man who had been demon-possessed begged to go with him. Jesus did not let him, but said 'Go home to your family and tell them how great things the Lord has done for you and has had mercy on you.'"*

Whatever our individual Christian experience has been, it is intended to also be shared with **others** as well. In this way, God's eternal love and power will continue to work through us, even though our faith may seem as miniscule as that little bottle of water on the mantle. God's love and power are boundless, infinite!

A **great** hymn was written in 1875 by a young man in desperate need. Samuel Trevor Francis stood on a bridge over the Thames River on a very windy, rainy night, watching the dark waters flowing by. He thought of ending it all right then and there. He came so close to the edge that he drew back in real fear and he later wrote; "Suddenly a message was borne into my very soul: You do believe in the Lord Jesus Christ. '"I do believe,'" he replied to the divine encounter, and **his life turned right around** in that fleeting instant. He went on to write a vivid picture of the" Deep, Deep Love of Jesus"- the immensity of Christ's liquid love, overwhelming and submerging us in the depths of His tender, triumphant heart. (Then SINGS my Soul by Robert J. Morgan)

Yes it is great to look out at the surface immensity of Lake Erie and understand a bit of its full power. But how much different is the experience of being **in the water**, just as being **in** the deep, deep love of God. This meditative question opens rich new thoughts as I walk along the southern shore of Lake Erie. It brings to mind the scriptural record of Jesus walking by, and on, the Sea of Galilee.

Now, these twenty centuries later our own **sea,** Lake Erie, provides the opportunity to meet the WORD and reflect on his continuing interest in our lives and concern. What happens within us at such times brings insight, healing and peace as we face future challenges.

 "Jesus sat by the lake, . . . and he told the multitudes many things in parables." Matthew 13:3 Many great new things happened for many people there. Great things can happen for us too, now in our time, here, by this **Great Lake.**

Stranger or Friend ?

MATTHEW 14:22-36

Living by the lake is very interesting, because of its constantly changing action and its influence on the soul. The basic idea of this book came from walking along its shore and letting the rhythms of nature synchronize the thought life. The old gospel song, "The Stranger of Galilee" by Leila N. Morris, often comes to mind as I consider the effect of learning about Christ. Walking by the water seems like life itself, sometimes very peaceful and other times very turbulent. Perhaps you have seen someone at a distance down the beach and wonder who it is. Then as you draw near you recognize a friend and find companionship instead of fear.

Jesus walked by, and on the lake Chinnereth (meaning harp shaped). We know it in the Bible as the Sea of Galilee. Many of his life experiences and teachings were shared there by the multitudes that followed him . . . The miracles of many fish and the calming of the storm were more evidence of his divine power. Many were healed by him near its shores.

The "Walking on the Water" scripture, in Matthew 14:22-36, speaks to our fears and anxieties in life. The disciples were afraid of capsizing in the lake that night, but then the Master came from his prayer time, walking to them on the water, and calmed the storm. Gloria Gaither once said about this miraculous experience, "Christ can walk on the chaos of my life."

Are you familiar with the hymn *FINLANDIA ?*

Be still my soul! Your God will undertake
To guide the future as He has the past.
Your hope, your confidence let nothing shake
All now mysterious shall be bright at last.
Be still my soul ! The waves and winds still know
His voice who ruled them while he dwelt below.
(Katherine von Schlegel)

The great lake is descriptive of God's grace ~ eternal, deep, wide, full of life and constantly active, expressing him in different ways and in all conditions. The lake is like our God who is trying constantly to get through to us who are limited, distracted and earthbound on the shore. His waves shape and cleanse our minds, always working to calm our fears and smooth off our rough edges. Through the WORD whom we know as Jesus Christ he offers us the help we need to fully become what he has created us to become.

He is not a stranger, though we may not recognize him at first. The disciples were scared out of their wits that night on the stormy Sea of Galilee. The storm was crashing all around them and they were battered by the waves. It was 4 a.m. and they must have wondered if that night would ever end. When they saw him coming toward them they cried out in terror, *"It's a ghost!" But Jesus was quick to comfort them.*

 'Courage, it's me. Don't be afraid.'"<u>TM</u>

This is the WORD at the shore, not a stranger after all.

Horizon

LUKE 5:1-11

A certain man who felt hopeless asked his doctor for medication. After the examination, the doctor wrote something out on his pad, handed it to him and said, "This should help." When he took the prescription to the drug store, the pharmacist handed it back to him and said, "I can't fill this one." It read, "Go to the lakeside for a whole day to watch and think."

Mystified, he went, studied the shoreline at his feet, and watched the waves and the rhythmic swell of the deep. At first it all seemed pretty dull and time was dragging, so he watched the sky, the clouds sailing by and the changing light. He began to look inward, remembering people and events that had greatly benefited his life. The list was long. Then, quite unexpectedly, he noticed the horizon, that apparent line that separates the earth and lake from the sky. He saw the distant offing about three miles away where the curvature of the earth limits more direct, distant sight. The horizon seemed hazy and vague. He thought about the obvious, but forgotten fact that our planet is constantly turning on its axis and eternally revolving around the sun.

Clouds temporarily obscured the horizon line, but then, to his wonder and delight, the disk of our sun seemed to touch the water and many brilliant colors of a glorious sunset enameled and gloriously sharpened the horizon line.

His heart beat quicker, hope rose again in his chest and he realized he, too, had a horizon in his own life, heart and soul. He was touched by the wonder of God as he remembered Jesus' words, *"The kingdom of God is **within** you."* Luke 17:21 He had a future after all, sometimes subtle and obscure, but very real. He remembered the words of Albert Schweitzer: "He comes to us, as he did to those disciples so long ago by the side of the sea and we shall know who He is in our own experience." Quest for the Historical Jesus

It seems that in our human ways, we may have seen the mighty works of God in past experiences but still wonder if he can do another great thing now. We may even feel that God has done enough for us and has no further plans or resources for the new challenges! How wrong could we be? Of course we trust him because we have seen great things in the past, but we may be blind to his ultimate power yet to be used. If it was true before, it is still true now and if it is his will and purpose, then even greater things are yet to be done.

 How's your internal horizon? *"The kingdom of God is within you."* Luke 17:21

Dawn

MARK 2:13-17

The winter of 2011-12 in Northeast Ohio was the warmest on record. As a result Lake Erie did not freeze over, leaving the shore unprotected and allowing the westerly winds, storms and waves to crash unimpeded, on the beach. Much of the sand was washed away to the east, leaving many piles and rows of small stones, a sort of **stone beach.** This was not an encouraging sign for barefoot time in the summer.

The dawn of March 24, brought a welcome northeastern stiff breeze and wave action, bringing some sand back and slowly rebuilding our shore. So this **non-winter** of 2012 actually resulted in a nice soft summer beach at Hallwood.

Seeing the **scripture of nature,** I was reminded of the truth of God's renewal for us. When we have felt vulnerable with cold darkness in our souls, it is the time to read the Bible again. As we do, we realize that it isn't just another good self-help book with suggestions for personal improvement. It is God speaking to us and is full of his power. It is a written record of his actions and as we put the words back into action, his power is at work healing and restoring our faith. A good example of that insight is found in Lamentations 3:23: *"Because of the LORD's great love we are not consumed, for his compassions never fail. They are new every morning, great is your faithfulness."*

Like the beach, our faith can be rebuilt even if devastated, as we prayerfully walk and study the WORD. It's a three-way conversation among 1. The written Word, 2. your inquiring heart, and 3. The living WORD who referred to himself as **Comforter:** *". . . he shall teach you all things, and bring all things to your remembrance, whatsoever I have said unto you."* John 14:6 <u>KJV</u>

God wants to do a new thing in your life today. Do you perceive it? What is it?

 Watching that sand being brought back grain by grain, I thought once again of God's great promise in Isaiah 43:18-19:

"Forget the former things; do not dwell on the past. See I am doing a new thing! Now it springs up; do you not perceive it?"

Forecast

I CORINTHIANS 15

It is mid-January of a very unusual winter on the north coast of Ohio. It has been mild and snowless, but today, finally, a big winter storm is predicted. A little snow is falling now and the temperature is slowly dropping.

Skye, our Collie, and I walked the beach, beautiful in its own way every day. Today the winds are rising and the waves are growing in size and sound, rolling and crashing in every few seconds. Clearly, the storm is coming from the west with rapidly increasing power. Yesterday the beach had long windrows of many small stones, brought in over the past month. Today, however, all are covered by beautiful slopes of new sand. It runs for hundreds of yards, widening here and there to accept the new offerings of the crashing sea.

The forecast is for wild weather coming in. This is important information, and contrary to Mark Twain's comment, there **is** something we can do about it. We can get ready! This is the **coastline code**. Safety depends on preparedness. Not a year passes that some unprepared boaters suffer, sometimes fatally, from accidents out there on the deep, perhaps because they ignored the warnings.

I love the power of the waves and stand in awe of them, as they roll in from as far as the eye can see. They are forming somewhere way out there, out of my sight. By the time they reach our shore, their foaming crests are 5 or 6 feet high. As just a speck of human flesh in this drama, I thrill to the prelude, in anticipation of the storm. Shivers! I remember the legendary story about the great environmentalist, John Muir. Somewhere in northern California a big storm of wind and rain came through. Muir is said to have forsaken the comfort of his warm fireside and cabin. Instead he went out, climbed a big tree and lashed himself to it so that he could be a part of the storm.

Isn't this our calling as Christians even when the world seems to be ending? Luke 21:25-26, records these words of Jesus: "*There will be signs in the sun, moon and stars. On the earth, nations will be in anguish and perplexity at the roaring and tossing of the sea. Men will faint from terror, apprehensive of what is coming on the world, for the heavenly bodies will be shaken. At that time they will see the Son of Man coming in a cloud with power and great glory. When these things begin to take place, stand up and lift up your heads because your redemption is drawing near.*"

Well I do not know about the timing of the end of the world, but I know that many people seem to think it is imminent and to be feared. As I watch the roaring and tossing of the sea this morning, I have a healthy respect for it, but I do not fear it as long as I am where I should be. It represents the Power of God to me, preceding and warning us of the storm to come. This Power is good, calling us to get ready. It is the knowledge that history has a purpose and that for those who follow the LORD, the big ending is really the **big beginning**. How will this happen and when? No one really knows, but we do know there will be surprises when our **redemption draws near.**

Are we fearful of that great day? Let us remember that the WORD calls us to courage, his courage. This kind of faith in him doesn't depend on always needing the strokes of others to keep it going. It doesn't acquiesce in the face of loud opposition. It doesn't fold under pressure, tarnish under time, die under duress, fade under technology or rot under moisture. This is not some phony life-style. Rather, it always lifts Christ up, knocks down barriers, marches over objections, overwhelms pessimism, gobbles up cynicism and tramples under skepticism. It always dares to challenge society's low standards and raises it up to God's Standard. It may never be popular, convenient, stylish or wealthy, but when the fighting is done, the battle over and the dust settles, it is the LORD who will remain standing. Let us be standing with him!

The world's forecast is usually gloomy. How is yours? Do you need courage? *"Wait on the LORD: be of good courage, and he shall strengthen thine heart: Wait, I say, on the LORD."* Psalm 27:14

Pure Water

JONAH 1

Lake Erie has been here for many thousands of years, according to geologists. Some say that 14,000 years ago its southern shore was our State Route 84 - South Ridge Road about 3 miles away. Probably Native Americans (Erie Tribe) and wildlife made the first walking trail along that gravelly shoreline. Over time it became a road for horses, wagons, stagecoaches and finally, automobiles and trucks.

Walking along the present lakeshore, I wonder where our shoreline was when Jesus walked by the Sea of Galilee where so many wonderful things happened. His shoreline changed also and recently a fisherman's house, probably from the first century, was discovered a few miles inland from the current water's edge. It is still a living sea, as it was when Andrew, Peter, James and John made their living as commercial fishermen there.

Sometimes our lake is very cloudy and opaque, other times very clear. In either case, environmentalists wisely instruct us about PURE water and the dangers of occasional impurities. Unless you are a fish, don't drink the water!

These facts remind me of Jesus' well-loved words, *"Blessed are the pure in heart, for they shall see God."* Matthew 5:8 It's a wonderful core value in our lives as Christians, with a lot of personal meaning for each one. <u>The Message Bible</u> phrases it this way: *"You're blessed when you get your inside world - your mind and heart - put right. Then you can see God in the outside world."*

Or to put it yet another way, to the impure person, life is like a stained-glass window seen from the outside and it seems opaque. In contrast, the pure hearted person sees it from the inside with glorious sunlight shining through. He sees this from a transparently true and sincere motive.

We are all fortunate to know people of the pure heart perspective. Among other benefits, it is a great cure for boredom and cynicism. Learning to have a pure heart brings many new and interesting experiences to you. It's a great blessing when you suddenly can see things **with new eyes.**

Even in a long cold winter when the lake ices all the way over to Canada and all the world seems dull and unchanging, **purity of heart** can bring new enthusiasm and fresh insights. One surprise for me was to read a totally unfamiliar verse in the Bible, *"Who despises the day of small things?"* Zechariah 4:10

Truly, any of us can become bored with the mundane, such as days when nothing out of the ordinary happens. We may think we want excitement but real life teaches us the wisdom of appreciating those days when nothing unusual happens. These are days of **small things.** These are better, after all, than days of serious accidents or loss. There are many blessings in these **ordinary days.**

Tina, a friend of many years, has battled serious cancer for a long time. Recently she wrote saying that her last tests were **unremarkable and that's great news.** "I'll take **unremarkable every time, gladly,"** she said.

Well, God loves us and wants us to enjoy a truly abundant life with the **pure** heart and outlook Jesus taught about. Perhaps you have heard this parable by Bruce Barton that appeared in <u>McCall's magazine</u> in 1928:

"There are two seas in Israel. One is fresh and fish are in it. Splashes of green adorn its banks. Trees spread their branches over it, and stretch out thirsty roots to sip of its healing waters. Along its shores the children play, as children played when He was there. He loved it. He could look across its silver surface when He spoke His parables

"The river Jordan makes this sea with sparkling water from the hills. Men build their houses near to it, the birds their nests, and every kind of life is happier because it is there.

"Then the river Jordan flows on south into another sea. Here is no splash of fish, no fluttering leaf, no song of birds, no children's laughter. Travelers choose another route unless on urgent business. The air hangs heavy above its water and neither man nor beast nor fowl will drink.

"What makes the mighty difference in these neighbor seas? Not the river Jordan. It empties the same good water into both. Nor is it the soil in which they lie, nor the country round about.

"The difference is this. The Sea of Galilee receives but does not keep the Jordan. For every drop that flows into it another drop flows out. The other sea is shrewder, hoarding its income jealously. It will not be tempted into any generous impulse. Every drop it gets it keeps. The Sea of Galilee gives and lives. This other sea gives nothing. It is named The Dead and it is the lowest place on earth.

"Yes, there are two seas in Israel, and there are two kinds of people in the world."

"Each of us is now a part of his resurrection body, refreshed and sustained at one fountain - his Spirit- where we all come to drink." I Corinthians 12:13 TM

Ships

JONAH 2

Reading the Bible by the lake limns the reality of God's presence which we may forget but is always with us. Think of our Lord as he lived by his lake, the Sea of Galilee, his experiences, his friends, his miracles there. It is a new, wider doorway of thought into the newness and fullness of life that he always wants us to have.

Recently I looked up from the gospel of Mark and noticed a small rowboat drifting on the water. No passengers, no motor, just dragging a rope and drifting aimlessly wherever the wind and waves took it. It finally beached over by the break wall.

Then looking further out, I saw a Great Lakes freighter, fully loaded, headed west with a clear purpose. It had a destination, propulsion and a plan how to get there. It was an interesting contrast. **Drifting or driving? Aimless or purposeful?** Sometimes there are both kinds of voyages in our lives.

I looked down and read again Mark 4:3: *"That day when evening came, he said to his disciples, 'Let us go over to the other side.' Leaving the crowd behind, they took him along, just as he was, in the boat."* There are two things at work here. First, he needed time to rest for the next challenge. Secondly, the next challenge was on the other side of the lake, over there at the Gerasenes.

Out in the middle of the lake he could find some peace and quiet, **a sacred space** for the inner life of body and soul. We all need to take our rest before the next big challenge comes along. As someone has noted, even Jesus had to go and put a stout fence around some corner of time and space. A life that is too crowded to do that cannot be renewed and cleansed or fortified.

Did you ever notice how often Jesus says, *"Let us go . . ."*? For example, in Mark1:38, *"Let us go on to the next towns that I may preach there also, for that is why I came forth. And he went throughout Galilee."*

Are we not all tempted to stay right where we are spiritually? "This is good," we tell ourselves. "I have done enough. Let's just keep repeating the same stuff as before. It's so easy. I don't have to learn anything new. Why take any risks when you have a sure thing?" Some would call this the **hamster wheel** of a stale and very predictable life.

No doubt those disciples were running a successful fishing business, but when the Lord said, *"Let us go to the other side,"* they did so and life was never the same. Even when Peter tried to go back to the old life of fishing after the crucifixion and resurrection, the Lord was waiting for him on the shore.

What **other side** do you think of when you pray? What, or who is over there needing to hear or see the good word of the gospel from you? Yes, rest is good and necessary but its purpose is to gain strength for new tasks. Are you keeping your mind and heart in motion? Or have you put walls around the WORD, shutting Jesus into some little prison? It is his call to each of us, *"Let us go . . ."* He has new work and adventures for you and it will be a great experience, so when you have rested, get up and be ready to learn new things. Will you put up the sails and pull on the oars to take him to the other side?

> In simple trust like theirs who heard
> Beside the Syrian sea
> The gracious calling of the Lord
> Let us, like them, without a word
> Rise up and follow Thee.
> (John Greenlief Whittier)

 *"Do not conform any longer to the pattern of this world, but be transformed by the renewing of your mind. Then you will be able to test and approve what God's will is – his good, pleasing and perfect will."* Romans 12:2

Night Ship

JONAH 3

It's a gusty winter's night on the lake. High westerly winds are driving 4 foot waves to our southern shore. The sun has set by 5:45 leaving serrated trails of golden clouds which gradually surrender somberly to the blackness. Far out on the deep is a brightly lighted freighter - an incongruous sight of man's invention riding God's darkening sea. It is an amazing sight - that light out there in the distance. What a curious experience it must be for those sailors on their small lighted island of steel, in the midst of immense darkness on the swelling waves.

If I were out there on that ship on a night like this for the first time, (after my great desire to get off), I think the pessimistic musings of Matthew Arnold would come to mind:

> *Most men eddy about*
> *Here and there, eat and drink*
> *Chatter and love and hate,*
> *Gather and squander, are raised*
> *Aloft, hurled in the dust*
> *Striving blindly, achieving*
> *Nothing, and then they die,*
> *Perish and no one asks*
> *Who or what they have been,*
> *More than he asks what waves*
> *In the moonlight solitudes mild*

Of the midmost ocean have swelled
Foamed for a moment, and gone.

<u>Rugby Chapel</u>

That is existential despair, the hopeless feelings that some people sometimes have when discouragement or fear overwhelms them. "What's the use?" is the question, down deep in the soul.

Believe it or not, there is **secret strength** in such a feeling. When you **touch bottom** like that, you can learn new things about yourself and your situation. It is then that you are most open to the LORD who has the WORD of hope and truth for you. It is then that you are really ready to receive the help that you need.

Our earliest Christian brothers and sisters faced great dangers. It was to some of them that the letter of I John was written, saying: "*God is light; in him there is no darkness at all.*" And the answer we need continues: "*If we walk in the light, as he is in the light, we have fellowship with one another, and the blood of Jesus, his Son, purifies from all sin.*"

Isn't it true that you can only know what light is, after you have been in darkness? Everything may look alike and quite indistinguishable in the darkness, but light reveals the truth, it exposes whatever exists, whether it is good or bad. Just as darkness cannot exist in the presence of light, so hopelessness will not continue to exist in the LORD'S presence.

 Are you in the darkness of discouragement or fear? "*Walk in the light as he is in the light.*" I John 1:7

97

Storm

JONAH 4

We have been waiting for gentle spring for weeks now but the weather continues to be chilly and wet. Last night a most unusual, huge cloud moved easterly across the lake. Some said it looked like a giant whale, dark gray and right down on the surface. Then the wind began to blow hard bringing in a riveting cloudburst with frequent bolts of lightning stabbing the waves. This morning, however, there is an opposite strong wind from the northeast and the waves are crashing very high up on the beach. It is littered with driftwood and miscellaneous trash resting on new, multicolored sand. It is like the sea has finally gotten tired of waiting and decided to clean house.

As Skye and I dodged the rushing waves, Psalm 96 came to mind, *"Let the heavens rejoice, and let the earth be glad; let the sea roar and the fullness thereof . . . fear before him all the earth."* Even nature, or perhaps **especially** nature, knows and worships its Creator.

The time does come for housecleaning - and soul cleaning too. Duties long delayed suddenly must be dealt with. Do you know this? Suddenly inertia becomes high energy, procrastination becomes too burdensome to bear and good things happen! Neglected tasks become fun to check off the list and a fresh view of life springs to soul and mind, even if the weather is not balmy. It's a sea change of attitude.

There was a great day of fellowship here recently. Our whole big county has just one half-way house for women in recovery from substance abuse. It is a faith based work in one of our poorest neighborhoods. The few Christians who keep this work going love the Lord greatly and try to do his will in their corner of the world. Their director applied for a grant which was given, along with the proposal that an ecumenical work day do as much of the volunteer labor as possible.

The word went out and over 20 new friends showed up. There was laughter along with the scrubbing. Conversation empowered the paint brushes. Applause rang out as an old storage building surrendered to demolition. Good new fellowship was enjoyed along with nourishing food. It was a fun and productive day, an unusual day for us all as we worked and fellowshipped together with new friends.

It could be called a storm of high energy praise to the Lord, as the psalmist wrote, *"Great is the LORD, and greatly to be praised."* Like a good housecleaning, this **soul cleaning** was most enjoyable once we got started. Wouldn't it be great if everyone could read that twelfth chapter of Romans about the many abilities God has given to be used?

I guess even people of faith need a good bolt of lightning once in a while.

"In his grace, God has given us different gifts for doing certain things well." Romans 12:6

WWJD?

I PETER 2:21

It's a clear morning along the shore. Yesterday there was heavy snow and blowing, but today the sun is out. A foot of snow is melting away. Hundreds of dazzling white gulls are hanging out at the channel, finding some breakfast there, I guess. They look like a starched collar.

The lake is open water and some say it probably will not freeze over this year. It looks very unusual out there today. Most of it is ruffled with a textured look, caused by small sections of very thin ice that has not formed into sheets. However, along the shore the water is very smooth with gentle swells coming in. Here and there the smooth water extends out into the deep, looking like pathways through the ice. It is an interesting contrast, the determined effort of the cold air to freeze and immobilize the warmer water.

While watching this, a friend called, asking for prayer in dealing with cold financial realities which were threatening to take his home away. "What would Jesus do?" he asked.

This is not an easy question and many people are facing hard choices in their lives, financial and otherwise. Even turning to the Bible, we may not find specific literal answers to specific problems. What we can find however is a relationship with the greatest person who ever lived, and who can help us solve any problem. Speaking to the crowds, he said, *"Who of you by worrying can add a single hour to his life?"* Matthew 6:27 I often wish we could hear the tone of his voice and his accented words.

In our modern, pressure cooker world with its complex situations, we know that worry can really wear us down, weaken our immune systems and lead to illnesses. The cold and realistic demands and concerns that confront us can lead to paralyzing stress, freezing out the warmth we need to live productively and joyfully.

Researchers say that a little stress can be a good thing as motivation for new learning. It can sharpen your focus and make you more alert. We need just enough of it to prevent boredom and to find new creative ways to meet our challenges. This balancing of stress and faith might be seen as pepper and salt, the pepper of challenge matched with the salt of our response. Just as salt and pepper shakers are controlled by your hands, so are stress and faith controlled by your choices.

So I think the WORD is teaching us that we should not worry about the things which God will supply. We can really trust him but if worry interferes with that trust, we **ice up** and faith freezes.

Even when there are times that stress comes from sources beyond our control, we can still change the way we respond to it by **rebalancing**. There are ways to resolve your conflicts that you have not thought about yet. It is often said that solutions come to us when we are not thinking so hard about the problem. Also, we can help ourselves by eating right, being more realistic in our goals and breaking down big challenges into smaller elements. We can become more honest with ourselves about activities or habits. We can rediscover how helpful good exercise is to feeling better and thinking more clearly.

Mark Twain is credited with saying that a rut is **just a grave with the ends kicked out.** While our routines enable us to get a lot of important things done every day, let's be flexible enough to know that there is always a better way to get things accomplished. One man I know drives a different route to his office every day because it helps his brain see and think of new options to his business challenges. We all need to see new things and old things in new ways every day.

Looking at the lake again after writing these thoughts, I see that the ice is gone. The smooth, warmer more active water has won the battle and it is all flat out there now.

"But seek first his kingdom and his righteousness and all these things will be given to you as well. Therefore do not worry about tomorrow, for tomorrow will worry about itself. Each day has enough trouble of its own." Matthew 6:33

Icebergs

GALATIANS 5

In the summer, the sandy beach along our lake is warm and inviting but in the bleak midwinter it looks more like Barrow, Alaska, inhospitable and cold. The water begins freezing along the shallow shoreline. Then as winter winds drive in large waves, they dash up higher and higher, freezing into hummocks several feet high.

Walking along this winterscape, one can see large chunks breaking off and becoming isolated, drifting icebergs. No swimming today! Seeing this, and thinking about how to walk more closely with the Lord, I named some of those icebergs that can freeze your life: selfishness, discord, hatred, envy and the rest of the sorry list found in Galatians 5. Certainly, if we are to be friends with the WORD, we must acknowledge and deal with any obstacles that stand between us.

Of course, the obstacle may not be a big, serious character flaw. Sometimes we just get too far away from him, going it alone by neglecting our priority of prayer and meditating on his written word. If we lose touch with God, we lose the wonderful benefit of knowing his plan for our lives.

Zeal is a wonderful old word from the Bible. It means having an intense enthusiasm for something. When Teddy Roosevelt was a boy he was very close to his mother, Mittie, who faithfully took him to church. Then one day he became afraid of going inside the building. After some gentle questioning, Mittie learned that he had heard the minister read from the Holy Bible, *"The zeal of thine house hath eaten me up."* Psalm 69:9 No way was the little boy going to get caught and eaten by **zeal** whatever that was!

It's a fact of life, that over time we may tire and lose our zeal for the Lord's work. The New Testament deals with this situation in many places. What can you do when your energy and enthusiasm for the Kingdom are fading?

Recently I became aware of the weariness and burden of 'going it alone' and learning once again that we just cannot be all that God calls us to be when we freeze him out, relying only on our own strength and effort. Then, at an appointed time of worship, I gathered up many tangled loose ends and just handed the snarls to God. Great peace came into my heart once again as the icebergs melted. I felt **touched by his grace**.

Communion was served. Forgiveness touched my soul once again and relaxation eased my troubled mind. For a long time I simply walked in God's gentle and loving presence. If he could forgive my poor efforts, then I could see the future gradually opening up, with energy and hope.

"But he gives us more grace . . . Come near to God and he will come near to you." James 4:6-8

Shipwreck

ACTS 27:27-44

100 years ago, the Titanic sank in the North Atlantic, going down into the depths with 1500 passengers. Personal recollections of the survivors or their relatives recount a terrible night of fear and loss of life. Named after the Greek god, Titan, the enormous ship was thought to be unsinkable. It was a great tragedy and the retelling of it, along with a fictional love story, has made millions of dollars for the entertainment industry.

It is difficult to fully imagine the depths of the great bodies of water in the world. Looking out at the flat surface of Lake Erie, one might imagine it is all the same depth, but of course it is not. The surface is like your visible conscious mind, and below, is the invisible, powerful subconscious mind of deep mysteries and concepts.

Erie is the shallowest of the Great Lakes, being the farthest south when gouged out by the great ice sheet that moved southward from the frozen north. The northern Great Lakes are much deeper and hold the greatest collection of shipwrecks per square mile of any body of water in the world, with many hundreds of lives lost.

Many of the wrecks here have never been found, including the 1909 sinking of the M & B No. 2 railroad-car ferry somewhere between Conneaut and Port Stanley, Ontario. Down there somewhere, the 350 ft. steel ship with lost passengers still waits to be found.

For all of the Titanic love story and our romantic inclinations associated with the weather and these glorious lakes, we also must treat them with great respect for their sometimes dangerous power. Just as we enjoy the circus because it helps us deal with our fears as we watch others taking the risks, so is the lake fascinating. It reminds us of our human desire for adventure, and the healthy respect for danger that we must exercise while pursuing our dreams.

A certain man known to be caring and responsible became very troubled by family problems. It had been a buoyant and happy group but now a teenage child was giving a lot of grief and seemed to enjoy hurting his parents. This led to the further problems of bitterness and despair. The former good relationships were like a fearful, hopeless Titanic going down, down into the fathomless depths of loss. Other family relationships began to lose faith and sink as well.

The father was unable to sleep late one night after a particularly difficult evening. He was really at the **end of his rope** and dark thoughts of his own death began to form. He walked into his back yard and looking up at the stars cried out from his soul to God for help. In the mysterious way that God works, a quiet peace came over him. He went back inside, opened his Bible seemingly at random and read, ***"For God hath not given us the spirit of fear, but of power, and of love, and of a sound mind."*** II Timothy 1:7 KJV

The sense of God's presence and peace increased as he opened his life more and more to him. He described it as beautiful music and comfort as he realized how much more important this new relationship was than anything else in his life. His fears began to subside and his mind became **sound**, filling with strength and a new kind of love. He was renewed in spirit. He gained strength over his fears and troubles. In other words, he was healed.

As he learned to be at peace with himself, he researched more scriptures that opened that same door to the peace of God. He wrote them down on cards and carried them around with him every day. Whenever the old anxiety began to rise up again, or when tough confrontations threatened, he would take out a card and **pray** it. He returned again and again to the *"peace of God that passes all understanding."* Philippians 4:7

These verses became his mainstay and platform for living. He grew stronger and stronger in his faith, able to handle tougher problems than he ever had before. Here are some of his **lifeboats** when it seemed the ship may be going down:

 *"Fear not: for I have redeemed thee, I have called thee by thy name; thou art mine. When thou passes through the waters, I will be with thee; and through the rivers, they shall not overflow thee: when thou walkest through the fire, thou shalt not be burned; neither shall the flame kindle upon thee." Isaiah 43:1-2*

"Thou wilt keep him in perfect peace whose mind is stayed on Thee." Isaiah 26:3

"Rest in the Lord, and wait patiently for him: fret not thyself." Psalm 37:7

"Come unto me, all ye that labor and are heavy laden, and I will give you rest." Matthew 11:28

"Let the peace of God rule in your hearts." Colossians 3:15

"Let not your heart be troubled, neither let it be afraid." John 14:27

"Remember ye not the former things, neither consider the things of old. Behold, I will do a new thing; now it shall spring forth; shall ye not know it?" Isaiah 43:18-19

Sand

LUKE 6:47-49

What's not to like about sand castles? Getting down on your knees, close to the earth, digging with spoons, cups and toy tractors with the youngsters is great fun. Then go and find stuff like feathers for flags on the turrets and small red stones for the road to the drawbridge over the moat. This is great!

And did you know that for really creative adults, it has even become a niche eco-industry with national contests? Really good castle builders can make a living from it, creating unique, elaborate sculptures for business seminars, parties or weddings. **Sandcastle Days** at South Padre Island, Texas, draws 70,000 spectators. Each creation starts with about a 10- ton sand pile. One 8 -hour day is allowed for artists to finish their works of art. One such artist says, "This is art in its purest form. You can't buy it, you can't sell it, and you can't take it with you."

Then what happens, either to the child's simple castle or the elaborate sculptures? Along come winds, rains or waves and it's back to plain ordinary sand again.

Seeing these sandy creations on the shore brings to mind the Master's words, *"Therefore everyone who hears these words of mine and puts them into practice is like the wise man who built his house on the rock. The rain came down, the streams rose, and the winds blew and beat against that house, yet it did not fall because it had its foundation on the rock. But everyone who hears these words of mine and does not put them into practice is like the foolish man who built his house on sand. The rain came down, the streams rose, and the winds blew and beat against that house and it fell with a great crash."* Matthew 7:24

What a perfect story, told by the Carpenter who must have known the right ways and places to build a solid house. A place with smooth sand, maybe in a lovely canyon might look ideal in good weather, but unless you dig down to the shelf or rock beneath, it will not withstand the storms that will certainly come. Jesus requires two things for the right life structure. First, that we really listen, and secondly that we do put the knowledge into action: ***"Everyone who hears these words of mine and puts them into practice . . ."***

He was an expert craftsman and an expert in life. He knew what he was talking about and only on His truth can a well- built life endure.

George Buttrick expresses it so well : "A man's character is like a house . . . every thought is like a piece of timber in our house of life, every habit like a beam, every imagination like a window, well or badly placed; and they all gather into some kind of unity, seemly or grotesque. Of the two builders one is a thoughtful man who deliberately plans his house with an eye to the future; the other is not a bad man, but he is thoughtless, and casually begins to build in the easiest way. The one is earnest; the other is content with a careless and unexamined life." Interpreter's Bible volume 7

Near our sandy beach is **Resurrection House**, a faith-based residence where formerly addicted people can step down half way from professional treatment before returning to regular society. The director works and prays with them to rebuild their foundations on solid rock for the future. She says, "They cannot build a new life on the mess of the past. They need to become new creatures in Christ."

It is likely that most of us have some sand in our foundations, areas that are not as strong as they should be.

Paul wrote to the secular Corinthian church, *"For no one can lay any foundation other than the one already laid, which is Jesus Christ."* I Cor. 3:11

Remember the great old hymn by Edward Mote?

When darkness veils his lovely face
I rest on his unchanging grace;
In every high and stormy gale
My anchor holds within the veil.
On Christ the solid Rock I stand
All other ground is sinking sand,
All other ground is sinking sand.

<u>The Solid Rock</u>

Words in the Sand

JOHN 8: 1-11

The beach sand is constantly changing. Its colors composition and surface arrangements are always a work in progress, being rearranged frequently by the wind and waves.

Sometimes it is interesting to write words on the sand only to watch them be washed away. Secrets, ideas, names, regrets, questions can all disappear in a few brief moments. It is an interesting group topic to discuss **what** Jesus wrote on the ground, twice. Someone remarked that this was the only sermon Jesus ever wrote. It was when the Pharisees were trying to trap him in that touchy situation in John 8. What do you think? Some good artwork by Liz Lemon Swindle shows a compassionate Jesus writing with a strong, muscular hand on the ground. He looks deeply thoughtful, saying, *"Neither do I condemn thee, go and sin no more."* John 8:1-11 KJV

Writing words in the sand can be a healthy exercise. It helps to get something down in writing that you would really like to forget. **Write your worries in the sand but carve your blessings in stone.**

Walking barefoot on the sandy beach sends new ideas from the sensitive soles of your feet all the way up to your brain. Sometimes it seems you can actually feel them percolating like really good coffee, up through your body! It is a good time to reflect about your past decisions in your life experiences. Everyone has times of reflection, when we think about disappointments or missed goals and question why did this or that happen? Times when we wonder if we had made a different decision how things would be. I wish I had done that! I wish I had **not** done that! I wish I could do that again! **If I only knew then what I know now!** Yes, there is some of that in every life.

However, we need to keep it from becoming the dominant theme of our everyday living. If not, we will become pessimistic, always expecting the worst, which in turn can become the famous **self fulfilling prophecy.**

The great Gospel news is that we can get beyond those painful memories. In fact, we can learn a great deal from them by realizing that poor decisions may have been the best we could do at the time. Perhaps we didn't know any better. The important thing is to get it fully expressed and find the forgiving and understanding release of the WORD - *"Go and sin no more."*

One day I was doodling in the sand with my walking stick and created this grid which can be helpful in thinking through the decision process.

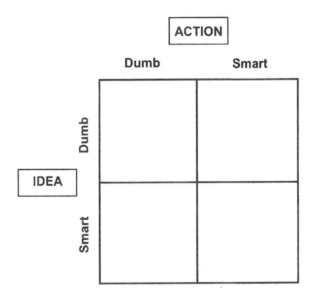

In each of the four squares, write **with a pencil that has a big eraser** the few words that capture the strongest impression. This works for any event past, present or future.

Example: Upper left - what would be the dumb idea and dumb action. Upper right - what would be the dumb idea and smart action. Lower left - what would be the smart idea and dumb action. Lower right- what would be the smart idea and smart action.

Just as in John 8:1-11, the critics or condemnation will disappear and your course of action will become plain.

President Theodore Roosevelt is credited with these powerful words: "It is not the critic who counts; not the man who points out how the strong man stumbled, or where the doer of deeds could have done them better. The credit belongs to the man who is actually in the arena, whose face is marred by dust and sweat and blood; who strives valiantly; who errs, who comes short again and again, because there is no effort without error and shortcomings; but who does actually strive to do the deeds; who knows the great enthusiasms, the great devotions; who spends himself in a worthy cause; who at best knows in the end the triumph of high achievement, and who at worst, if he fails, at least fails while daring greatly, so that his place shall never be with those cold and timid souls who neither know victory or defeat."

Dune

ECCLESIASTES 4:9-10

There are some small sand dunes along the shore, many of them with tall green and brown beach grass rustling in the breeze. One dune is a very good place to sit and watch the pastel sky above, the waltzing of the sea and to let the mind feast on great possibilities. The dune is a big comfortable box seat that shapes itself to you in this **theatre of nature**. This morning small lingering waves are curling in, with little white caps. The hollow tubes of water just keep rolling, smoothly unfurling from east to west, with tassels of golden sunlight on their crests.

The wind has crafted some small ridges on this particular dune revealing that two adult barefooted people were here recently. There are words and symbols drawn in the sand around their toe prints. I wonder what they were talking about? Who were they? Was it a good conversation? Big decisions? Problems solved? Plans about the future? When were they here? Daytime? Night-time? Where did they go? Will they be back sometime? Well, it's none of my business, but I like to think they were **in the moment.** Were these two here together, sensing the goodness and eternal life of our universe?

I picked up a handful of sand and let it slide through my fingers. How many grains of sand are there in the world? Uncountable, of course, as it says in Psalm 139:17 about our Creator: *"Your thoughts – how rare, how beautiful! God, I'll never comprehend them! I couldn't even begin to count them, any more than I could count the sand of the sea."*TM

How incredible to know that the persons who sat here, when first conceived, were as small as grains of sand. Yet they developed and were born. Now they have life and breath, plans and hopes.

Yes, God is good, and you can reflect that when there is faith, **believing that something you deeply want will come true,** that God loves us and will help when we ask from the heart. When we attune ourselves to nature's rhythms on this dune or any **sacred space**, a great conviction is known.

We understand deeply that all the passionate surges of our souls are evidence that we, too, are a part of God's creation. We are alive to the fingertips! God understood us even before we were born.

 Then magnificent thoughts like these rise up in our hearts: *"Hast thou not known? hast thou not heard that the everlasting God, the LORD, the Creator of the ends of the earth fainteth not neither is weary? There is no searching of his understanding."* Isaiah 40:28 KJV

Stones

PSALM 118 : 22 - 29

The huge storm that passed through here last night left a few new banks of pebbles and larger stones along our north coast of Ohio. They are varied in size and shape, some very plain, others beautifully striated with layers of color. A few of them, I am told, came all the way from Canada. As they crunched under foot, I remembered that stones are mentioned frequently in the Bible, as in the Old Testament question, *"What mean these stones?"* Joshua 4:6 As Israel crossed the Jordan into the Promised Land, Joshua had 12 stones brought from the middle of the river for an altar. It was a memorial to God's faithfulness to them so that future generations would not forget the nation's deliverance into Canaan

In the coincidental cycles of daily life, it so happened I had recently watched a vintage foreign film entitled "LaStrada," ("The Road"). It was popular in the 60's as were many other black and white foreign films. As seminary students in Boston, we would go downtown to a small theater to see them. "8½" by Frederico Fellini was another one. They were quite abstract and philosophical. I guess we thought they made us serious about life. Why they were popular I do not know, because as someone said, they were **99 percent despair and 1 percent hope.**

Anyway, La Strada came back into my thoughts and I recall only one hopeful line in it. The main character (played by Anthony Quinn) spoke one day to his simple assistant (played by Fellini's wife) when she was very sad and lonely. He picked up a common pebble from the road they were traveling and said, "Even this stone has a purpose."

She believed this and somehow it gave her comfort. As I considered the many thousands of new stones on our beach, it is true that I may not know what their ultimate purposes are, but they are here for a reason. It's a fascinating mystery, similar to our own search for life's purpose, short term and long range. The enormous popularity of the book <u>The Purpose Driven Life</u>, by Pastor Rick Warren, proves the massive interest in finding a great reason for living.

Recently an urban legend type of e- mail came around. Someone had lost a contact lens at a picnic on the beach. Everyone was on hands and knees looking for it when someone saw it moving along, seemingly by itself. On closer inspection, they discovered an ant carrying the lens! This caused great laughter, amazement and discussion as they imagined the ant's reasoning, "I don't know why I am supposed to carry this darn thing but it's my job and so I will do it to the best of my ability." Did he want a window in his anthill?

Who has not wondered about his purpose in this life? What teenager has not agonized about the choices he or she must make and what their life's trajectory should be? What adult, in later life, has not wondered about career changes or other commitments during the closing chapters of his life?

It can be a puzzle that calls for deep thought and interesting new explorations. Yes, it is important to know yourself and your abilities, but even more so to know God. As you learned in English 101, **every subject needs an object.** We cannot find the answers to our searching to be all we should be without a good relationship with God. Jesus taught us, *"God is a Spirit and those who worship him must worship him in Spirit and in truth."* John 4:23

An interesting verse for us is I Peter 2:4: *"As you come to him, the living Stone rejected by men but chosen by God and precious to him, you also, like living stones are being built into a spiritual house."*

Living stones! This means that the varied talents a person has can be assembled and reassembled into a life of joyful fulfillment if Christ is the capstone, holding it all together. The little stones on the beach are each unique and different individually seeming to lack a larger purpose. When integrated together under a single purpose however, just like your various skills, they have a unified, structural usefulness in the world.

So it can be in our lives. It's a thrilling discovery when someone prays and finds that they have an ability they never realized before. And it is an even greater discovery when the truth dawns on us that: *"It's in Christ that we find out who we are and what we are living for. Long before we first heard of Christ . . . he had his eye on us, had designs on us for glorious living, part of the overall purpose he is working out in everything and everyone."* Ephesians 1:11 <u>TM</u>

Are you looking for your future pathway? Here is a prayer for your journey.

> *In the castle of my soul*
> *Is a little postern gate*
> *Whereat when I enter,*
> *I am in the presence of God.*
> *I am where God is. This is a fact.*
>
> *When I enter into God*
> *All life has meaning.*
> *Without asking, I know*
> *My desires are even now fulfilled.*
> *My fever is gone*
> *In the great quiet of God.*
> *My troubles are but pebbles on the road,*
> *My joys are like the everlasting hills.*

So it is when my soul steps through the postern gate
Into the presence of God . . .
Big things become small, and small things become great.
The near becomes far, and the future is near.

Walter Rauschenbusch

You can find the right path by becoming good friends with the WORD.

 "I am the way, the truth and the life. No man comes to the Father except through me." John 14:6

Skipping Stones

I SAMUEL 17:32-58

In midwinter, the shore is bordered with millions of small stones. They are all sizes, shapes and colors. The winter storms roll them in from their ancient origins in the north. The heavier ones are on the fringe of the lake, the smaller ones farther up the shore and finally the sandy beach completes the seascape. It is Pebble Beach this time of year. Later, nature will build a slope of new sand over the rocky foundation.

One of the simple shore pleasures for people of all ages is skipping stones. Remember? You find a flat stone right sized for your hand, and with a strong side arm pitch send it across the surface of the water. It skips, 1, 2 3 or more times. Our grandson's record is 23 skips!!

The fascinating story of the shepherd boy David killing Goliath *"in the name of the Lord of hosts"* I Samuel 17:45 <u>KJV</u> *always* stirs new courage within us. He did this with a simple slingshot and five smooth stones which he picked up from the brook. Rereading this wonderful story I Samuel 17:32-58, while sitting by this stony shore, brings the thought that these ancient stones probably existed back when David accomplished his divine mission. So I picked up five smooth stones.

One was flat, so impulsively I skipped it out over the water - 5 skips! David had five in his arsenal, but only needed one. It was his weapon of choice rather than the King's armor and sword. **Each generation must find its own spiritual weapons.** For David it was a slingshot and one simple stone, which in the name of the LORD of hosts, did the work of five.

Everyone has their Goliath to deal with. He has many names, too numerous to mention but can always be described as a giant who stands in the way of God's total victory in our lives. He may be a bad habit, an insensitive heart, deliberate disobedience to God or something else. He is nine feet tall and carries huge weapons with which he has killed many. He is shouting curses at you. We can never match his size, weapons or ferocity, nor do we need to. Our approach is to run straight at him in spiritual warfare inspired by our certain knowledge that God will prevail.

Let us pick up 5 smooth stones and use the one that will drop the giant in his tracks and allow us to cut off his head with his own sword!

1. Submit yourself willingly to God. This is the starting place, for without God in your life, it will be **restless** as described in Deuteronomy 28:65-67 "*. . . you will find no repose, no resting place for the sole of your foot. There the Lord will give you an anxious mind, eyes weary with longing, and a despairing heart. You will live in constant suspense, filled with dread both night and day, never sure of your life. In the morning you will say, 'If only it were evening!' and in the evening, 'If only it were morning.'*"

2. Find a version of the Bible that you understand best and begin reading it as a priority. This may be called **praying the Bible** and will bring good new truth into your thoughts. *"For the word of God is living and active. Sharper than any double-edged sword, it penetrates even to dividing soul and spirit, joints and marrow; it judges the thoughts and attitudes of the heart."* Hebrews 4:12

3. **Pray naturally** from the heart as a way of life. *"Don't fret or worry. Instead of worrying, pray. Let petitions and praises shape our worries into prayers, letting God know your concerns. Before you know it, a sense of God's wholeness, everything coming together for*

good, will come and settle you down. It's wonderful what happens when Christ displaces worry at the center of your life." Philippians 4:6-7 <u>TM</u>

4. "We are not just human beings having a spiritual experience; we are spiritual beings having a human experience." We often hear this and know that we do live in both dimensions which need care and feeding. **Make sure your physical health is as good as possible.** Get balanced sleep, eat the right foods, and exercise every day to enhance your brain neurotransmitter activity. Actively engage with life and friends.

5. Every day, **overcome some fear** and develop your awareness of where God wants you to grow. He loves you so listen to him and when you are nudged by his spirit, go forward. Believe the fact that, "What lies behind us, and what lies before us, are tiny matters compared to what lies within us."

6. Here's an extra stone. What would you add ?

Beach Glass

"No discipline seems pleasant at the time, but painful. Later on, however, it produces a harvest of righteousness and peace for those who have been trained by it." Hebrews 12:11

What's with this beach glass? Is it really valuable treasure? It can be found all over the world but the northeastern United States lakes are said to be some of the best places to find it. This is due to the population concentrations over the past 300 years. Villages, then towns, then cities grew up around large bodies of water during the same time that commercial products became available in glass containers. Combing our lake shore is a growing hobby and has even become a minor cottage industry. Broken glass shards from bottles and other sources are naturally tumbled along the lake bottom and worn smooth. Some people say it's kind of exciting to find these among the many stones along the shore.

Wikipedia reports that the most common colors are green, brown and clear. The more rare colors are jade, amber and soft blue. Even more rare are purple, cobalt (as in Milk of Magnesia bottles) and aqua. Extremely rare beach glass includes gray, pink, teal, black, yellow and red (as in old Schlitz beer bottles). Orange is really scarce, found only once in about 10,000 pieces. I am not sure who keeps track of all this information, but it is said that these glass treasures are becoming rarer due to modern No Littering laws. Personally I doubt that the laws work very well, judging from all the plastic waste around the shore.

I confess that I, too, have spent time looking along the shore and have found a few pieces. I have learned, that one disadvantage of this is missing the rest of creation while always looking down! Why miss the sunrise while looking for pieces of broken glass? Which, after all, is greater? Well, there is room for both in life.

Perhaps you have heard the legend about the man who heard that a certain stone on the beach would magically turn ordinary metal into gold. All day long, day after day, he would pick up a stone, touch his metal belt buckle and then throw the stone into the sea so he wouldn't pick it up again. He grew weary and bored after days of effort and on returning to his lodging one night, discovered that sometime during the day it had worked! But when? And which stone? And where was it now? Somewhere out there in the pounding surf. He had forgotten to check every time and his treasure was lost.

Well that's just a fable so now turn your thought to the treasure of character in your life. Jesus spoke often about the important values which are at the heart of true happiness, ***"For where your treasure is, there will your heart be also."*** Luke 12:34 The treasure of knowing genuine love can result from the consistent and persistent tumbling of your emotions over the many challenges of life. It is a good discipline. It is far more than feelings or simply saying that you will do the right thing. It is **actually doing it,** even when it means sacrifice on your part. Sacrifice is a discipline and is usually irksome; only true love can make it a pleasure.

Let's face it. Selfish desires, sharp edged emotions, and various personal wishes can usually be worn smooth and manageable **only with the LORD's help.**

Father Michel Quoist in <u>Prayers</u> eloquently captures the conversation we might have with God when it comes to making the valuable treasure of character out of personal wishes, desires and temptations.

"Lord do you hear me?
I am suffering here, dreadfully, locked in myself. Prisoner of
myself.
I hear nothing but my own pathetic voice.

"Silence

"Lord do you hear me?
Deliver me from my mind and thoughts so full of myself, my
ideas, and my opinions. It cannot carry on a dialogue because
no words reach it except my own.

"Silence, and then he **hears** God's response.

"Son, I have heard you. I have long been watching your
closed shutters. Open them and my light will come in and
you will find me on the threshold. Why have you chosen
to be a prisoner of yourself? You are free. It is not I who
has locked the door. It is not I who can open it. For it is
you, from the inside who persist in keeping it so firmly
barred."

Yes, praying to the Lord for help is good, but he can only deliver us when we truly want him to, accept the discipline and make the needed changes.

Do you want great character? Then really give God something to work with, whatever it is, even the broken pieces of your life. The Lord will surely help you make quality character out of every desire and temptation. He can do it if you will let him, but you must open the door from the inside.

"At the time, discipline isn't much fun. It
always feels like it's going against the grain.
Later, of course, it pays off handsomely, for
it's the well-trained who find themselves

mature in their relationship with God. So don't sit around on your hands! No more dragging your feet! Clear the path for long-distance runners so no one will trip and fall, so no one will step in a hole and sprain an ankle. Help each other out. And run for it!" Hebrews 12:11-13 <u>TM</u>

Beach Paraphernalia

"I have loved you, my people, with an everlasting love. With unfailing love I have drawn you to myself." Jeremiah 31:3

How much stuff do we really need?

Lake Erie is sparkling like diamonds, there is a warm breeze, the sun is shining, and the sand is finally clean and inviting after a long cold spring. The waiting is over and people are arriving for their hours at the shore. Some bring just a towel, wearing a swim suit and flip-flops. Others, however, need wagons to lug all their stuff: umbrellas, chairs, coolers full of beverages, sand toys, picnic baskets full of food, armloads of firewood (or charcoal grills with charcoal and lighter fluid, of course), blown up rafts, blankets, games such as volleyball, snorkels, flippers, portable boom boxes and lots more of this hedonistic machinery. People think they will need all this stuff for a good time at the beach. I say, to each his own, but a wonderful motto for our modern consumer society should be **LESS IS MORE.** Remember the round "Three Blind Mice?" Here are some new words:

Too much stuff
Too much stuff
More than enough
More than enough
It's out of the closets and filling our space

It's growing and spilling all over the place!
We're tripping all over a terrible case of
Too much stuff! ***Too much stuff!***
Janet Lindeblad Janzen

Hey, I don't mind a few things to make life more fun, I do like Frisbees. I don't mean to be a wet blanket, but Jesus' words to that *"innumerable multitude by the lake"* in Luke 12:15 fit our American excesses very well: *"Watch out! Be on your guard against all kinds of greed; a man's life does not consist in the abundance of his possessions."*

As usual, his wisdom is opposite the generally accepted way of the world and its many advertisers and consumer products. We are all under a constant barrage of enticements to buy things to make us, and our lives more, more . . . what? I truly believe that wealth and ownership are good things only when they serve the natural purposes of God's Kingdom. Possessions fall in that category as well, but honestly, wouldn't you agree that many of them simply complicate our lives unnecessarily?

Much could be said about the excesses of our time such as the hoarders featured on television. And, I must admit, I sometimes like to watch "American Pickers" on the History channel, but I notice that the buyers actually buy very few things out of those old overflowing barns.

It is depressing to live in a neglected mess and God surely does not mean for us to do so. *"For God is not the author of confusion, but of peace . . ."* I Corinthians 14:33 <u>KJV</u>

Elisabeth Elliot, the iconic Christian missionary, was accustomed to living on, and with very little, while on the foreign fields of God's work. Someone once asked her if she collected anything? "Far from it," she said. "I am too old to be accumulating anything. I regularly attack closets and drawers with three boxes; PUT away, GIVE away and THROW away. It is great fun to clear the clutter from the closets and at the same time from my mind."

On any given weekend, there are about 30 garage sales in our town. Elisabeth continues her thoughts:" I'm all for people having garage sales, but I'm not much of a customer. As I survey what's for sale I wonder what it tells us about American life. Restlessness. Discontent. Ceaseless activity. Short attention span. All those cute but unnecessary gadgets, the expensive, unused exercise machines, the tables loaded with useless bric-a-brac. Yet the sales are popular, mostly I think, because people love to find a bargain, even if they don't really need the items.

It is a short step from this line of thinking to recalling the fourth commandment in Exodus 20:8: *"Remember the Sabbath Day to keep it holy."* It is about really resting from work and discarding the unnecessary distractions from real life. It is about cleaning our cluttered lives and returning to the sincere worship of God. *"**Therefore the LORD blessed the Sabbath day and made it holy.**"* It is a spiritual focus, time really given back to God and to focus on him who gave us all that we have or ever will have. It is a time to deepen our relationship with God and forget about the paraphernalia in our lives.

It is always an interesting conversation starter to ask someone "If your house was burning down and you could only save a few items, what would they be?" People who know the true values of life usually would not pick possessions like furniture, unless they had tremendous sentimental meaning. Scrapbooks of photos and heirlooms from their family saga usually top the list.

Helen Keller once described what she would want to see if she had three days of perfect eyesight. Her answers were wonderful. She would have chosen the faces of her loved ones, the church where she worshipped, and her beloved teacher Annie Sullivan as the most important choices she would make.

As I write this, I am watching a multicolored, beautiful sunset over Lake Erie. The sun is a brilliant orange orb dropping into a gray-blue, misty horizon. A shining golden pathway stretches from the western horizon to the shore just below our bluff. It is indescribable, yet there are many looking at their movies or magazines or sleeping instead of watching this day dying in the west.

That seems to be the prevailing way of life in the modern world. I was amused at the idea of a TV show like Wheel of Fortune giving away a week of silent, spiritual retreat in remote mountains rather than money or automobiles. No advertisers would support it and probably no one would watch it.

"A life lived without reflection can be very superficial and empty. That emptiness must be filled. It is a vacuum of not knowing the One who alone can fill the heart, so that man grabs repeatedly for some new stimulation, sensation, satisfaction to fill his time and slake his restlessness. His enjoyment is short-lived. What he got for Christmas or bought at a garage sale last year he soon tires of. It only furnishes him with goods for his own garage sale. He is like the man who wrote, *I denied myself nothing my eyes desired, and I refused my heart no pleasure. Yet when I surveyed all that my hands had done and what I had toiled to achieve, everything was meaningless, a chasing after the wind."* Ecclesiastes 2:10-11 Elizabeth Elliot Newsletter

Do you have the contentment of God's presence in your heart? Have you discarded any unnecessary paraphernalia lately?

How much is enough? Who needs anything more than what God has given us, and continues to give? *"Godliness with contentment is great gain."* I Timothy 6:6

Erosion

PSALM 51:15 -17

If you want to get lakeshore dwellers excited, just ask about erosion. It will always stir up opinions and stories, almost as much as whether the state or the residents really own the shore. Costly shore erosion happens but can be delayed, halted or reduced with thoughtful planning about our environment. There is one area just west of here where spring rain runoff from the bluff is directed down a stone filled gully and runs toward the lake. When it reaches the beach, however, it erodes away the sand which is carried away into the lake. But then eventually the lake returns it.

When we find ourselves alone with God in the wilderness times of our lives, it is natural to fear the process of erosion that works on our hearts and minds. We may wonder where our faith has gone, along with the high inspiration we have felt in times past. We all face this sometimes and through it we can learn that erosion is not only a breaking down process, but also a sustaining force that can restore and build up in a different area. It can be seen as one way that God builds us up through loss and a deepening friendship with him.

Sometimes very difficult changes come into our well-ordered lives. Health challenges, changing relationships, lost employment, diminished freedoms, are a few that can happen. When securities are lost, we may think, **I didn't sign up for this!** Why is this happening to me? We may wonder how a loving God can require such adjustments to our lives.

This is a good time to read again Jesus' words: *"If anyone would come after me, he must deny himself and take up his cross and follow me. For whoever wants to save his life will lose it, but whoever loses his life for me and for the gospel will save it. What good is it for a man to gain the whole world, yet forfeit his soul?"* Mark 8:35-36

God is always at work in our lives in hidden ways that we do not always understand, or like. We may watch physical certainties being eroded away, and struggle in our own way to find the reasons for that. We may be looking in only one direction for answers, but his response may come from a completely different place.

Probably you heard about the man searching on the ground at night for his car keys under a streetlight. A passerby stopped to help and asked, "Exactly where did you drop them?" "Over there," said the man. "Then why are we looking here?" asked the other one. "Because the light is better here!" he replied. How like us that is. We want to find our answers **where we want to find them**, instead of where they really are.

Jesus always spoke the truth, and also said **he was the truth.** John 14:6 Our plans and expectations are of own making in this society that worships overachievement. However, when we really follow the WORD, we find that he may have very different ways and ideas for us. Are you aligned with God's purpose for your life, regardless of what happens to you physically?

That is the saving knowledge for his disciples all through the ages. We are not in control as much as we like to think. There is a big difference between **existing and living**. If we just exist, that means that our lungs are working and our heart is beating. To **live** means to be alive in the world, knowing joy, fulfillment, peace and purpose. The WORD has told us how to have life, rather than just existing. *"I am come that they might have life, and that they might have it more abundantly."* John 10:10 KJV

If erosion comes into your life, it can be the opportunity to find life in Christ even richer than ever imagined. It is then that we can realize that our only possible gift to Christ is our life, just as his was to us. We can be like the sports team who lost a big game but held the attitude, "We were outscored, but we are undefeated!"

A friend, who has faced much erosion in her life, holds a great truth in her heart. She still can say, *"My grace is sufficient for you. For my power is made perfect in weakness. That is why, for Christ's sake, I delight in weaknesses, insults, hardship, persecution, difficulties. For when I am weak, then I am strong."* II Corinthians 12:9-10

If your life is suffering from erosion by fears, believe that God is building you up somewhere else, for your eternal benefit. Don't be afraid. To be habitually afraid of something may set the mental stage for it to become a reality that repels the positive work of God in you. Why not memorize the **whatsoever** scripture below and repeat it to yourself every waking morning?

"Finally brethren, whatsoever things are true, whatsoever things are honest, whatsoever things are just, whatsoever things are pure, whatsoever things are lovely, whatsoever things are of good report; if there be any virtue and if there be any praise, think on these things." Philippians 4:8 <u>KJV</u>

Driftwood

"He heals the brokenhearted and binds up their wounds. He determines the number of the stars and calls them each by name. Great is our LORD and mighty in power, his understanding has no limit. The LORD sustains the humble but casts the wicked to the ground." Psalm 147:3

Driftwood along the lakeshore comes and goes. Sometimes there is a lot of it after a storm, other times it has been picked clean, usually for bonfires to bring comfort and maybe s'mores to a gathering. Each piece of wood has its story if it could talk. In Japan, where wood is scarce, it is said those very special social evenings may be enjoyed around a fire. Each person brings a piece of wood and tells the story behind it, such as, "This wood was once part of our home where the elders were honored and respected by the young." I can imagine such evenings are very entertaining as the stories are woven and the wood is consumed in the flames, giving warmth and new thinking to the group.

Some pieces of driftwood are quite unusual and attractive. Their twisted shapes, great strength and colors suggest certain art forms and their smooth surfaces testify to the constant working of the currents and waves. Where have they been and what brought them here? Now they may be crafted into furniture or settings for useful items such as candles or clocks. I once saw a beautiful walking stick made from a weather-beaten limb of a cherry tree. Some pieces reveal beauty that was never evident in their original form. Now they are useful in their **second life due to the scripture of nature's relentless power.**

Such pieces can also reflect what Christian maturity is all about. Most people have interesting life stories to tell of their walk with the Lord, through many experiences of different kinds. They can speak of the Lord's help and correction and of his grace even when undeserved and unexpected.

A man recently told me that in his youth he had stolen several hundred dollars from an employer. A year later it was that man who suddenly sat down next to him, sending chills up his spine. There was silence for a few moments, and then the kid said, "I stole the money. I don't have it now, but I will pay you back." It was one of those really serious confessions when you fear retribution and your throat is dry. "I know," said the man. "Don't worry about paying me back. Just go out and really make something of yourself."

Can you imagine the impact on the boy? 30 years later as a successful businessman himself, he still shakes his head with tears in his eyes at the huge change that happened to him in those two minutes. Now he works to bring such goodness out of the many drifters he meets.

How true it is that God is in the transformation business. Our brothers and sisters in Christ in the church at Ephesus many centuries ago became strong in their faith through trials of many kinds. Paul wrote eloquently to them about becoming mature through tough times, *". . . so that the body of Christ may be built up until we all reach unity in the faith and in the knowledge of the Son of God and become mature, attaining to the whole measure of the fullness of Christ. Then we will no longer be infants, tossed back and forth by the waves, and blown here and there by every wind of teaching and by the cunning and craftiness of men in their deceitful scheming. Instead, speaking the truth in love, we will in all things grow up into him who is the Head, which is Christ . . ."* Ephesians 4:13-15

No doubt we have all been subject at some time to distorted teachings, bad habits or deceitful influences. Being tumbled through these experiences is nothing compared to learning the faith and knowledge of Christ! He supersedes every mistake we ever made. He teaches us how to speak the truth in love, both to ourselves and to others whom he brings into our lives.

He also teaches us how to really learn from the past, how to consider our previous life as a resource library that is as useful now as a reference. It can be of great help to others to see what we have learned. Our lives can become more purposeful and productive, because while we may have been pounded, now we have found new purpose.

When there is a real sense of the **continuity of life**, patterns emerge that reveal the ultimate purpose of your life. It's like a puzzle being assembled. When your life is not stagnant, but is constantly **becoming** through growth, you can comprehend the direction God wants for you. You need a sense of history if you are to make sense of life. Like driftwood, if you look only at the point where you are, your history and your future do not make much sense.

It is exciting beyond measure to know that *when we are weak, he is made strong* and that knowing and following Christ brings you to your destiny of maturity.

 "But (the LORD) said to me, "My grace is sufficient for you, for my power is made perfect in weakness. Therefore I will boast all the more gladly about my weaknesses, so that Christ's power may rest on me. That is why, for Christ's sake, I delight in weaknesses, in insults, in hardships, in persecutions, in difficulties. For when I am weak, then I am strong." II Corinthians 12:9-10

Shelter

ISAIAH 25:4-5

The lake is wild today. The waves are 4 - 6 ft. with big, whipped cream whitecaps as far as the eye can see. Standing on the break wall, I can watch waves crashing against the red and green marker tower lights, spume flying above them 15 ft. or more. The beach has been cut deep, and now there are 6 ft. sand cliffs along the shore. The wind is strong from the northeast and there is a sudden staccato of rain on my rain hood. These elements are very stimulating today, but I am very glad not to be out there in a boat!

Wanting to fully sense the drama even more for a while, I found a dense thicket on the shore. It is a thick bush forming a small leafy cave that gives shelter from the wind and rain. It's a good place to watch the powerful weather out there. It's a cozy and safe feeling, to be warm and dry but close to the action. It is somehow a wonderfully **young** feeling. I remember the words of Psalm 61:3, *"For you have been a shelter for me, a strong tower from the enemy."* It is a hint of grace, and a glimpse of heavenly peace that comforts the soul.

When I was young, our youth group would go to summer Camp Harmony on Millsite Lake near the Adirondack Mountains. It was wonderful in so many ways, summer youth camp at its best. It was a transition week of a sheltering faith to be developed as we faced the challenges of growing from childhood to the teenage years. Each morning started with an hour called "Alone with God." A scripture was read to us and then each would find a solitary place to meditate and journal our thoughts. Here and there over the wooded mountainside could be seen the campers writing in their journals. For most of us, this was an acquired skill.

In a few days, you could see unselfishness growing among us. In the shelter of God's care we learned more about thinking of others. I remember one older camper who was chosen captain on a softball team. He surprised everyone by choosing the smallest and youngest players first instead of the more physically developed. They were shocked!

The life and work of Dr. Albert Schweitzer was one of our studies. He accomplished tremendous things, which started in a sheltering faith in his youth. He wrote; "Grow into your ideals, so that life can never rob you of them. If all of us could become what we were at fourteen, what a different place the world would be! All work that is worth anything is done in faith.

"The great secret of success is to go through life as a person who never gets used up. That is possible for him who never argues and strives with men and facts, but in all experience retires upon himself, and looks for the ultimate cause of things in himself . . . I still remain convinced that truth, love, peace, meekness and kindness are the violence which can master all other violence . . . All the kindness which a man puts out into the world works on the heart and the thoughts of mankind, but we are so foolishly indifferent that we are never in earnest in the matter of kindness. We want to topple a great load over, and yet will not avail ourselves of a lever which would multiply our power a hundred-fold." Memoirs of Childhood and Youth.

Good things like that happen when you place yourself in God's sheltering presence and honestly seek His will. In the book of Acts we see this priority among those Christians living in dangerous times. They were **weak before God but strong in the world** and they turned the world upside down. It is amazing in these modern times that so many people will look everywhere else first to find themselves, rather than seeking the face of God. They somehow believe they will find some inner wonderfulness about themselves, without meeting their Creator.

How greatly we err if we do not understand that true worship is directed toward God and not our own egos. In the shelter of **that** faith we witness the mighty power of God.

"For I can do everything through Christ who gives me strength." Philippians 4:13 <u>NLT</u>

Alone?

PSALM 103

The lake, sky and shore are surreal today - singular in their unique appearance after the big winter storm that passed through yesterday. Today, all is cold, desolate and very still. No one is around here. The sky is laden with stratus clouds, dark on the underside, but glowing with white and golden sunlight above. Here and there are windows revealing the heartbreaking blue sky above. The surface of the lake is pearl gray, with a shimmering quality as very gentle wavelets rise and fall, like beautiful, kinetic art. The water caresses the shore's edge which has a crusted snowpack about two feet thick, stretching about 30 feet up to the exposed sloping beach.

The beach looks like an environmental recycling center. It is littered from one end to the other with tree branches, a few plastic items large and small, old tires, a camper gas canister, a couple of flipflops, some old toys and a few pieces of usable lumber. They could, in a pinch probably be used to build a small shelter. At the far eastern end of the beach, the wind driven snow, sand, litter and small stones actually ramp all the way up to the top edge of the breakwater. It's a natural mess. A good workday by friendly neighbors will probably be needed in the spring to clean it up. The hard work will be made fun and satisfying by laughter and a cookout.

But today there is one word that describes this scene, **lonely,** beautiful in a rough way, but **lonely.** It reminds me of Robinson Crusoe who became so lonely that he ran to a valley and shouted the 23rd Psalm into the void so he could hear the echo of a human voice.

This landscape today seems a parable of life. It is very good to have friends and family, but often we must face our challenges alone. We must deal with ourselves and our problems if we are to find purpose and joy in our living. The TV personality Jack Paar once said; "I know there are many obstacles in my life, but I am the chief obstacle." Knowing what our lives can be and how to live those means confronting ourselves down deep, where only we know our own souls.

Sir Wilfred Grenfell, medical missionary to Labrador with winter landscapes much more harsh than this one, spoke of his work with people who had never found peace with themselves. He said they reminded him of the little barnacles at the sea shore. When first born they gave promise of being free swimming sea animals. Very early however, they learned to live alone and attach themselves to dock pilings, to grow a hard shell and spent the rest of their lives just hanging on and kicking food into their mouths with their back legs.

The good news is that even in the deepest, darkest cellar of our lives, God is there waiting for us. Psalm 139:7-10 expresses the fact of our faith: *"Whither shall I go from thy spirit, or whither shall I flee from thy presence? If I ascend up into heaven, thou art there. If I make my bed in hell, thou art there. If I take the wings of the morning and dwell in the uttermost parts of the sea, even there shall thy hand lead me and thy right hand shall hold me."*

This is what the WORD knew on the worst day of all human history. On the cross he said, *"Father, into thy hand I commit my spirit."* This is the ultimate and final decision that we can ever make. He has gone before us **through** the valley of shadows and so we do not need to fear what happens to us, now or later. He is always with us. When you have looked yourself full in the face in the loneliest times you have ever known, his eternal faithfulness to you is the final reality.

Sometimes in lonely situations people of faith can really help each other. Several years ago the <u>Los Angeles Times</u> reported that a screaming woman was trapped in a car dangling from a freeway transition road in East L.A. The 19-year-old woman apparently fell asleep behind the wheel around midnight. The car plunged through a guard rail and was hanging by its left rear wheel. A half dozen motorists stopped to help, securing the car with a rope until the first fire units arrived. A ladder was extended up from below to stabilize the car, while the tow trucks hooked up with chains and cables. "Every time we would move the car," said one of the rescuers, "she would yell and scream, she was in pain." It took over 2 hours and 25 people, police, firemen, tow truck drivers to secure it and pull it to safety. L.A. County Fire Captain Ross Marshall said, "It was actually kind of funny. She kept saying, **'I'll do it myself!'**"

Yes, we should solve our own problems as best we can but there certainly are times when self-sufficiency can be taken too far. Sometimes we really need the help that others can gladly give. Let us not be too proud to admit we are open to suggestions or even outright direction. In the fellowship of believers, there is no reason to suffer alone.

Returning to all that driftwood on our beach today, I am reminded of the man shipwrecked alone for a few years on an island. Finally he was rescued and was showing his new friends around. "What is that building?" they asked, seeing a rude hut made of driftwood. "That's my house," he said. They saw another structure. "What's that?" they asked. "That's my church," he replied. "I go every week." They saw yet a third hut. "And what's that?" they asked.

"Oh," he said, **"That's the church I used to go to."**

Certainly, we can find the LORD in anyplace we are, for he is waiting everywhere we may go, waiting, for us to accept his love and truth that will set us free.

"Even though I walk through the valley of the shadow of death, I will fear no evil, for you are with me; your rod and your staff they comfort me." Psalm 23:4

Log

ROMANS 15:1 - 6

For several months we have watched a large drifting log with a forked trunk as it floated back and forth along the shore. In the winter it was a beautiful ice sculpture, armored with an icy shield and long sharp spears. Finally a big storm deeply anchored it in the sloping sand right at the edge of the water. It seems to be a hardwood tree, now ruggedly beautiful, stripped of bark, smooth and bleached creamy white by the elements. One side of the fork is buried deep in the sand with old roots pointing to the sky. The other fork presents a perfect natural bench, cantilevered out a couple of feet above the water., You can easily sit there and dangle your feet in the crashing surf.

It is a very peaceful space, where a waiting expectant soul can be touched by grace. It can be a place of watching in speechless prayer. Where did this old tree come from? What was its previous life? It is a real beauty. I think it is oak; therefore it once was only an acorn full of potential.

Sitting there one beautiful summer morning, large, warm waves swept in and swirled around my feet. They roared in fiercely with scalloping designs, an overture of crashing sound and foam. Then having had their say, they retreated quietly back into the deep.

I thought of our human ways and moods, the highs and the lows of our existence, the crashing initiatives and the subtle reconsiderations.

Looking sadly back over her life, one friend said, "If only I had known then what I know now!" Who would not agree? It is a core skill of living successfully; to know and fully understand our emotions as they are happening **now**, instead of later after actions have been taken.

Equally, if not more important, is to know the firm, unchanging center; in other words, to understand that there is something more important than our feelings. When change is happening all around us, when old securities are swept away, when former certainties are gone, we can still know the ultimate certainty of God's eternal goodness and presence with us.

How can we know this indescribable truth? It is as factual and eternal as the natural laws that govern the universe, like those waves that arrive with such drama to our shore. Malachi 3:6 confirms it, *"For I am the LORD, I change not."*

Somewhere in your own DNA, this knowledge is just waiting to be recognized again. Give it a chance. Do it more than once! Spend some time ardently pursuing it and the abiding peace of God will speak to you, down deep where it really counts. John Greenleaf Whittier composed these lines:

> *Yet in the maddening maze of things,*
> *And tossed by storm and flood,*
> *To one fixed trust my spirit clings;*
> *I know that God is good!*
> *I know not what the future hath*
> *Of marvel or surprise,*
> *Assured alone that life and death*
> *His mercy underlies.*
> *And so beside the Silent Sea*
> *I wait the muffled oar,*
> *No harm from Him can come to me*
> *On ocean or on shore.*
> *I know not where His islands lift*

Their fronded palms in air,
I only know I cannot drift
Beyond His love and care.

<u>The Eternal Goodness</u>

"Whatever I have, wherever I am, I can make it through anything in the One who makes me who I am." Philippians 4:11 <u>TM</u>

Hawk

COLOSSIONS 1:15-20

The lake is a good schoolroom with many lessons for us, and for the creatures that live around it. I watched a hawk recently, sailing against the strong westerly winds, not making any headway. Then he circled back and flew through the trees along the bluff, able to make his destination by using the windbreak they provided.

There are times when we should all just sit down and reconsider the ways we are trying to do God's work. Someone once said the seven last words of the church are, "We have always done it this way!" Truly there is a lot of security in following the same traditional patterns, but let's not forget the word of the Lord in Isaiah 43:19, *"Behold I am doing a new thing. Do you not perceive it?"*

If we are faithful, even discouraging times can actually mean that a greater time of personal enlargement is coming. So let us place everything, the past, the present and the future in God's hands and **get into His stride.** We can learn again, believe it or not, that there is great strength in discouragement and that this may actually be required of us, if we are serious about letting God lead us into his plan for our future. Doing things his way requires humility.

The hawk by the lake learned and accepted the natural help of nature to find his way easier. It's often the same deal for us when we are struggling in our faith. God always has a better plan for us and we can find his way, even, or maybe especially when, we are discouraged and fighting an uphill battle. Then it is time to sit down and think clearly about our methods and God's plans.

"May he give you the desire of your heart and make all your plans succeed. We will shout for joy when you are victorious and will lift up our banners in the name of our God. May the LORD grant all your requests" Psalm 20:4-5

If you happen to be working in a church that is seeking a fresh understanding of God's plan, perhaps these new words to a familiar hymn will be helpful. If you can, take a walk along a lakeshore and think about the WORD walking by his lake.

You walk along our shoreline
Where land meets unknown sea.
We hear your voice of power,
"Now come and follow me.
And if you will still follow
Through storm and wave and shoal,
Then I will make you fishers
But of the human soul."

You call us, Christ, together
The people of the earth.
We cannot fish for only
Those lives we think have worth.
We spread your net of gospel
Across the water's face
For all out there who are found by your grace.

We cast our net O Jesus;
We seek your promised reign.
We work for love and justice;
We learn to hope through pain.

You call on us to gather
God's daughters and God's sons,
To let your judgment heal us
So that all may be one.

Chautauqua Lake / Institution
Music – <u>The Church's One Foundation</u>

Ordinary Andrew

JOHN 2: 1-11

"Good morning Rachel. Shalom. Beautiful day at the sea isn't it? Thank you for coming to our tent today. Please excuse the smell. The fishing business isn't the perfume business, for sure! But we can deliver very good fish for your wedding feast. Oh excuse me, my name is Andrew. My brother Peter said you would be coming by. Our father is not here today because it started raining again early this morning - another wasted day. If it lets up later, a few of us will go out because the fish are usually hungry on a day like this, cloudy and wet.

"Simon says he met you at the market yesterday. He does most of the selling since he knows everybody and is a good talker. I know the nets and boats and I like it here by the lake. So we work as a team. He looks for business and I organize the equipment. We go out there on the water together and we both clean the catch. Peter is a good thinker and makes the decisions, but I don't mind. It works and we even get some of our catch into Jerusalem on the big feast days.

"OK. When is your wedding? How many guests do you expect? Do you like a certain kind of fish? No problem. We can do everything you want. Oh, you were at the wedding in Cana that day? So was I! Wasn't it amazing? I am not one for big events or meeting important people but I have to say, that day changed my life. No, I don't know if Jesus will come to your wedding or not. He does seem to enjoy people and to like being at good parties. When I saw that water turned to wine, I was amazed. I couldn't believe it but I can't deny it either. It really did something to me - water into wine like that. (Snaps fingers) I began to think that since he could do that, he could change my life too.

"And even more happened later. I began to follow Jesus around, learning something new every day. I watched him baptize people in Judea. I was never an upfront type of person you know. I like the background life. Simon is the guy if you want a good speech or a dynamic plan. Oh, sometimes it's not easy to be his brother, watching while he gets all the attention and credit for things that I did. I wonder sometimes if he realizes how my life makes his life possible. I went back to my hometown of Bethsaida to sort things out for a while; I kept thinking and thinking about the way my life could be.

"I began to feel new and wonderful things. I began to think and to dream about the kind of life Jesus talks about. I wondered if it could be true for me. Just the other morning we were out on the lake and I was thinking about all those things, sort of drifting off I guess, listening to the waves lapping the side of the boat. I kept thinking of the things the LORD has said when Simon yelled at me to 'Wake Up!' The net needed to be pulled in or the catch was lost.

"So, something new and very exciting has been happening to me. I never knew what life could be like until the Master came along. He cared about me and what I would like to be. And you know what? I no longer am afraid to speak up! I have found that I can introduce people to the LORD. It's simple and in fact, that's all I really want to do now. It doesn't matter that I can't make speeches or cut big business deals or be wealthy enough to wear fine clothes. All I want to do is make the connection, and bring people to meet the One who can change their lives too.

"Hmm. I never used to talk this much! Guess you are a good listener! The rain has stopped and the sky is clearing, and . . .

"*Look*! Here comes the LORD now! Why don't you ask him to come to your wedding? Don't worry, we will catch you the finest fish in the sea for your wedding - but now I have to run! The first thing I have to do is to find that brother of mine, rough and tough Simon, so that he can get over here and meet the LORD today!"

"His mother said to the servants, 'Do whatever he tells you.'" John 2:5

Eloi, Eloi

EXODUS 20 :16

It is Good Friday, March 22, 2013. Temperatures are in the high 40's. Skye and I are walking along the shore of Lake Erie. It is very flat out there, with a soft breeze ruffling lacy patterns randomly here and there. It is fascinating to watch as the breeze, like the breath of God, touches down and then rises and moves on to caress the surface elsewhere. *"The wind blows wherever it pleases. You hear its sound, but you cannot tell where it comes from or where it is going. So it is with everyone born of the Spirit."* John 3:18 Winter is ending and all seems right with the world. It is a beautiful and worshipful morning, a natural call to prayer.

There is, however, another reality here today. The winter kill of fish was extensive. Thousands of Gizzard Shad of all sizes line the beach. Known as a 'junk' fish, they are not considered a commercial loss, because they are only used as bait. Their habitat is near the surface of the water making them very vulnerable to this winter's fluctuating temperatures. It is not a pretty sight nor is it fragrant. Vultures and sea gulls are circling all up and down the shore.

These two strong impressions collide in the mind and nose. The lovely presence of God and the unlovely, odorous death of many fish compete for my attention.

Thoughts move along to a sad conflict raging in a friend's family. They are devoted Christians known for leadership and prayer, yet harsh, scalding words were flung at each other. Long held reservations about their opposing viewpoints boiled over. Feelings were trampled. Relationships were crushed. How can this be?

It may be a modern problem in these hectic times, but it is not a new one. We may think of the earliest Christians as saints, but a close reading of James 3 tells us otherwise; *"With the tongue we praise our Lord and Father, and with it we curse men, who have been made in God's likeness. Out of the same mouth come praise and cursing. My brothers, this should not be. Can both fresh water and salt water flow from the same spring?"* v. 9

How often would we prefer to just bask in the loving embrace of God, ignoring problems and not growing up and out of childish behavior?

In our friends' problem, the angry words were followed by a cold, wintry silence. It was approaching the point of no return, in spite of their individual faith in the Lord. What to do? Which was going to win, the forgiving grace of God or the stink of thoughtless anger?

Have you ever been there?

Each of our friends was miserable, struggling to reach the forgiveness that needed to be given and received. While the silence between them was deafening for two long days, it was also acting as a suction cup to pull the poison out.

Two things happened that showed wonderful maturity. He appeared with a colorful note pinned to his shirt. She ignored it as long as she could but finally simply had to know what it said. It read: "I am a real dope to think I could ever live without you. Please forgive me." A silent embrace and favorite meal followed. They began to talk, haltingly at first, then more and more freely. They committed to communicate and listen more candidly, right up front on any issue. God's grace had won again in both of their lives.

So on Good Friday, I looked again over the smelly, disintegrating fish along the shore and knew that soon they would be gone, but the Spirit of our gracious Father will never forsake us. We can always come down to earth from our blissful trust in him and know "*. . . the wisdom* *that comes from heaven is first of all pure; then peace-loving, considerate, submissive, full of mercy and good fruit, impartial and sincere. Peacemakers who sow in peace raise a harvest of righteousness.*" James 3:17

We are not meant to be alone always. It is not the WORD's way. Is there someone you should be speaking to, with kindness today, candidly and in the Spirit of Christ?

Being Baptized

LUKE 3:15-22

It was a sunny July day, a nice time to be at the beach. It was especially so because most of our family (30 or more) were at our lake house for a little vacation. It doesn't happen often anymore, that we are all able to be together in one place, so it was a special time for us all.

The lake was warm so there was a lot of swimming and the Waverunner got a good workout. There was a lot of laughter and good conversation. It was a good day.

Our kitchen was picnic central with plenty of food and supplies. We had finished eating when Katy asked if she could talk to me. She is my niece's daughter-in-law, a delightful and enthusiastic mother of two. She really loved the beach and had gathered many colorful stones from the shore. We stepped outside and smiling, she asked, "Would you baptize me?" It was a moment of beautiful enlightenment when a younger person wants to take the serious step to make a new commitment to personal growth. "Joy" is the word for it.

A half hour later we were all at the shore, appropriately clothed for the occasion and in grateful prayer for God's goodness. Katy and I went out into the lake where I asked her if she had fully accepted Christ as her LORD. "Yes," she replied, and with shining eyes and big smile, she was immersed and raised to new life in Christ. The family on the shore sang and applauded.

155

Great! Just as it should be for all who believe, accept and are ready to grow into Christian maturity. It is vital to know how important this personal choice is. It is not just a onetime event. Baptism appears frequently in the Bible as an active verb, **being baptized**. It is an ongoing process of being filled, many times over, with the Holy Spirit Who gives us his gifts.

Luke 3:15-22 expresses this ultimate reality. John the Baptist was baptizing people in the water as a sign of repentance from their sins. He told them, *"But one more powerful than I will come, the thongs of whose sandals I am not worthy to untie. He will baptize you with the Holy Spirit and with fire."* When people have seriously made the decision and invited Christ into their hearts and are baptized, the Holy Spirit enters their lives. They may be aware of it, or he may only become known to them later. As they grow in their faith, and when the time is right, the Holy Spirit reveals more and more, giving gifts to the willing new believers.

These gifts may be either **sign** gifts of impressive display, or **service** gifts which quietly build up and strengthen the body of Christ. Both kinds are important enough to be listed in several places in the New Testament.

We may not know all about the Holy Spirit, but since he is from God, we know that he is good and should be invited and welcomed. How else will we know more about him? In some churches, it seems that people find security only in predictable experiences of conversion. However, we cannot control God or the Holy Spirit. Thankfully they are outside of our human and limited way of seeing things

There is one way in which we could control the work of the Holy Spirit in our lives. That way is to choose to shut him out. To make that choice is to miss the full meaning of BEING baptized, to settle for Kindergarten instead of going for the very most you can learn.

I love reading the book of Acts, because it reports many details of the work of the Holy Spirit, empowering and growing individuals and the church. A very interesting account is given in the nineteenth chapter, verse two about **incomplete Christianity**. Paul meets a group who knew only the baptism of John and, "*. . . they never even heard the Holy Spirit exists.*" Paul laid his hands on them and they were baptized in the Holy Spirit.

I cannot express it any better than William Barclay who writes: "First, there is the stage in which we awaken to our own inadequacy and our deserving of condemnation at the hand of God. That stage is closely allied to an endeavor to do better that inevitably fails because we try in our own strength. Second, there is the stage when we come to see that through the grace of Jesus Christ, all condemnation may be taken away. That is the time when we find that all our efforts to do better are strengthened by the work of the Holy Spirit, through whom we can do what we could never do by ourselves." <u>Barclay's Commentary on Acts</u>

Without the help of the Holy Spirit, our faith will always be a thing of struggle, but with him, it will be a thing of peace. There can be no complete Christianity without the Holy Spirit. Make him welcome, and enjoy!

"Instead, be filled with the Spirit."
Ephesians 5:18

Waterspout

PSALM 42

It doesn't happen very often but on a recent warm spring morning, several of us on the common watched as a small waterspout moved slowly west to east across the lake. Then we watched as two more formed and followed, drawing water up from the surface of Erie into the whirling cloud above. I asked our neighbor, Julie, what it made her think about. She replied, "Every day has its surprises."

How true. No day is ordinary; there is something unique about each one. Henri Nouwen wrote, "Real life takes place in the here and now. God is always in the moment, be that moment hard or easy, joyful or painful." Many days have a mixture of all of them.

Watching that waterspout, Psalm 42:7 came to mind, *"Deep calleth unto deep at the noise of thy waterspouts: all thy waves and thy billows are gone over me."* KJV

The Psalms are interesting because they are not religious mumbo-jumbo, and are so honest about our human situations. They are prayerful conversations with God, our best and trusted friend. Talking with him, you can lay your heart bare and be open about anything that is on your mind.

Psalms 42 and 43 express the human despair and depression that results from feeling separated from God. The **waterspouts, waves and billows** are overwhelming, swamping the writer into helplessness and discouragement. In these modern times, we hear a lot about depression

158

and how difficult it is to determine its cause. The good news in Psalm 42 is that this writer not only can express it, but he also knows the solution!

Not to oversimplify the real debilitating effect of such sadness on many people, we learn from this Psalm that real **worship** can lift our spirits. We can meditate on the great, good things of God in past experiences. We can rejoice in His faithfulness to us in other difficult times. Remember and relive those!

Dean Trotter in seminary would often say, "The modern psychosis of many people would be solved if they could find and believe in our transcendent God." And as an old cowboy once told me, "I couldn't afford a psychiatrist so I just went to a good, friendly church instead."

The Psalmist was writing from captivity: "*These things I remember as I pour out my soul: how I used to go with the multitude, leading the procession to the house of God, with shouts of joy and thanksgiving among the festive throng.*" Psalm 42:4

We can find solid footing and strength when we **mine past great experiences from our lives.** These are historic events that cannot be changed and serve to help us in the future. The storms will pass, then this wonderful fact of our faith comes alive once again.

"Why art thou cast down, O my soul? And why art thou disquieted within me? HOPE THOU IN GOD: for I shall yet praise him, who is the health of my countenance, and my God." Psalm 42:11

Undertow

PSALM 18: 1-6

"un-der-tow/n – a strong seaward bottom current returning the water of broken waves back out to sea from the beach. If channelized by obstacles on the bottom, may become rip currents of exceptional force." Webster's Dictionary

This description was tragically proven true recently when a highly respected businessman in our town drowned in the ocean as he attempted to save his grandson, who survived. There can also be spiritual undertows in life that occur to us, pulling us far out from our securities.

"It really happened many years ago but there are still people along the Eastern Shore of Maryland who remember the legend of Dr. McAlister, the so-called weeping physician of the Eastern Shore.

"As a young man the doctor had taken as his bride a lovely, charming young woman. He was deeply in love with her, and then suddenly she died. The shock of her death plunged the young doctor into a deep depression that caused him to withdraw totally from life. He would neither eat nor talk with anyone. He became suicidal, and to protect him from himself, friends had him guarded day and night. Three nurses, serving eight-hour shifts, were his ever- present companions.

"Denied a means of killing himself, the doctor's melancholia deepened. He became an emaciated shell of his former self. He had to be lifted from his chair to his bed and was forced to eat enough to keep him alive. Despite their efforts on his behalf, he hated the three nurses with a passion that was beyond mere contempt.

"As the years went on a certain resignation seemed to set in. He was biding his time until one day he would have the opportunity to end it all. There was one thing he liked to do: in the summer he was taken to the seashore, where he enjoyed sitting in his wheelchair on a bluff overlooking the sea.

"On one of those visits he surprised his nurse by suggesting that she go for a swim. 'You can watch me just as well from the water,' he told her. The nurse should have suspected what he was up to, but she did not, and decided to accept his invitation. As she made her way down to the water, the doctor quietly watched her, and then started inching his wheelchair close to the edge of the bluff, where he would throw himself on the rocks below.

"Just as he reached the edge, he heard the nurse scream. She was caught by a sudden undertow and was drowning. What happened then is a matter of historical record. Without hesitation the doctor stood up, made his way to the water, dove in and swam out to the floundering nurse. There he gripped her with his right arm and swam back to the shore, where he worked over her, drawing on some inner reservoir of strength, until she revived.

"That was the end of Dr. McAlister's melancholia. In restoring life to the nurse whom he had thought he hated, he lost all desire to die. A few months later he opened his practice again, and thereafter lived a normal life." <u>Bits and Pieces</u>-undated

As the old saying goes, "The life you save may be your own."

 "Be strong and take heart, all you who hope in the LORD." Psalm 31:24

Heliograph

"For by the grace given me, I say to every one of you: Do not think of yourself more highly than you ought, but rather think of yourself with sober judgment, in accordance with the measure of faith God has given you." Romans 12: 3

One of the interesting sights on the lake during the boating season may take you by surprise. The pleasure boats with windshields may be cruising so far offshore that they are out of sight. Sometimes the sun reflects off the windsheild glass with a bright flash so quickly **here and gone** that you may ask, "What was that?" Then as the boat rocks, it catches the solar rays again and it sends a heliograph message to shore. Heliography has been used effectively by different cultures, including early military, to convey quickly important information.

This is of interest today as we heard the news of the death of yet another famous celebrity. Whitney Houston, award winning vocalist and film star has died at age 48. Prescription drugs were mentioned as one cause, as are the attractions and needs of celebrity energy. Her brilliant star of entertainment rose extremely high for several years. Then her career and voice and marriage all collapsed. How soon the arc of success can fall!

The Cleveland Plain Dealer newspaper graphically eulogized her, saying: "Long after the stories of her death at 48 and her years in a drug-defined personal wilderness have faded, the strong, beautiful voice - the instrument that drew millions of fans to her and made her one of the recording industry's brightest stars - will soar on . . . her songs are themselves about loss and promise unfulfilled. Years from now, those songs and that powerful and expressive voice will remain accessible (in recordings). But they will also be there as a reminder of what can be lost when addiction and personal demons get in the way of a beautiful talent and a promising life." (February 13, 2012)

Thousands are mourning her death for she was greatly admired and loved. A private memorial service was held in the church of her childhood completing a life gone full circle. There need not be any judgment of her now so let there be new wisdom and precautions as the best way to honor her achievements. Her death was tragic. For hers, and many deaths of those far less known, the grieving can include a fresh awareness of the very brevity of life, like an instantaneous flash of sunlight in our eternal universe.

Indeed, she was a person of tremendous gifts, discipline and achievement, who no doubt knew and believed the words of the WORD: *"What good will it be for a man if he gains the whole world, yet forfeits his soul? Or what can a man give in exchange for his soul?" Matthew 16:26*

Think of a significant event in your life from 10 years ago. Time goes by so much faster than we realize, doesn't it? How we live our brief span determines our eternal destiny.

 "For a thousand years in your sight are like a day that has just gone by, or like a watch in the night." Psalm 90:4

Lenten Campfire

JOHN 14:17

Lent is a time of reflection and deep thought about our spiritual lives and is a good time to go for long walks in favorite places.

Sometimes when Skye and I are the only ones on the beach, he is allowed to go off exploring by himself for a while. This evening he was ahead of me, checking out some brushy territory on the bluff slope. I was meandering east thinking of Lent and Easter while watching the Lake Erie swells. Then I couldn't see him and wondered if he had gone home, back up the stairs? I turned around to scan the western slope and sure enough, as so often happens, he was right behind me. This always amuses me. I never seem to learn that he often just patiently waits for me.

I looked up to the western sky and saw an unusual sunset. Walking east I would have missed it. It was not filling the whole sky as it sometimes does. It was more contained, a long, flat, smokey layer of clouds seeming to rest on a lower layer of brilliant burnt orange and glowing deep red. Beautiful! It looked like a bed of burning coals, the remains of a huge dying campfire. Billowing clouds above the colorful embers resembled ascending smoke. As you know, campfires can inspire deep and peaceful emotions. It can be a time of honest reflection and new resolutions. I asked Skye, our collie, if he knew the old Chautauqua hymn, "Day is dying in the West." Not receiving an affirmative bark, I sang what I could remember of it to him -

Day is dying in the west.
Heaven is touching earth with rest
Wait and worship while the night,
sets her evening lamps a-light
Throughout the sky.

Holy, Holy, Holy, Lord God of Hosts!
Heaven and earth are full of Thee.
Heaven and earth are praising Thee
O Lord most high!

Wagging his tail, I guess he liked it OK.

We continued walking toward that amazing **campfire in the sky.** I remembered that both the gospels of Luke and John recount a campfire at night in the High Priest's courtyard right after Jesus was arrested. This is very interesting and deserves our concentration. *"Simon Peter and another disciple were following Jesus. Because this disciple was known to the high priest, he went with Jesus into the high priest's courtyard, but Peter had to wait outside at the door. The other disciple, who was known to the high priest, came back, spoke to the girl on duty there and brought Peter in. 'You are not one of his disciples, are you?' The girl at the door asked Peter. He replied, 'I am not.' It was cold, and the servants and officials stood around a fire they had made to keep warm. Peter also was standing with them, warming himself."* John 18:15-18

Some historians have research that concludes why John was well known to the high priest's household. It is thought that his fishing business provided preserved salt-fish to customers in Jerusalem, and therefore he could vouch for a friend, the stranger Simon Peter, who was then allowed in. He was unknown there, a stranger by the fire warming himself, because if he stood off alone somewhere, it would be even more suspicious. The three pressing questions to him, **Do you know Jesus ?** are well known to all of us, as is his triple denial. What a spot to be in, and he cracked under the pressure, lying his head off, I presume out of fear for his own life by crucifixion.

Truly, we all may make cowardly mistakes, and even think, "When I do something wrong, no one forgets. But when I do something right, no one remembers." When failure happens to us, it may be hard to rise above it, to become stronger in our faith in ourselves and in our loving God. It doesn't help if others keep reminding us of the mistake. There is a legend that says people imitated the rooster crow whenever Peter passed by. However, one important fact is this; he followed Jesus much farther than the others who ran away.

What are your thoughts on being courageous for Christ?

Dr. William Barclay's helpful insights on these **campfire verses** are so appropriate for Lent. "The essence of the matter was that it was the real Peter who protested his loyalty in the upper room; it was the real Peter who drew his lonely sword in the moonlight of the garden; it was the real Peter who followed Jesus, because he could not allow his Lord to go alone; it was NOT the real Peter who cracked beneath the tension and denied his Lord. *And that is just what Jesus could see.* A tremendous thing about Jesus is that beneath all our failures he sees the real person. He understands. He loves us in spite of what we do because he loves us not for what we are, but what we have it in us to be. The forgiving love of Jesus is so great that he sees our real personality, not in our faithfulness, but in our loyalty, not in our defeat by sin, but in our teaching after goodness, even when we are defeated." <u>Commentary on Luke</u>

 "If the Son therefore shall make you free, you shall free indeed." John 8:36 <u>KJV</u>

Benediction

PSALM 100

Some experiences are so surprising and awesome, that speaking of them only diminishes their full meaning.

This November evening by the Lake is like that. The waves are 3-4 ft. high, constantly rolling and crashing in, one right after the other. The powerful energy of their **BOOM** overwhelms normal speech. The water sprays high as the waves foam, rise, curl and fall in upon themselves. Then they quietly flow, oh so smooth and slick up the sandy slope of the beach, each one sighing in a different whisper as though they are saying a quiet hello. Then, returning, the tamed water flows back out and under the next incoming undulation. Their brave statement made and brief existence over, they leave a legacy of shining sand, washed clean. It is now a glowing pathway down a long stretch of beach, accompanied by the percussion of the impulsive sea.

There's more. The darkening sky is curtained with low clouds drifting eastward, with only a small window here and there revealing the cobalt sky above. Off to the west, the huge brilliant sun is setting. The sky there is filled with a **van Gogh palette with broad strokes of sunflower yellow, crimson tulips, and the bronze of ripened harvest fields.** Like an archer's upward flying arrows, these colors paint the lower layers of clouds, brightest now in the west and gradually spreading east.

Can you see it? The clouds are drifting over the crashing sea, resembling a burning fire, with the darker clouds above like rising smoke. It is all passing so quickly, the slanting shafts of all that color now mirrored in the shining sands of the shore's edge. It takes your breath away even though you have seen hundreds of sunsets. It is a glorious and surprising benediction to the day, fleeting moments in time.

I think it could have been like this by the Sea of Galilee where so many met the LORD. Their eyes and souls were opened to new thoughts and great possibilities. He himself is an extraordinary surprise that brings wonderful change into your life. Throughout the Gospels we read that people were **greatly astonished and marveled** at his words and actions. In Matthew 19, his disciples were **exceedingly amazed** at the new horizons in their lives because of him. They asked him how these ideas and new ways of looking at things could be true. His reply is an eternal fact, *"Jesus looked at them and said, 'With man this is impossible, but with God all things are possible.'"* Matthew 19:26

No man or government could create the beauty, energy and power of this November **benediction sunset** at day's end. God can do what we cannot. He can create and change us in ways we cannot do by ourselves. Consider this cooperative partnership with God. Philippians 2:12-13 tells us, *". . . work out your own salvation with fear and trembling. For it is God which worketh in you both to will and to do of his good pleasure."* Some might think this is to lose personal independence, but in fact, it increases and deepens it many times over. He will take us from human aimlessness to his divine purpose and strength.

Yes, this incredible sunset is a great benediction to this day and calls forth pangs of longing in our human souls. Truly, *". . . with God, all things are possible."* And truly, God longs to give a powerful benediction to our lives, even greater than the pounding surf, setting sun and glorious sky.

The Message version says it this way, *"Be energetic in your life of salvation, reverent and sensitive before God. That energy is God's energy, energy deep within you, God himself willing and working at what will give him the most pleasure."*

Sunrise

JOHN 21: 1-14

Sunrise at the lake is a wonderful meeting of eternity and today. The western horizon is shrouded in a dark gray fog while the eastern horizon reveals a faint strip of golden, pink light. Gentle waves are making love to the shore. Here and there a fish jumps, breaking the placid surface of the water. A fishing boat with eight men in it is being rowed, gliding quietly out of the mist, their night torches extinguished. A few gulls quietly and hungrily follow them. The rhythmic splashing of oars is the only overture to the new morning's arrival. They had returned to their routine profession while trying to absorb the power of the resurrection. The sky brightens gradually, and like a golden blade, the eastern horizon sharpens its edge against the receding darkness. One high cloud drifts silently eastward, its ragged prow fringed by red and gold glory.

A solitary figure stands on the beach. Next to him is a small fire, smoke rising in a single, straight column. The boat is now only about a hundred yards from shore. Then we read these facts in John 21:4; "*Early in the morning, Jesus stood on the beach, but the disciples did not realize that it was Jesus. He called out to them, 'Friends haven't you any fish?' 'No,' they answered. He said, 'Throw your net on the right side of the boat and you will find some.'*"

This was met with some skepticism since they had fished all night and caught nothing. However, thinking this stranger must have seen something, they did as he said. Their newly folded net was opened again and thrown. It belled out in the air and fell so precisely on the water that the small lead weights hit the lake at the same moment making a circular splash. The stranger's advice was astounding! We read that, *"When they did this, they were unable to haul the net in because of the large number of fish."*

By now the sun's rising has layered the eastern sky with violet, indigo, pink and bright gold. The morning spreads its glory across both the sky and the lake. The top edge of the burning disk rises on the eastern horizon as a great day fully dawns. Truth is dawning too, on the disciples. John says to Peter, *"It is the Lord!"* Not waiting for the boat to crunch up on the beach, Peter plunges into the water in the ecstasy of joyful reunion. Who can describe this fully?

The others in the boat haul it all to shore and find 153 fish in the net. Ancient scholars wrote that there were 153 kinds of fish in the Sea of Galilee, meaning that these **fishers of men** could extend the good news of salvation to all people of all backgrounds. The unbroken net symbolized the church, that even if all the **fish** were caught, the church still could hold them all.

We continue to read that Jesus said, *"Come and have breakfast. None of the disciples dared ask him, 'Who are you?' They knew it was the Lord."* It was one more real proof of his bodily resurrection. This had really happened and there was a new and real future ahead. The conversations that followed that breakfast on the beach were specific. **Don't worry about the task that is given to someone else. Your job is to follow me.**

It is one thing to see things with the **eye of the mind**, and quite another thing to see with the **eye of the heart**. Both are possible if we want to walk fully into a new day with the Lord. Many things may seem to conspire against this newness of life. The disciples caught nothing all night and in our modern times, we also know disappointments and lost opportunities. If there is to be a new dawning of faith in our lives, we must see him, both with the mind and the heart.

The time comes to leave the lake and the beach for our regular tasks, but wherever we are, in the turning of a thought we may stand right next to the Lord, because the presence of his resurrected body knows absolutely no limits. It is the greatest friendship we may ever have in all of life.

"Rejoice in the Lord always. I will say it again: Rejoice! let your gentleness be evident to all. The Lord is near. Do not be anxious about anything, but in everything by prayer and petition, with thanksgiving, present your requests to God. And the peace of God, which transcends all understanding, will guard your hearts (feelings) and minds (thoughts) in Christ Jesus." Philippians 4:4

Divine Rush

 "And the Spirit of God moved upon the face of the waters." Genesis 1:2 <u>KJV</u>

Walking by the quiet, still waters of Lake Erie this beautiful St. Patrick's Day morning, the 1949 prayer of Dr. John Baille, Chaplain to the Queen of Scotland came to mind. The British Isles, with their great seafaring explorations, fully understood the power, importance and use of all the seas in all the world.

"Almighty God, who art ever present in the world **without** me, in my spirit **within** me, and in the unseen world **above** me, let me carry with me through this day's life a most real sense of Thy power and Thy glory.

"O God **without** me, forbid that I should look to-day upon the work of Thy hands and give no thought to Thee the Maker. Let the heavens declare Thy glory to me and the seas Thy majesty. Let every fleeting loveliness I see speak to me of a loveliness that does not fade. Let the beauty of earth be to me a sacrament of the beauty of holiness made manifest in Jesus Christ my Lord.

"O God **within** me, give me grace to-day to recognize the stirrings of Thy Spirit within my soul and to listen most attentively to all that Thou hast to say to me. Let not the noises of the world ever so confuse me that I cannot hear Thee speak. Suffer me never to deceive myself as to the meaning of Thy commands; and so let me in all things obey Thy will, through the grace of Jesus Christ my Lord.

"O God **above** me, God who dwellest in light unapproachable; teach me, I beseech Thee, that even my highest thoughts of Thee are but dim and distant shadowing of Thy transcendent glory. Teach me that if Thou art in nature, still more art Thou greater than nature. Teach me that if Thou art in my heart, still more art Thou greater than my heart. Let my soul rejoice in Thy mysterious greatness. Let me take refuge in the thought that Thou art utterly beyond me, beyond the sweep of my imagination, beyond the comprehension of my mind, Thy judgments being unsearchable and Thy ways past finding out.

"O Lord, hallowed be Thy name. Amen."

A Diary of Private Prayer

The WORD In The Country

Homeward Bound

In the quiet misty morning when the moon has gone to bed,
When the sparrows stop their singing and the sky is clear and red,
When the summer's ceased its gleaming, when the corn is past
its prime,
When adventure's lost its meaning, I'll be homeward bound
in time.

Bind me not to the pasture; chain me not to the plow.
Set me free to find my calling and I'll return to you somehow.

If you find it's me you're missing, if you're hoping I'll return
To your thoughts I'll soon be listening, in the road I'll stop and
turn.
Then the wind will set me racing as my journey nears its end,
And the path I'll be retracing when I'm homeward bound
again.

Bind me not to the pasture; chain me not to the plow.
Set me free to find my calling and I'll return to you somehow.

Words and Music by MARTA KEENE THOMPSON
COPYRIGHT 1991 ALFRED MUSIC

Are you ready ?
MATTHEW 13: 1-23

If you were to describe your idea of a perfect day, what would it be? Probably you have had some perfect days in your lifetime that you like to recall and enjoy again. They may involve something new and exciting, the fulfillment of a dream perhaps, or time spent with someone you greatly admire, respect and love. Perhaps there was an element of surprise in it.

An elderly friend of ours recently received a phone call on her birthday from her daughter in Florida. It was especially nice to get the call since she had no desire or plans to celebrate the day all by herself. While she was on the phone, her doorbell rang. She opened the door and there stood her daughter, cell phone in hand, smiling at the surprising pleasure she brought her mother on that special day.

When we read Matthew 13, we sense the setting of a perfect day. *"At about that same time Jesus left the house and sat on the beach. In no time at all a crowd gathered along the shoreline, forcing him to get into a boat. Using the boat as a pulpit, he addressed his congregation, telling stories."* TM

It is a very picturesque description and what a great experience it must have been to be there. Imagine the day! The WORD is by the beautiful lake and his popularity is increasing more and more, because he has the words of Eternal Life.

Many, many people come from all around to hear what he has to say and to see the miracles of God. It is so crowded that he has to get into a boat and push off so he can be seen and heard by all. Imagine the hush over the crowd as they listen and pay attention to what he says. He begins telling these stories, four of them reported here, of the thirty that we know about.

He knows why the multitudes are there. They have multitudes of problems. In our own time, Billy Graham, who called many thousands to faith in Christ, says he always knew 5 things about the large audiences at the crusades, paraphrased here;

> "1.) He knows their life's needs are never totally met by social improvement or material wealth;
> 2.) He knows that there is an essential emptiness in life without Christ;
> 3.) People are lonely;
> 4.) Most people have a deep sense of guilt about something;
> 5.) There is a universal fear of death."
> <u>Breakfast with Billy Graham</u>

The LORD starts where we are, knowing that only there can we be ready for new and deeper understanding of God. That's part of a perfect day, this being ready for a fresh experience and to take needed steps to **get the real answer to our needs.** It is God's new important thought entering our open minds that really deals with the troubling factor and leads to a life changing decision and greater happiness.

Perhaps Jesus looked up to a field on a nearby hill where a person was sowing seed for a crop. He speaks about four kinds of soil: hard pathways, rocky, thorny and finally good ground. The good seed is sown on all of these.

Now if any or even all of those five factors are at destructive work in a life, think of what it means when they are all resolved in one meeting with Jesus Christ. We call this conversion and it is the only perfect

179

solution to our many human dilemmas. Think of that perfect day by the lake, with the perfect WORD teaching the perfect truth of God. Think of being at a new place to experience something so liberating to your soul . . . The whole being is healed; body, mind, and soul are filled with the comforting Spirit of God. That is conversion.

Perfect days are possible when we are really ready to listen, wherever we are, to the WORD's words of eternal life.

One nearly perfect day for me, now long ago but still vivid, was hearing the great scholar Dr. Paul Tillich speak. I was really ready, and feasted on his words. I will never forget the emotional and intellectual impact as he closed with the powerful words of Dr. Albert Schweitzer:

"He comes to us as One unknown, without a name, as of old, by the lake-side; He came to those men who knew Him not. He speaks to us the same word: 'Follow thou me!' and sets us to the tasks which He has to fulfill for our time. He commands. And to those who obey Him, whether they be wise or simple, He will reveal Himself in the toils, the conflicts, the sufferings which they shall pass through in His fellowship, and, as an ineffable mystery, they shall learn in their own experience Who He is." Quest for the Historical Jesus

"Jesus said, 'You're absolutely right. Take it from me. Unless a person is born from above, it's not possible to see what I'm pointing to-to God's kingdom." "How can anyone," said Nicodemus, "be born who has already been born and grown up?" John 3:3-4 TM

Pigs in Church

Pigs in Church

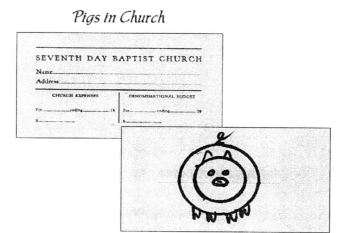

The many living memories of my parents include sitting with them in our hard wooden church pew near the front and next to the colorful Warner window. This was for at least an hour every Sabbath morning in the grown-ups' church. Our farm was near that white clapboard country church which was comprised mainly of other farm families. We were all there rain or shine, summer and winter, without exception. Sometimes my mother would play the piano for hymns, most of which I can still remember.

The formal service was led by a dignified Pastor in a black suit and it seemed VERY long. I would watch the play of colors from the sun shining through the stained glass as the sun passed overhead **in its freedom**, moving the red and amber colors slowly over my hands.

181

Finally the benediction from Jude would be spoken, *"Now unto him who is able to keep you from falling (asleep?), and to present you faultless"* . . . *etc.*

This was serious, important stuff for all of us. It was hard to sit still, no figiting or talking or any other malefactions. It was not much fun then, but I am eternally grateful now, for that family experience. **You can pay attention to God's Word for one hour of the week** was the wisdom of those times, and we did.

There is one fond and memorable exception, however, that has persisted in my memory all these six decades. It was a beautiful summer day, a peaceful and restful Sabbath. I was sitting next to Dad who was trying to stay awake, and I was restless too. He looked over at me, then took one of the little manila offering envelopes and the short yellow pencil (no eraser) in his brawny hands and began to draw something, using the Service Hymnal for support.

Three concentric circles, then the ears, nostrils, eyes, feet and curly tail of a pig seen head on. Hmm. Even I could do that. I practiced pigs until the final hymn and sometimes I still doodle it today just for fun, remembering Dad's kindness.

I am surprised to observe that I have used three concentric circles most of my life for various things, including my college paper on Freidrich von Hegel's philosophical dialectic ; Thesis, Antithesis, Synthesis (without the porcine features).

There's more! In a scholarly study by Cajete, it is stated that drawing a picture of concentric circles is a natural thing for people of all **past cultures and languages worldwide.** Why do all human beings do this? It is a mysterious activity preserved in prehistoric cave art which they used as education, conveying important knowledge. It is an ancient religious art form used to permanently establish important events and rituals.

Such ancient cave art might be dismissed as idle doodling if it weren't for the fact that working in stone takes time and concentrated effort. Only critical events such as discovery of game, or a good sheltered place to live would justify the effort. Big news was focused and immortalized this way and remembered in community chambers.

Concentric circles! Imagine that you are in an unfamiliar landscape and turn yourself in a 360 degree circle looking all around you. That would be the first, innermost circle. As you repeat the turning action, you are learning more and deeper things about your surroundings.

The theory is that every circling turn deepens and informs your impressions, eventually arriving at a total, holistic grasp of your new experience. Each expanding circle represents expanding knowledge.

The first turn gives first impressions of the **physical** characteristics and first emotional responses to them. The second turn evolves the **social meaning** and connections by putting the pieces together. The third turn is deeper yet being metaphysical, meaning the intuition of what we perceive beyond our own intelligence. We ask, **what is God saying to me?** This may be called **revelation** and is how the human mind grasps the deeper, abstract meanings of the events of our lives.

Such knowledge is so mystical and valuable; you want to **carve it in stone**, establishing it as a sacred experience where something **BIG AND SIGNIFICANT** happened. Such ancient circles were combined with other artwork such as wild game or other humans in various activities.

So, who says you can't learn good stuff in church? I am sure my father would laugh his head off if I tried to explain my excitement about drawing pigs in church. Try it sometime!

I want to take this one step further. One of the most beautiful and helpful scriptures I have loved is Romans 5: 1-5. It is about the way that God brings us through the hardest times that we face in our life's journey.

"Therefore since we have been justified through faith, we have peace with God through our Lord Jesus Christ, through whom we have gained access by faith into this grace in which we now stand. And we rejoice in the hope of the glory of God. Not only so, but we also rejoice in our sufferings, because we know that suffering produces perseverance, perseverance: character, and

character: hope. And hope does not disappoint us, because God has poured out his love into our hearts by the Holy Spirit, whom he has given us. You see, just at the right time, when we were still powerless, Christ died for the ungodly . . ."

If suffering is the innermost event/circle such as a **broken heart** which happens to someone, we know the first question is **Why?** We have to try to understand why it happened so that we can move on. This process takes perseverance, a second circle. Eventually this can bring about a change in our character and finally we can find hope *that does not disappoint us.* How? Because we have peace with God through Jesus Christ who suffered and died for a future destiny which includes us.

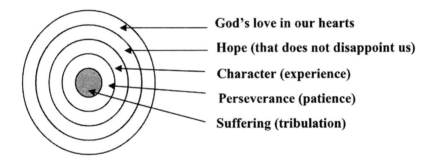

God's love in our hearts

Hope (that does not disappoint us)

Character (experience)

Perseverance (patience)

Suffering (tribulation)

In God's time and strength, these can be redemptive opportunities for growth in the WORD – forward and outward; ever forward and outward into the hope that *"does not disappoint us."*

Can you remember how God has brought you through difficult times and where you are today because of his faithfulness and grace toward you?

"The first place that I can well remember was a large pleasant meadow with a pond of clear water in it."

PROVERBS 21

So began my father's favorite book. I can still see him with his reading glasses after a day's work in the farm fields, opening <u>Black Beauty,</u> by Anna Sewell. He reread it again and again. As you probably know, the title page tells us that it was "Translated from the Original Equine," and was told in **first horse narrative.**

Black Beauty had many horse friends and their horse sense conversations about life and people were always interesting. Reviews of the novel expressed the importance of good 19th century animal welfare for English carriage horses. The book also taught the value of treating people with kindness, respect and sympathy. It still is a gem, in the tradition of <u>McGuffey's Reader</u> of that era.

This English novel was first published in 1877 and was a best seller. My father's first copy was probably given to him when he was 7 or 8 years old. He could, until the end of his life, start telling the story himself, saying, **"The first place that I can well remember was a large meadow and flowing stream . . ."** It became one of our family phrases to lighten the day.

My Father loved horses and had a strong natural ability to care for their health and training. Draft horses were the way of farming in America in the early 1900's. He also saw their great work value in the digging of the Barge canal with slip scoops. The canal bordered our farm and was a major engineering feat, following a parallel route of the much smaller Erie Canal. These opened the water route from the Hudson River and New York harbor to the Great Lakes.

Horses were always a big part of our lives. Their pictures festooned with fair prize ribbons adorned our farmhouse walls. At fair time, the harness leather and brass were polished, the draft horses were groomed with tails braided, and often ribbons were placed in their manes. Of course they had names, as all family members do. Sandy, Chubb, Nell, Cherry, Jim, Guard (with one eye), Mac, Mabel, and Kit were some of the gentle giants. Firefly was one of Dad's first horses and an old family story tells that he brought the colt into the kitchen one winter morning, just for fun. Then there were our saddle horses too, Little Red, Sally, Skipper and Nick to name but a few.

My father had become the primary farm worker at age 14. Later he was able to go away to Alfred Agriculture School for a few months. One of his text –books was **Practical Lessons in Agriculture** published in 1915. Page 66 teaches us that; "In treating a horse, firmness and kindness are the two essential qualities. Never let a horse conquer you, but have him understand you are the master. This can easily be done without resort to cruelty of any kind. If obedience is taught early, the horse will never give you any serious trouble. The best way to train a horse is to train yourself; keep control of your own temper and never lose your self-control. Patience is the cardinal virtue in overcoming opposition upon the part of your horse. A good horseman seldom strikes his horse with a whip or other instrument of torture. The human voice is sufficient in most cases to bring about desired results. Everything you do about a horse may easily be associated with your tone of voice. Very soon the animal comes to understand what you want and how you want him to do it. It is surprising how quickly a horse understands every tone of your voice."

How true that was. I can still see the team standing patiently waiting for dad's trusted voice command to **giddap** or **whoa**. They knew their names, their master's voice and his kindness and care for them.

So it is with us who listen for the WORD to teach and instruct us in our tasks. We are not horses, but it matters even more how we think and behave.

*"We pray that you'll live well for the Master, making him proud of you as you work hard in his orchard. As you learn more and more how God works, you will learn how to do **your** work. We pray that you'll have the strength to stick it out over the long haul-not the grim strength of gritting your teeth but the glory-strength God gives. It is strength that endures the unendurable and spills over into joy, thanking the Father who makes us strong enough to take part in everything bright and beautiful that he has for us."* Colossians 1:10-12 <u>TM</u>

That's good horse sense. It means that God wants to produce his character in us. But to do this, he demands our discipline and effort. As we happily obey Christ, who guides us by his Spirit, we will develop self-control over our actions and also over the wild horses of our emotions.

I want to obey the WORD the way those good horses willingly obeyed my father. Usually no whip is necessary, just strong, kind authority, caring hands and a gentle voice.

We are a team and so important work gets done!

 "And the servant of the Lord must not strive; but be gentle to all men, apt to teach, patient." II Timothy 2:24 <u>KJV</u>

One Horsepower

PROVERBS 13

One of the big summer jobs on the farm in the '40s was the haying. Before tractors were in common use, we worked with horses to get the crops in the ground and then in the barn.

Haying was a big job, dependent on the ripening of the crop and the weather. Before mechanized cutting and baling, the hay was cut with our horse- drawn mowing machine. This had a cutter bar of sharp teeth that could be manually raised or lowered. It was gear driven by the traction of the heavy steel wheels with cleats as they turned. Depending on the heaviness or thickness of the standing hay crop, the length of the cutter bar was usually 5 feet, but some were 3 feet, others 4 feet.

After being mowed and cured in the field, the loose hay was loaded by the mechanical hay loader, also gear driven by the wheels and hooked to the back of the flat wagon being drawn by the team. Often the hay was also pitched on the wagon by hand. These hot days were good for haying, but called for plenty of cold Switchel to quench our thirst. (Switchel was a homemade power drink in glass gallon jars. It included water, vinegar, brown sugar, ginger and some other forgotten ingredients.)

When a wagon was heaped high it would be taken to the barn, avoiding the woodchuck holes in the field which could dump the whole thing. The wagon was parked on the west end, under the big drop down door above. My father would set the four large harpoon type forks into a big bite of hay. A rope ran from the clevis joining the forks up to the barn peak, then through a pulley and was attached to the small track car.

Another rope called the return rope ran from the car the full length of the barn, through another wooden reverse pulley at the far end, and then down to the outside to where I stood with Cherry, our harnessed draft mare. The rope was attached to the singletree and when Dad called "Ready," we walked forward, **one horsepower** pulling the load up, up into the barn. The forks would catch the track car, rolling along the steel track in the peak into the chosen bay. Whoever had the job of working up there in the heat and dust would yell **Whoa** and we would stop. The mare would almost do it all herself, stopping at the **whoa** and knowing to turn around and walk back, being ready to go again. She really knew her job and did it patiently hour after hour. I believe she could have done it without me, but the drag rope had to be kept untangled and clear.

My father would then yank the trip rope which opened the forks, releasing the load of fragrant, cured hay. It would drop and my brothers there would then mow it away by hand, fork by fork. The trip rope could then pull the little car and forks back to the open door, releasing the forks to drop down to the wagon. Cherry returned to her position and waited, sometimes stamping a hoof and switching her tail at a few flies. I would pat her neck and sometimes lean against her for a while. She was a nice horse.

This may sound complicated but it worked well, and depending on weather, July 4 was the goal to be done with haying. If we made it, we might get a 50 cent speed boat ride some evening on Oneida Lake. Later in the summer there might be a second cutting, a richer blend of hay that was desirable if it could be brought in. Some years there was even a small third cutting, but that was unusual.

One dramatic memory recalls a hot day when the afternoon sun was beating off the western face of the barn and my father tumbled off the wagon. He whacked his head on the steel wagon pole, opening a gash on his temple. My watchful mother saw this from the nearby farmhouse and came rushing out with a pan of cold well water which she deposited twice on his face. He considered that unnecessary help, but it sure did bring him around! He was embarrassed to have fallen. She bandaged up the gash, saying it needed stitches, but he said he was all right and there was still an afternoon's work to get done. After a brief rest in the shade it was back out to the field for another load.

In that fearful moment of his falling, striking the pole and seeing the blood, I stood there unbelieving. He was briefly knocked out and I held the horse close and tight in all the noisy excitement, more for my benefit than hers, I guess. In the simple and well ordered days of summer work, unexpected things were not, well, expected. Hard physical work was the acknowledged way of life, the right way to live. We were always taught to be careful and safe. How could such an accident happen?

There is no simple answer to that question, which most people must face when suffering or an accident comes their way. **It is a hard test of faith which in the end does not blame God.** When trouble comes, it can bring us into a closer walk with the WORD. Reading the Psalms with eyes newly opened by suffering draws us closer and closer to our loving God. We find in him the strength and comfort needed to distinguish between the hazards of our earthly lives and his divine presence.

I believe that we are never stronger than when we are tested.

The WORD has always been aware of the conflict we feel when trouble comes and challenges our trust in him. He is there for us when that happens, wanting to see us through the deep waters.

"These *things I have spoken unto you, that in me ye might have peace. In the world ye shall have tribulation: but be of good cheer; I have overcome the world.*"John 16:33KJV

The Roundup

PROVERBS 12

I wish every kid could grow up on a working farm. The intimate relationship with nature and accomplishing things with your hands are enriching experiences beyond measure. It creates a lifelong sense of belonging as you learn about partnership with God. The tasks and responsibilities from an early age somehow teach you about faith in God as new challenges arise every day.

Yes, I wish that every kid could grow up on a working farm. It confirms that you are a part of something good. Working with the land and animals helps answer the important questions about the meaning and purpose of life. Watching nature's rhythms and the life cycle of animals gives a deep sense of life itself.

It is not all easy! Early morning hours and hard physical labor can be a demanding way to live, without much leisure (wasted) time. I loved it, and I will always love it. If I could, I would do it all over again.

And then there is the Fall roundup to consider. We raised black and white Holstein milk cows. After weaning, the young heifers were left out to pasture for most of the summer as they matured. When fall and winter were approaching, it meant getting them into the barns. After a full summer of complete freedom they weren't interested in this, having grown strong and partly wild.

One such roundup included a few that had sometime broken through the summer pasture fence and were living in the dense woods bordered by the Barge Canal. I remember the day clearly; my dad and brothers on horses and our good neighbor big Jim Finn coming over to help.

The trees were too thick for the horses to help much. Jim was afoot, waving his arms to head one of the girls toward the makeshift corral. I can still see her white face, big strong chest and wild glaring eyes. She did not like this whole idea, not knowing that it was for her own good. She charged Jim, hammering her big thick skull directly on his chest. Jim went flying, knocked out cold. It took him a few hours to recover and to even know what day it was.

It was a scary experience – one that stays with you a long time, teaching you lesson after lesson about life.

Here is one of them.

The wild heifer did not know that this was for her own good so she took violent action. She was wild, totally selfish and immature. Often, in our human ways, we too may want to do only things that we want to do, but they may not be for our own good. We need to know and to follow the teachings and presence of our LORD. His ways run counter to the wild impulses of people and the world. He wants us to see all things from God's plan and point of view, since he desires the best possible life for us. He calls us to unselfishness and full maturity.

> *"Brethren, do not be children in your thinking; be babes in evil,*
> *but in thinking be mature."* I Corinthians 14:20 RSV

The Life Application Study Bible includes an interesting chart of The **Choices of Maturity** as follows.

Mature Choices	**vs.**	**Immature Choices**
Teaching others		just being taught
Developing depth of understanding		struggling with the basics
Self evaluation		harsh self criticism

Seeking unity	promoting disunity
Desiring spiritual challenges	desiring only entertainment
Careful study and observation	opinions & halfhearted efforts
Active faith	apathy, doubt and fear
Feelings and experiences evaluated	experiences closely evaluated

Are you finding the joy of growing up into Christ?

 "If you love learning, you love the discipline that goes with it – how shortsighted to refuse correction!" Proverbs 12:1 <u>TM</u>

Sabbath Picnic

"Remember the Sabbath day by keeping it holy. You have six days each week for your ordinary work, but the seventh day is a Sabbath day of rest dedicated to the LORD your God. On that day, no one in your household may do any work. This includes you, your sons and daughters, your male and female servants, your livestock, and any foreigners living among you. For in six days the LORD made the heavens, the earth, the sea and everything in them, but on the seventh day he rested. That is why the LORD blessed the Sabbath day and set it apart as holy." Exodus 20:8 <u>NLT</u>

It must have been around July of 1948 after haying season and before grain crop harvest, when a special picnic was planned. My Dad and his lifelong friend, John Williams, knew how to have a good time with their families. They were farmers who were very skilled with horses, especially the big draft work horse teams. They enjoyed them immensely and of course the horses all had names like Sandy and Chub.

I clearly remember that warm, sunny Sabbath afternoon. After church we drove to John's farm where they hitched his team to a hay wagon. We all climbed aboard, along with the picnic baskets, lemonade, switchel, table service and everything needed, including apples for the horses.

John's farm was on a long sloping hillside, beautiful country near the aptly named Mt. Hope. It wasn't really a mountain, just a very large hill, but I like to think of it as a mountain.

Anyway, up we went, up and up, looking toward the level meadow near the top. For some of us, this was a first, a real change from the lower bottom lands where we lived and worked our dairy farm.

Arriving, we turned and viewed the midsummer landscape spread out before us. To me, at age eight, it seemed the top of the world with miles and miles of country below. Farms with their animals, buildings and silos dotted the panorama. It was a great new view of things, a real treat when seen from my 4 foot perspective.

Of course, before we ate, there was a prayer blessing the food "and the hands that prepared it." The dessert pies were special and the simple games, a lot of fun. I think of it today, 65 years later, as perhaps the first time it dawned on me that there really are times and ways you can see the big world in a totally different way. This was not a **virtual** experience. It was the real thing. It was fun, memorable and a very thoughtful day.

"Fun" and "thoughtful" are good threshold words to exciting growth. A new world opened up that day, a day which was **pleasing to the Lord** and to me. To be a real part of something like this opened me up to discovery of more of myself because we were together that day with the WORD in the country.

The Bible is clear that the LORD traveled around a lot as in, "*One Sabbath Jesus was going through the grainfields . . .*" Luke 6:1 Now, whenever I read a scriptural segue about the WORD moving from place to place **in the country**, I think about the exciting growth that was going to happen to those he would meet next.

I have been on a lot of much higher mountains since that 1948 picnic, but nothing compares to that first experience. I remember with great affection and wonder that special day, the folks, the horses and the picnic on John and Millicent Williams's mountainside (well, big hillside) farm, and I feel again the entrance of **Kingdom Country** in my 8 year old soul.

"No eye has seen, no ear has heard, and no mind has imagined what God has prepared for those who love him." I Corinthians 2:9 NLT

Plowing and Promises

"Behold, the days come, saith the LORD, that the plowman shall overtake the reaper . . ." Amos 9:13 <u>KJV</u>

It was the annual two **cylinder plowing day** and the putt-putt of 25 John Deere vintage tractors were pulling 2, 3 and even 4 bottom plows down a quarter mile stretch of rich Ohio land. The competitors had come from near and far to enjoy the way farming was done in past times. It was a field day of big tires, yellow and green colors and lots of laughter among friends.

Redwing blackbirds were following the freshly carved furrows, picking up an easy lunch. Listening to their excited songs recalled the bird music of my grandmother's backyard in many years gone by. It was a fun **throwback** day of sight and sound that stirred the ancient hope and faith of farming in the spring.

There is something very inspiring about a plowed field. It is the first step in the harvest cycle when the earth is opened up to be planted, cultivated and harvested. It is the first step in fulfilling the potential of the productive soil. It is a unique experience well known to farmers. Observing the huge amount of work those plows accomplished brought to mind the ancient origin of the simple plow and primitive hoes many thousands of years ago. That basic idea has evolved into the sophisticated tools of production of today. When oxen were domesticated in

Mesopotamia around 6,000 B.C., plows could be pulled by their power. **OXPOWER** was a big step forward in crop production.

The Bible, of course, has many good lessons drawn from agriculture. Watching those plowshares turning the soil, I thought of the WORD's words, *"No man, having put his hand to the plough, and looking back is fit for the kingdom of God." Luke 9:62* KJV This is about plowing a straight furrow, looking to the future and faithfully completing the task at hand. Another version is, *"No man who puts his hand to the plough and looks back is the right kind of man for the Kingdom of God."* Barclay's Daily Study Bible

These encouraging words are good promises to be taken seriously by anyone who is starting out on a new course in life. We may have ambition, dreams, and high aspirations, but the WORD teaches that we must **finish** the job. That means going beyond the original enthusiasm. Procrastination and weariness may tempt us to stop, or we may decide to substitute our good feelings and emotions for completed action. The WORD urges us to act rightly when his Spirit inspires our hearts, and not excuse ourselves with laziness or doubts.

While a plow appears to be a simple tool it is comprised of several parts. Let's compare a few of them to our spiritual promises from the WORD.

Chisel - This is the first point of the plow that penetrates the earth at a chosen depth below the visible surface.

When we realize that we want a deeper understanding of ourselves, who we are and can become, the WORD tells us that we are the children of God. He loves us and has a plan for our lives. This truth penetrates the hard surface topsoil assumptions of our lives. We discover that this love of God deals with the defects and errors of our lives no matter how deep they may be. We then begin to understand that **with God all things are possible**. This new birth brings a genuine humility and we understand that this living relationship with the WORD will come through the expression of our own best personality. That single spark of his divinity as expressed in the way we live makes us unique from every other living being. It is "**Christ in you, the hope of glory.**" Colossians 1:27

Share – This is the slicing edge of the plow that cuts the earth below the sod, loosening the deeper soil for the next step.

When we have first understood that God loves us, we want to grow in the knowledge of what this means in our everyday lives. It means positive changes in habits, commitments or relationships and in the way we are living.

Scriptures tell us, "So *we have stopped evaluating others from a human point of view. At one time we thought of Christ merely from a human point of view. How differently we know him now! This means that anyone who belongs to Christ has become a new person. The old life is gone; a new life has begun!*" II Corinthians 5:16-17

This new view of life may take some courage and new thinking. Well brought up people accustomed to their own way of life and social contacts may shy away from any experience that seems uncharacteristic of their own self regard. However, this is the only kind of experience that is truly new and alive, leading them to new, worthwhile goals.

Such brand new experiences happening at just the right time are one of life's greatest adventures. They are as necessary for new growth in a person's life as a newly sharpened plowshare opening a neglected, overgrown field. Note that the **plowed under vegetation** becomes decomposing mulch, nourishing the new crop that will come. "*. . . old things are passed away; behold all things are become new.*" II Corinthians 5:17

MOLDBOARD - This is the broad curved part of the plow that turns the sod over, flopping it upside down and exposing the new soil for the planting. This changes the appearance of the earth. It is the preparation for new productivity and an eventual generous harvest.

In the first century, Christians were learning how to live by the new ways of the Kingdom of God. They obediently waited for the Holy

Spirit to empower them before going out into the world. The result was the presence and power of God's Spirit in their living, and they were known as *"These that have turned the world upside down."* Acts 17:6 <u>KJV</u>

That is what a living, dynamic relationship with the WORD can do – not in a destructive way, but as a new exciting dynamic in life. God's own power is involved in our faith, energizing and bringing about the necessary plowing in order that the new planting and harvest will be possible.

In the hard work, duties and sometimes difficult challenges we face in life, we can find real hope and encouragement in the promises of God. *"Behold the days come, saith the LORD, that the plowman shall overtake the reaper . . ."* Amos 9:13 <u>KJV.</u> Ultimately the harvest will be so great that it will not even be out of the fields before the new plowing for new crops is being done.

Hitch – Well this is obvious I guess. A plow without mobile power can't get the work done.

I like this description: **God is the force that is pulling us into the future.** He is all about the fulfillment of his purpose and plan in our lives and in the world. He will help us at every single opportunity that we give him. It is a happy and hopeful personal decision that brings music in our souls.

A popular song in past years was, **Without a song, that field of corn would never see a plow!** What is your song today? Sing it while you turn the earth of your life over for the new, unbounded possibilities of the good new harvest God has planned for you.

 "The seed cast on good earth is the person who hears and takes in the News, and then produces a harvest beyond his wildest dreams." Matthew 13:29 <u>TM</u>

The Law of Abundance

"Then the LORD your God will make you most prosperous in the work of your hands . . ." Deuteronomy 30:9

I bargained with Life for a penny
And Life would pay no more.
However I begged at evening
When I counted the paltry score.
For Life is a just employer
He gives you what you ask,
But once you have set the wages,
Why, you alone will bear the task.
So I worked for a menial's hire
Only to learn dismayed,
That any wage I had asked of Life
Life would certainly, gladly have paid.

The anonymous author of those lines knew that **genuine enthusiasm is an essential part of success.** It inspires new, fresh ideas and brings energy to the vision and quality to the effort. It sets your goals high enough to fulfill the possibilities of your life.

This is the Law of Abundance. Our Lord said, *"Seek ye first the kingdom of God and his righteousness; and all these things shall be added unto you."* Matthew 6:33 <u>KJV</u>

If you know in your heart that God wants something done and that you are the one called to do it, there will always be enough resources.

He provides the vision and the means to achieve it. You provide the willingness to work it out his way and in his time.

When you go out to your work with this attitude, great things happen. Your desk, your truck, your work station can be an altar, not for worshipping work, but as a place where you can honor God.

A design engineer for a major tractor builder in the Midwest has created some of the most innovative agricultural machines in the world. Behind his office is a large warehouse filled with old farming equipment from over the years. There are horse drawn plows, mule treadmills, steam powered threshing machines and hand tools such as hay forks and threshing sledges. He likes to study them, he says, because "This is where I get all my **new** ideas." How can this be? By remembering their original, primitive purposes, he is able to adapt modern designs to the same, but greatly improved, function. In some ways this seems to be proof of the old saying, "There is nothing new under the sun."

In our modern challenges to witness to Christ, it is tempting and easy to think we must adapt new technology to the gospel. Sometimes such decisions can actually obscure the message. People still need to hear it in human voice, person to person, just as Jesus did before the electronic industry.

As I reflect on the interesting work I have been privileged to do in my life, I know that a personal spiritual life is important to success. This was true for the WORD who stressed his relationship with God, *"My Father is always at his work to this very day, and I, too, am working."* John 5:17 It is good to pray for your business associates and for their success.

When we truly desire good things and success for others, we find that we are twice blessed. As we pray for them and take a real interest in their needs, **we ourselves are aligned with God's purpose in this opportunity**. We become open to his timing, learning patience and new ideas that we had not thought of before. That is a good definition of **faith**.

If you love people, at least most of the time, and pray for them, they somehow know they are valued and respond accordingly. President Abraham Lincoln is credited with saying, "All I know about prayer is that when I stop praying, good coincidences stop happening." I add to that the comment from my honored boss in authority at work; "If you work hard for your customers, you get lucky."

When we seek and receive the **pre-approval of God for our plans and hopes, he is faithful to answer.**

"Commit to the LORD whatever you do, and your plans will succeed." Proverbs 16:3

Straight to the goal

LUKE 9:61-62

In Luke 9:61-62, Jesus has made his commitment to the cross and is on his way to Jerusalem. On the road, a man says to him; *"I will follow you Lord, but first let me go back and say good-by to my family"* Jesus replied, *"No one who puts his hand to the plow and looks back is fit for service in the kingdom of God."*

This calls to mind when as a farm kid, I was plowing a long field. The temptation is to look back over your shoulder to see if your furrow is straight for the entire world to see. This almost guarantees a crooked line. Instead, by focusing on a certain white rock at the other end of the field, the plowshare sliced open the first furrow, straight and true.

Two things stand out in Jesus' words. First is his candid honesty. **You won't be able to do this if your heart is really in the past, because to follow me is to be moving into the future. It is an adventure that will include some unknown changes.**

Secondly is the immediacy of the decision to follow him. It is urgent. **You must act on your choice.** It is common sense that every time we have an inclination to do something good, but do not act on it, the less likely we are to act on it at all. We become satisfied with the comforting emotion and intention, but disregard the action. Delaying only strengthens our resistance to the doing of it. "I always meant to do that," we say when it is too late.

Think about those people in your life who have given you hope and courage when you needed it. You probably have seen the tracks of their lives, their accomplishments and their values. Their witness brings helpful power and influence into your own decisions and actions. Perhaps they are still a living presence in your own journey. It would be a good thing to sit down today and make a list of those who have really strengthened you in your own challenges over the years. It will cheer them if you send them a message about their importance in your life.

Then, consider the **tracks left by your own spiritual autobiography**. Is it straight? Is it what you truly desire? What are others learning from your journey?

Paul Gilbert expressed it so well;

> *You are writing a Gospel,*
> *A chapter each day,*
> *By deeds that you do,*
> *By words that you say.*
>
> *Men read what you write,*
> *Whether faithless or true;*
> *Say, what is the Gospel*
> *According to You?*
>
> <u>Your Own Version</u>

"But one thing I do: Forgetting what is behind and straining toward what is ahead, I press on toward the goal to win the prize for which God has called me heavenward in Christ Jesus." Philippians 3:17

Whump!

ACTS 9:1-19

Mid-January is usually very cold and snowy in the country along the shore. This year is very different and some are calling it **unwinter.** This late afternoon is sunny with temperatures in the high 50s. The pampas grass is doing the hula, swaying in the warm breeze to the music of the waves. The beach looks almost like summertime, but way out over the lake, however, there are heavy, slate gray stratus clouds. Curtains of rain are sweeping along the northern horizon. It's nice now, but change is expected and usually quite sudden.

To the far west is yet another drama. A vanilla sky is trying to hold its own against a low ceiling of indigo clouds that resemble a rumpled, heavy winter coat not needed today. It is a descending shroud of winter, bringing strong westerly winds. It is an awesome day, but an hour later the pleasant breeze has turned into 50 mph wind gusts which are driving the rain horizontally eastward. The waves are now 4 ft. high and crashing continuously with a loud "WHUMP." There is power there and it's no wonder that people are searching for ways to harness wave energy for society's benefit. Then, in the curious way our memories work, that seems a very familiar sound. WHUMP! What was it that sounded like that?

I close my eyes and listen to several of them, and suddenly I remember. It is almost the same sound as that of 55 years ago when we were blasting stumps out of our farm fields. I remember the good neighbor who brought wooden boxes of dynamite, pushing the brown sticks deep into holes under the stumps. Then, running the wire and waiting until all were clear back out of the way, he touched the wires to a battery and – **WHUMP!** The stump and plenty of dirt were blown into the air. More good land was cleared for productive use. The farm memories persist and I will never forget that experience, the fun and especially that sound.

Uprooting obstacles to productive living is a good and often necessary thing. In Matthew 15 we read that Jesus was confronted by the Pharisees who often challenged his unique words and teaching. It was often a harsh exchange. He quoted the prophet Isaiah, calling them hypocrites, following the traditions of men rather than the revealed truth from God. The Message Bible-A Contemporary Version, expresses the concern of the disciples about this and his reply to them. *"Later his disciples came and told him, 'Did you know how upset the Pharisees were when they heard what you said?' Jesus shrugged it off. 'Every tree that wasn't planted by my Father will be pulled up by its roots. Forget them.'"* Matthew 15:12-13 TM

This is a clear statement that defines what really matters in our lives of faith. It is not our ritual observances, as good and helpful as they may be. What matters the most is the state of our hearts towards God. Going to church, supporting it and keeping its schedule of good events are all good things, but they are external. They only exist to help us get our hearts right with God. Anything that is not of God's true purpose for us should be rooted out. As the LORD quoted: *"These people honor me with their lips, but their hearts are far from me. They worship me in vain; their teachings are but rules taught by men."* Isaiah 29:13

Sometimes we need some **divine dynamite** to get our priorities straight. We once knew a medical doctor who came from a very demanding childhood. If his school grades dropped, his father would take the boy to work with him. All day long he would stand next to his father at a machine that stamped out hundreds of identical parts, over and over. At the end of a long, weary day the father would say, "If you don't want your life to be like this, you had better get your grades up." It was tough love and it worked. His grades brought him to the top of his class. The same drive continued through college and then into medical school which he said was "six years of hell."

Upon graduating he set up a successful practice in a wealthy community. In his spare time he turned his compulsive habits into many activities; underwater photography, biking, running, and swimming, doing many laps every noon at his club. He had no use for the church, seeing it as a boring, unproductive place of meaningless obligations to be avoided. However, he still felt a growing need in his life for more meaning.

Then one day leaving his club, he met one of his patients in the parking lot. The man was very ill so the Doctor helped him find his car and sit down. To his great dismay, the man died right there before other help could come. This was a big, unexpected turning point in the doctor's life. Later he described it as **walking into a totally dark room and turning on a very bright light.** He found the LORD, or as he would later say, "The LORD found me." He realized that he did not have to prove himself to himself, over and over for all his life. He was touched by the grace and mercy of God and became a Christian. It was not in church but in a public parking lot where a personal, large obstacle of pride was uprooted in a way that he understood.

It was the real deal. As he grew in the knowledge and love of God, his ability to help others increased many times over. All those recreational skills he had learned became ways of reaching out and communicating with other people about the grace of God.

It was a real **WHUMP** experience in his life, and while it may not be as clear-cut for everyone, the **effective change** can be the same. God is able to change us from being so obsessive about our human habits, our ways of seeing and doing things, when we truly ask him to. It is **deeply**

different from just going to church. It is the attitude of your life which starts at your deepest roots.

All the outward observances and religious routines of the world cannot and will not atone for a heart that is riddled with boredom, bitterness and hate.

 "The LORD does not look at the things that man looks at. Man looks at the outward appearance but the LORD looks at the heart." I Samuel 16:7

First Snowfall

ISAIAH 1: 17-19

There is something about the first snowfall that stirs the emotions. I was wandering along the edge of a large field of corn stubble when the first few flakes came gently floating down. There was a touch of white frost between the cornrows. I could see a set of farm buildings at the top of the neighboring slope. It was not very cold at all – in the mid- thirties. A fine Thanksgiving feast was just finished, wonderfully old fashioned and shared with close family ties. Then a few flakes of white snow came just silently floating down. It was one of those blissful moments of **sacred space with the WORD** as I walked through a living picture of my best country memories.

Such rare moments bring order and peace in the Kingdom Country of our inmost souls. I wondered as I wandered, if the WORD had ever seen snow? Northern Israel, being of higher elevation, reports occasional snow, but it is much less likely in the south. However, there are photos of modern day Bethlehem blanketed in a light snow, an unusual sight. These weather observations are sometimes considered by people who debate the accuracy of the December 25th celebrations of Christ's birth.

There is something far more important than that to think about. It is the realization of returning to God and accepting the confirmation of his peace touching our deepest souls. There is nothing better. *"Come now, let us reason together' says the LORD. 'Though your sins are as scarlet, they shall be white as snow; though they are red like crimson, they shall be like wool.'"* Isaiah 1:18

Well you don't have to be watching the snowflakes drifting down after a great family time to get the true meaning of those words. It isn't always possible to have beautiful conditions around you to know the peace of God in your heart. Sometimes it's a storm, making life more difficult.

The important thing is to know that whatever is going on in your life, it is possible and desirable, to turn toward the LORD. You can **return to him** and know he is always waiting to help you out with your life. Yes, he is always there, tapping on the door, or maybe just silently waiting for you to open up.

A man I once knew was troubled about many things going on in his life. He worried that he couldn't see around the next corner of events. Then he gave the LORD a chance to help him. He found his way when he read and really believed these words:

 "Do not be anxious about anything, but in everything, by prayer and petition, with thanksgiving present your requests to God. And the peace of God, which transcends all understanding, will guard your hearts (emotions) and minds (thoughts) in Christ Jesus." Philippians 4:6

Less is More

PROVERBS 15

Hogback trail in northeast Ohio is described as a beautiful and remarkable place, but I must say today it's pretty dreary and common. The leaves on the trees are very still, no breeze at all. It is dull and gray and very overcast with no sailing clouds or sunshine. There aren't even many birds, just a very still morning with no visible natural drama. Are we so accustomed to noise and traffic in our world that we don't know what to do with the silence?

Much of life does seem ordinary and unexciting. As I walk along; the only sound is my feet crunching on the gravel path as I watch for today's lesson from Professor Nature. I think of Einstein's remark; "Look deeply into nature and you will understand everything better."

What would the disciples say about this very ordinary day when nothing very notable was happening, as they followed the WORD ? More than that, what would the WORD himself say? Would it be something about endurance, whatever our circumstances or complex problems may be ? *"Have faith in God."* Mark 11:22

Quiet simplicity is good and is certainly at the root of our honest commitment to Christ. The austerity of our early Christian American settlers is still a good way to live. "Use it up! Wear it out! Make it do! Or do without!" When Jesus empowered and sent the disciples out to preach the Kingdom of God and to heal the sick, they were to take the message and the power but *"Take nothing for the journey-no staff, no bag, no bread, no money, no extra tunic."* Luke 9:3

It sounds like the **straight edge minimalist** movement that some practice today. No distractions from core values are allowed from owning too much stuff, excess equipment or complicated gear. (They shop at the Salvation Armani thrift stores.) Sounds good to me and I wonder sometimes if young people today are growing up with so many electronic gadgets that they will not know how to do things for themselves? Will they know how to really think for themselves and find the right answers? When writing something original, for example, it is pulled from within yourself, learning and thinking a progressive line of thought rather than always asking someone else what to say.

It is important to have ordinary stillness to feel the impulse to think originally and create solutions. I heard of two adult fishermen trying to cast their lines into a very promising water hole under a fallen tree. They failed over and over, tangling their lines until a barefoot young boy came along and observed their efforts. Then he showed them how to float their baited hooks on a large leaf, right into the target area, no fancy equipment needed!

There is always a better way to do things, and the fun is going through the steps of simple discovery, rejoicing in the passionate experience of your own learning.

Christians especially should practice simplicity and stay close to the LORD who apparently owned very little. I have read and believe that he did wear an expensive (seamless) robe and enjoyed good parties.

Whenever I think about these things I remember an ordinary evening vesper service with a large group of urban young people high in the Rocky Mountains. It was a simple campground in sight of the Continental Divide. As we watched the sunset behind the Rockies, someone was routinely reading: *"As the hart panteth for the waterbrooks, so panteth my soul after thee O God."* Psalm 40:1 <u>KJV</u>

Just then, in one of those rarest of moments, an adult stag with large antlers and 2 does walked into the clearing, not 50 feet from our group. Total silence came over the group - with barely contained excitement. The deer calmly looked at us, grazed a little then slowly moved off into the pine forest. The simple, living, natural beauty of that experience was greater than anything that could be preached or seen on a virtual screen. We sat in silence for some time and then, one by one, the campers rose and went to their cabins. An ordinary day had been touched by unforgettable grace.

So, when dreary days come along, as they surely do for everyone, we can nurture our souls with those 8 great words from the Bible, *"Be still and know that I am God."* Psalm 46:10 KJV

And if you meet someone who is having a down and dreary day, you will help yourself as you pass along to them this message from the greatest man who ever lived: *"In the world ye shall have tribulation: but be of good cheer; I have overcome the world."* John 6:33 KJV

Can you think of some ways to simplify your life? *"Don't hoard treasure down here where it gets eaten by moths and corroded by rust or – worse- stolen by burglars. Stockpile treasure in heaven, where it's safe from moth and rust and burglars. It's obvious isn't it? The place where your treasure is is the place you will most want to be, and end up being."* Matthew 6:19-21 TM

Clouds

*"I tell you the truth, whoever hears my words and believes him
who sent me has eternal life and will not be condemned, he has
crossed over from death to life."* John 5:24

Sometimes the clouds over the farmland are beautifully defined, other
times very mixed. On some windy days it is possible to see cumulus,
stratus and cirrus formations at their different levels all at the same
time. They sail along at different rates of speed, making a **sky canvas,** a
dramatic backdrop to country life with constantly changing colors and
shapes. There are thousands of encouraging sermons up there if we are
listening and waiting for the WORD to teach us.

Our Grandpa used to recite an old poem:

> *White sheep, white sheep on a blue hill,*
> *When the wind stops, they all stand still.*
> *When the wind blows, they walk away slow.*
> *White sheep, white sheep, where do you go?*

Gradually the kids among us would figure out that he was talking
about the clouds over the farm fields where we grew up.

Perhaps you have watched the clouds too, and have imagined various
figures up there shaped by nature. A little imagination can see horses,
chariots, castles and other things. A Peanuts cartoon had the children
watching the clouds. One saw a ducky but Linus saw the classical

sculpture, "The stoning of Steven," by Michelangelo. What we see up there reveals our own thoughts, backgrounds and expectations.

Consider then the words of our Lord who said, *"And then shall they see the Son of man coming in a cloud with power and great glory. And when these things begin to come to pass, then look up, and lift your heads; for your redemption draweth nigh."* Luke 21:27 <u>KJV</u>

He was not talking about imaginary things, but about his direct return and our need to be ready.

An advertisement in the <u>Cleveland Plain Dealer</u> newspaper screamed out in ink: "JUDGEMENT DAY! MAY 21, 2011! THE END OF THE WORLD! OCTOBER 21, 2011!"

This is not the first time some religious group has declared that they know when Christ will return. Apparently they have not read Jesus' reassuring words, *"Be ye therefore ready also; for the Son of man cometh at an hour when ye think not."* Luke 12:36-40. Truly, no one knows the day or time of his return.

Whenever it is, it will be the greatest event of all history. Imagine the sky splitting open, clouds rolling back, great trumpets announcing his final victory over all sin and death! It is not ours to know the how or when it will be, but **our faith tells us that history is going somewhere.** There is a goal and it is that Jesus Christ will be LORD of all. That is all we know and all we really need to know.

Believing this brings us to another important and personal question. Are we ready for this? If so, then we are living in the shadow of eternity and therefore in a constant, daily state of expectation.

Albyn Macintosh was a Christian architect who lived in this constant state of expectation that colored all his decisions about his life commitments. His belief was that **we should all live in the faith that Christ will return in our lifetime.** This brought joy and determination to his many accomplishments. His example confirmed that there is nothing as thrilling as living life in fellowship with the Lord. It changes everything and seasons your life with unspeakable joy and purpose.

Much of the modern world is in turmoil and the madness of war. We must acknowledge these distressing facts with open eyes. If we could solve these things, of course we would. Yet we remember that these conditions will continue to worsen until the LORD returns.

Therefore, let us never allow anything to come between us and the LORD. Then the distresses of our time can only press us closer to the LORD's plan and purpose for us.

May our daily prayer be the last words on the last page of the Bible; "*Surely I come quickly. Amen. Even so, come, Lord Jesus*" Revelation 22:20

Chariots of Fire

II KINGS 6:16-17

Six magnificent cumulus mustangs are racing toward the Canadian border, manes and tails streaming in the wind. Their coats are burnished to flame by the setting sun, sorrel, bay and strawberry roan. You can almost hear the pounding of their hooves. Rising high into the dark blue sky behind them is a giant white robed Elisha, his beard flowing over his shoulder. The judgment of God can be visualized in the skies over the blossoming vineyards of our county.

The moment passes quickly as the sun melts into the horizon which appears to reach up, embracing its arrival. It was a glimpse, just a glimpse of the horses and chariots of fire around God's prophet in his desperate hour; a vision of the heavenly hosts. In this crisis, Elisha's faith was renewed and he believed again, *"Those who are with us are more than those who are with them."* II Kings 6:16

There is not a single question that we may face in our lives, that cannot be found somewhere in the Bible. Elisha was confronting the unrighteousness of the warring Arameans with the righteousness of God. Spiritual warfare is nothing new. We find it throughout the scriptures. It is alive and well in the world today as well.

In a presidential election year when billions of dollars will be spent on the struggle for power, we will hear much in the media about social issues and the **perceived Will of God** regarding human life and religious behavior, (and of course the effect on the economy which seems to be all that most people care about).

In all of the debate about morals and the apparently insurmountable differences, it strengthens our faith in God to recall once again II Chronicles 20:15, *". . . the battle is not yours, but God's."* The war of words will go on endlessly as the armies of each ideology recruit others and struggle to win at the ballot box. In the end, whichever party wins the election, it still boils down to your individual conviction about God's purpose. Ultimately, the government does not and should not run your personal life. It is your responsibility. The decisions you make should be rooted and informed by your understanding of God.

When you are facing important personal decisions, take it to the LORD in prayer and He will answer. Open your eyes of faith and bring the questions of your heart before him. The power of God is invisible to the eyes of the unbeliever, but to those who know and trust him, insights and answers will come.

Every year we thank God for Easter with all of its meaning, beauty and promise. First, we must experience the darkness and fear of the garden of Gethsemane. Do you remember the words of Jesus there when he was betrayed and arrested? Peter defended him and fought back, cutting off a servant's ear with his sword, but the LORD said, *"Put your sword back in its place . . . Do you think I cannot call on my Father, and he will at once put at my disposal more than twelve legions of angels ?"* Matthew 26:52-54

The fact of our faith declares that God is doing more for us than we can ever realize through our limited experiences . . . If we can't see that in faith, we need to get our spiritual eyes checked.

 "Those who are with us are more than are with them." II Kings 6:17

Wind

JOHN 3 : 1 - 21

A visit to a restored farming museum such as Cooperstown, N.Y., reveals many illustrations of Christian discipleship.

There was a nice breeze blowing, swaying the tree tops as we watched the demonstration of **hand threshing, also known as tribulation.** The worker swung the **tribulum,** a hand held threshing flail with rake teeth that separated the wheat from the husks and chaff. The wheat and chaff were then tossed up into the breeze. The heavier grain fell back to the threshing floor and the wind blew the useless chaff away.

You can't see the wind but you can see what it does, just as what the WORD said to Nicodemas, *"The wind blows wherever it pleases. You hear its sound, but you cannot tell where it comes from or where it is going. So it is with everyone born of the Spirit."* John 3:8

During my working life in marketing, I was always interested in the personal touches in customers' offices, such as the photos on their desks. One sign over an engineer's drafting table really struck me. It read, "Only he who can see the invisible, can do the impossible."

I found that idea fascinating. Every new idea may be an incremental extension of an original invention, improving upon the earlier design. As I have thought about our work and living for the Lord, I realize the great diversity of gifts among all who follow him. No two of us are alike. Everyone has unique gifts and an individual approach *". . . as the Spirit gave them utterance."* Acts 2:4

However, in our diversity, there is always one great common reality and that is the essential work of the Spirit. First we must understand the simply basic thing that God wants done. Then when the invisible Spirit of God moves within the opportunity for witness, the results are of God's design.

Sometimes this means tribulation, which is no fun at all. The WORD has more to tell us: *"And I will ask the Father, and he will give you another Counselor to be with you forever, the Spirit of truth. The world cannot accept him, because it neither sees him nor knows him. But you know him, for he lives with you and will be in you."* John 14:16

Five times the Counselor is described as **him, not as it.** This personal pronoun is extremely important to grasp, for he is a manifestation of our personal God. We may not see him, but he is here, working out impossible things in a world blind to his presence. He works through our willingness to be his hands, feet, eyes, ears and tongues in the constant daily turning of planet earth.

As I watched the strengthening wind separating the good wheat from the useless chaff by the use of tribulation, I was overwhelmed once again at this amazing reality and wonderful words of our Lord: *"And I will do whatever you shall ask in my name that the Father may be glorified in the Son. If you ask me anything in my name, I will do it."* John 14:12

Incredible but true! Totally unselfish prayers offered humbly in his name, that conclude sincerely with, "Thy will be done," shall always be answered in God's way, in God's time. Yes, many unforeseen and invisible blessings are the result of your prayers when they come from the honesty of your inmost heart.

Even you? Yes, even you and all who believe. May this wonderful wind blow through your life today, eliminating the useless from the valuable.

"... so is everyone who is born of the Spirit"
John 3:8

Reverse, or Forward ?

ROMANS 5: 1-6

Consider that your life could be compared to the gears in an automobile; Low, Drive, Overdrive, Neutral, Reverse and Park. Every day we turn on the ignition of our lives and assume the authority of freedom and power to drive our plans and hopes.

Long before automobiles, however, people have known that not everything always goes as they hope. There are setbacks for even the most diligent efforts.

A most interesting story in American literature is <u>Giants in the Earth,</u> *by* Hans Rolvaag._It tells of the Norwegian pioneers who settled in the Dakota Territory in the 1800s. The main character, some reviews say, is the land itself which calls forth the hopes and dreams of ownership. The pioneers must contend with weather, squatters, plagues and many unexpected things.

The central figure is a man of great energy, hope and ambition named Per Hansa. Against his neighbor's warning, he joyfully plants his precious wheat seed much earlier than the rest of the farming community. This is soon followed by a freezing spring rain which seems to destroy the seed, casting him into deep depression and despair. He believes he has lost everything and truly does not know what to do. His promising future has disappeared, threatening his family's existence.

Days pass and his neighbors plant their crops in the traditional schedule. The weather warms, but in despair, Per Hansa is unable to rise to new mornings with any hope.

222

Then one day, his young son comes bursting into the prairie cabin with the exciting news that the crop has come up after all! Per Hansa rushes out to see that his seed has sprouted and the field is covered with green shoots quivering in the breeze. That moment of standing with his son is breathtaking and he is overwhelmed with emotion. **Reverse** has shifted into **Forward**! Everything is OK again ! In fact, everything is great !

Out of this close brush with total failure, their faith and future is reborn. He turns again to scripture. "Read us a chapter," he says to his wife, Beret. While this is a novel, I find myself wondering what Bible chapter would fit the occasion. Could it be Romans 5 ?

If some experience puts your life into **Reverse** or **Park**, you may be ready to learn and understand more deeply, our dependence upon God. In such devastating times beyond our control, our eyes may be opened to the absolute truth of Romans 5:8, *"While we were yet sinners, Christ died for us."* Acknowledging our human weakness is not politically correct in the modern world, of course. However, as someone has said, sometimes the way to God is down, not up.

The truth of how God brings us through these times, common to all of us, is found in Romans 5:1-6. It is God's sequence of recovering us from tragic experiences. I like to think of this as the chapter they read that fictional morning when, despite the freezing rain, the wheat had sprouted. Each step rises and overtakes the next one, as in faith we are restored, stronger and more realistically hopeful than ever before.

God's love in our hearts
Hope (that does not disappoint us)
Character (experience)
Perseverance (patience)
Suffering (tribulation)

We have challenges every day, don't we? In God's strength, they can be opportunities for growth – forward, ever forward into the hope that *"does not disappoint us."*

"Therefore since we have been justified through faith, we have peace with God through our Lord Jesus Christ, through whom we have gained access by faith into this grace in which we now stand. And we rejoice in the hope of the glory of God. Not only so, but we also rejoice in our sufferings, because we know that suffering produces perseverance; perseverance, character; and character, hope. And hope does not disappoint us, because God has poured out his love into our hearts by the Holy Spirit, whom he has given us. You see, just at the right time, when we were still powerless, Christ died for the ungodly . . ." Romans 5;1-6

Bucket List

PSALM 145

Evening chore time on the farm meant milking the cows. On a summer's late afternoon they would be brought into the barn to be fed. There's a certain peaceful atmosphere at that time, of the work routine and the secure rhythms of farm life. Clean milking machines were put together and the big sliding doors facing west were opened to let the setting sun shine in. The pulsating connectors and long rubber air hoses were attached to the vacuum line over the stanchions. The other end was fastened to the top of the DeLaval milking machine.

The cow's udder was washed, the cups attached and the milk drawn out to the pulsating rhythm. When done, the warm foaming milk was dumped into stainless steel buckets and carried, usually two at a time for balance, to the milk house. There it was strained and stored overnight in the cooler. Those were buckets of value not to be spilled or left out in the heat to spoil.

Such was an evening of a warm setting sun, quiet music on the old radio, cattle munching their supper and giving their milk. We fed and cared for them. And, in a sense, they fed and cared for us.

Do you have a **bucket list**? This phrase has become a standard comment in society due to the popularity of the successful movie by the same name. The concept is to enumerate the things **you would really like to do before you kick the bucket.** The idea has really caught on in a helpful way and makes for great conversation.

However, a Swedish proverb states, "Don't throw away the old bucket until you know whether the new one holds water."

Much has been made of what you still might want to do in your life. This is a good thing and may help maximize the time remaining. After all we never know what the future holds. However, it is possible that our buckets are already nearly overflowing with wonderful things from the past. The things we might list are too numerous to mention, but here are a few.

Family: Victor Hugo wrote: "A house is built of logs and stone, of tiles and posts and piers; A home is built of loving deeds that stand a thousand years." Practically everything that develops in your lifetime is based on the kind of family home life that you had. It is a shared servanthood within the home, a caring awareness of the others who live there. What are some things you still want to do with your family?

Love: The great theologian Paul Tillich said "The first duty of love is to listen." If you know how to really listen, love will be a continuing reality in your life, both in the giving and the receiving of it. What do you consider your greatest listening skill?

Friends: These are the ones with whom you have a natural, easy affinity. They are the ones with whom you can **speak the truth in love.** You enjoy being with them and even if a long time passes before seeing them again, you can pick up where you left off. A friend is a present that you give yourself, so choose wisely. Who is your best friend? To whom are you a good friend?

Faith: This is not just about a general definition of your religion. It is really all about your specific relationship with the LORD. When have you felt closest to God? Can you write it down, perhaps in a letter to a good friend or Pastor? What are you hoping to do to further your faith?

Work: Did you love your work or are you still working? Over your span of years perhaps you have done different kinds of work. Which was the most rewarding? Why was it so good? Do you want to do more work? If you were advising a young person about finding the right work in their life, what would you say? Do you know such a person who needs to hear from you?

Humor: This is not always telling contrived jokes so that you can be the center of attention. This is about the joy of our lives, the genuine fun that enhances our respect for humanity and appreciation of the good, friendly feelings among us. We are all human after all and should learn to laugh at ourselves. Some say that good country dancing, line dancing or square dancing is laughter in action to fun music. It can bring out the freedom and humor of our lives. Have you been dancing lately?

Community: Even when Israel was carried into captivity, God told them to pray for the prosperity of their captive city, and the benefits that would return to them when they were released. Instead of complaining, it is so much more rewarding to be a part of the solution.

One key thing that is usually needed in community work is fund raising. It is an art and must be done carefully, so if you decide to help there, first seriously ask: Does God want this done and how ? The first century church of Jesus Christ knew that work solely of men, would ultimately fail, but work truly of God, will always succeed.

Hobby: What do you like to do in your spare time? Does it help you grow personally and enrich your thought life? Is there an interest that you have pursued most of your life that you could take to a new level? Great things can come of it. It is said that great inventions like the wheel or the sail came about when someone was just leisurely playing with ideas.

What would you add? If your bucket is already too full for anything more, just pick up an empty one and see what the LORD has in store for you next. He has more blessings for you than you could imagine.

 What does the WORD want you to do next ? *"And let us run with endurance the race God has set before us. We do this by keeping our eyes on Jesus, the champion who initiates and perfects our faith."* Hebrews 12: 1-2. <u>NLT</u>

Frisky

PHILIPPIANS 4:10-13

That's not a word you hear very often anymore but it comes to my mind every April 4th. You didn't ask, but here's the deal.

The word **country** is now the name of a popular lifestyle. It is an urban identity that includes stylish country clothing, an accent, mechanical bulls, music and various accessories, including a cowboy hat. I recently saw an ad for a hat that cost $1200. We used to call these folks drugstore cowboys, often carrying a guitar they couldn't play.

My own earliest image of **country** is of a scrawny twelve-year-old kid wearing hand-me-down jeans rolled up to fit, a striped short sleeved shirt and scruffy hightop barn sneakers. He is standing in front of the old milk house with the little 4-H sign by the window. He remembers when Mr. Schrader built it, sticking the blocks together from a bucket of mortar reinforced by Beech-Nut brown tobacco juice which he regularly expectorated into it.

The boy is holding the halter lead that he braided from baler twine. He is working with his first calf, a spring heifer named Frisky, who was born on April 4. He is head and shoulders taller than she. Dreams of blue ribbon glory are in his head.

She is a Holstein, white with black markings, learning to stand with all four feet squarely underneath her, showing off her conformation and good grooming. If she is going to the school fair, she will need her shots, a clean, glossy coat and know how to behave in crowds.

What a great memory, so long ago. The old Kodak black and white snapshot with its scalloped edges has somehow survived 60 years, thanks to a family that still treasures those days before **country** was fashionable. Sixty times I have remembered April 4.

The **first calf** was a common tradition in those farm days. About the time a boy or girl was 11 or 12; adult responsibility began to mean something. You got baptized, immersed by Pastor Polan, either at Fish Creek or at Scheifle's farm pond. You may have gotten your first nice suit and tie from J.C. Penny's in Rome, N.Y.(It was fun to watch how the clerks would zoom the money from the main floor up to the mezzanine office via a little container on a wire that was spring propelled by a strong hand pull on the power handle by the clerk.)

If you were raised on a farm, you were seriously given your first calf as soon as you understood the responsibility. Your allowance was 25 cents most weeks, not always. You had specific work chores and were part of the adult schedule. Adults began to talk to you more, treating you with respect and asking about your progress and plans. It all hung together, so natural and right. You had no reason to think that any of this would ever change, that this life was always going to be, well, always.

Looking back, I appreciate now, those real country roots more than I can say, even without a $1200 hat, fancy boots or designer jeans. It is still a living world in my mind, almost like yesterday, embedded forever in my heart and soul.

 Even the gift of the Baptism Bible and special verse comes back loud and clear, *"I can do all things through Christ which strengtheneth me."* Philippians 4:13 KJV of course.

Frisky and I did pull down a blue ribbon or two, and then she grew up. And so did I.

229

Escape

PSALM 91

One of our cats, Cinnamon, likes to spend a lot of time outside because she is a hunter. The camouflage color of autumn leaves, she runs here and there and is one of the most alert and alive creatures I have seen. When in the house she is a good, relaxed domestic companion, but outside, she becomes a quick and total predator. Though small, she can arc those front legs in a wide sweep and her sharp claws mean the end for many mice and moles. Birds too, although one day I watched a red-winged blackbird narrowly escape, leaving a mouthful of feathers and humiliation for the mighty hunter.

All people, including Christians, at some time find themselves facing the sharp claws of capture in some area of life. It may be work dissatisfaction, physical addiction, relationship problems, or countless others. The Psalmist wrote, *"Surely he will deliver thee from the snare of the fowler."* Psalm 91:3 Yes, we believe he will, if we will entrust ourselves to him, and remember to act wisely.

If we have real faith in Christ, he is a strong resource when we are faced with the sharp claws of disaster. In the first place, we are making better, more thoughtful choices and commitments about these challenges. Secondly, even then if things go wrong, we find what Paul taught the Corinthian Christians about a *"way of escape"* to be true. (I Corinthians 10:13)

The good news is that we can also become captive to **good things** instead of bad. One term for this is **positive addiction**. For example, our efforts to be who Christ calls us to be opens up huge frontiers of service. Our LORD taught many things about being *"good and faithful servants."* Truly it can be the real pathway to fulfilling happiness. We admire the unselfish attitude of service that we often see in others. We seek to be the kind of servants who would be pleasing to God. This is the bread and butter of the life of faith, isn't it?

But who among us has not sometimes felt the need to escape from always thinking of others rather than ourselves? It is a rare condition but occasionally it's possible to become so consumed with other's needs that our own **emotional bank account** gets overdrawn. We feel burned out. Is it Christian to put ourselves first for a while? Of course it is! We read that the LORD himself sometimes needed to *"withdraw to a quiet place" to* pray and restore his strength. I believe it was the evangelist George Whitfield in the 1700s who wrote, "The LORD gave me a message and a horse to deliver it, but I killed the horse," speaking of his own physical body.

I admire the fictional character Demetrius, body servant to the Roman Legionnaire Marcellus in Lloyd C. Douglas' novel <u>The Robe.</u> As a manacled, purchased slave he was angry and dangerous. But when he and Marcellus both became Christians, servanthood took on entirely new power and meaning for both of them. It now was a **chosen** way of life, with respect for others because that was how Jesus would live. New, daily strength was drawn from the LORD, with wisdom in knowing when and how to help others.

Yes, at times we can become fed up with the demands others make on us because they think we will never say "no." We may long to escape from the LORD's perceived expectation of his followers. Even the first disciples seemed to struggle with this among themselves. In the last chapter of the gospel of John, even after the resurrection, Peter asked

Jesus *"What's John going to do?"* Jesus replied, *'What is that to you?"* John 21:21

In seeking to find the right balance in our everyday relationship to Christ, and our place in the world, we can find great help in his words, *"If the Son makes you free, you shall be free indeed."* John 8:36. Just as Jesus was the "free-est" person who has ever lived and faced death on planet earth; we also may become responsibly free. We must wisely evaluate our personal desire to escape from obligations, with the call to be his faithful servants on earth.

Dr. Ken Smith of my acquaintance years ago spoke about the rewards and risks of freedom. He bought a parakeet for his children and tried to teach it to talk, with very little success. One day they thought the bird would be happier if he could fly loose around the house, so they opened the cage door. Sure enough, Budgie flew out and in a flash banked a fast turn for the big picture window, seeking escape from his caged life. The result was predictably fatal, and the family thought sorrowful new thoughts about freedom.

Do you know that **the Son has made you free?** As you live with him daily, he will teach you to know when to say **yes** and when to say **no**. He wants you around for a long, long time.

> *Make me a captive, Lord*
> *And then I shall be free;*
> *Force me to render up my sword,*
> *And I shall conqueror be.*
> *I sink in life's alarms*
> *When by myself I stand;*
> *Imprison me within Thine arms*
> *And strong shall be my hand.*
>
> *My will is not my own*
> *Till Thou hast made it Thine;*
> *If it would reach a monarch's throne*
> *It must its crown resign:*

It only stands unbent
  Amid the clashing strife,
When on its bosom it has leant
  And found in Thee its life.

<u>Christ's Bondservant</u>
By George Matheson

 "I run in the path of your commands, for you have set my heart free." Psalm 119:32

Squirrels

PROVERBS 6

There are some tall oak trees along the fence line of the side pasture . . . In the top of one of those, way up there probably 75 feet, is a red squirrel's nest with a great view of the surrounding country . . . What an engineer and worker she is! Recently the northern winds reached 50 mph, taking down some branches but that nest is as solid as ever, while a man- made bird house by the well was blown away. The squirrel builder cut some green twigs 12 -18 inches long, carried moss and leaves in her mouth to that fork in the tree and wove it all together in such a way that it withstood the harsh winter. I imagine there are still acorns stashed in there. I have read that squirrels can actually carry their **lumber** in front paws over their head, and when necessary, even walk backwards to their building site.

My dad used to call the busy squirrels **sugar nervous** and they must have found some sweets somewhere to be so highly energetic all the time. The barn cats do a good job of keeping those squatters out of the granary.

I find no mention of squirrels in the Bible, but I do find strong and good teaching about work in II Thessalonians 3: 6: *"In the name of the Lord Jesus Christ, we command you, brothers, to keep away from every brother who is idle and does not live according to the teaching you received from us. For you yourselves know how you ought to follow our example. We were not idle when we were with you, nor did we eat anyone's food without paying for it. On the contrary, we worked night and day, laboring and toiling so that we would not be a burden to any of you. We did this, not because we do not have the right to such help, but in order to make ourselves a model for you to follow. For even when we were with you, we gave you this rule: "If a man will not work, he shall not eat." We hear that some among you are idle. They are not busy; they are busybodies . . ."*

When persons approach their work with the right attitude, it will be done in a way that will please the Lord. Great satisfaction and self-respect result. This **work ethic** is a foundation stone of our faith, and of our American culture. It is in the news a lot these days, about its value and sometimes about its absence in the modern world.

When did you first learn to work? Who was your first work teacher? What was your first real job? If you want a good conversation with someone, those are good starter questions to get the true personality coming forth. ! There are, of course, those who never have found work to be enjoyable. They may not have heard these anonymous lines:

> *Sitting still and wishing*
> *Will never make anyone great.*
> *The good Lord sends the fishing*
> *But we must dig the bait.*

No doubt you have heard the expression that, "Opportunity knocks on your door but once." There is a better one than that which I saw it at the Freightliner Corporation, "Let's go knock on opportunity's door!" Much better!

When a person knows the Lord and can pray honestly about his work, he will find a greater ability about his skills than he ever knew he had. Creativity blooms when the Lord is a key part of your vocational calling. You may not be in a Christian profession such as ministry, but you can even dig a ditch to the glory of God.

While on a youth mission in Alaska, Richard Foster was doing just that, digging a sewer ditch in the frozen earth. It was a very hard and long day, but a wise counselor said, "See every shovelful as a prayer to the Lord." He did and the job got done.

A person is most fortunate if he really feels his work is his passion. *"Work at it with all your hearts . . ."* is not just a good memory verse. It is a working, saving value in your human existence. It can be a great prayer connection to the Lord, and therefore will be ethical in the highest sense. You can ask the Lord about any aspect of your work and you will learn better and better ways of getting good tasks accomplished.

I recently retired and have had to learn about not going in every morning and checking up on the progress of business deals. This has not been an easy adjustment. I can understand those who refuse to retire because they can't see how to accept the future abyss of nothing to do. Dr. Paul Tournier observed that your working life might be compared with the cycle of a day; dawn, morning, high noon, afternoon, evening, nightfall. Inexorably, we reach the afternoon and evening of our life.

Then new questions of deeper significance arise. Have you kept your heart and your capacity to love? When you were in the morning of your life, you had the high ambition of choosing a meaningful work life, choosing one path over many. It is possible now to do that again, to remember the passion that is in your DNA. You can choose anew the most desirable path, now with a lifetime of skills and experience.

You know how to do this and you still have time to do it again, to be that person again, except now without the controls of set specifications, or the same obligations, or the confining limits imposed by economic and social obligations.

Come to think of it, I never have seen a retired squirrel sitting around drinking coffee with other grumpy squirrels complaining about the state of the world. Have you?

You can work at something with all your heart, as working for the Lord and learning in a fresh new way the meaning of these words:

"I pray that out of his glorious riches he may strengthen you with power through his Spirit in your inner being, so that Christ may dwell in your hearts through faith. And I pray that you, being rooted and established in love, may have power together with all the saints to grasp how wide and long and high and deep is the love of Christ and to know this love that surpasses knowledge-that you may be filled to the measure of all the fullness of God. Now to him who is able to do immeasurably more than all we ask or imagine, according to his power that is at work within us, to him be glory in the church and in Christ Jesus throughout all generations forever and ever!. Amen." Ephesians 3:16

Wild Strawberries

SONG OF SOLOMON 7

Out by the apple tree and honeysuckle bush is a generous patch of small wild strawberries. They are rare and sweet, even more so as they are hidden among the tall grass and usually undiscovered. They remind me of the **pleasant and tender fruits** described in the Old Testament book known as "Song of Solomon." It is a passionate, explicit love story, using highly sensuous and suggestive imagery. At first, it is kind of hard to understand why it is in the Holy Bible. It certainly arouses new interest in scripture.

It follows Ecclesiastes, which is about the meaninglessness of life without God. Then it precedes the major prophet Isaiah, the very serious and lengthy book which is all about God's judgment and salvation. Right there it is like a refreshing interlude, right in the middle of despair, separation, anguish, sorrow, death, suffering, moral outrage, paganism, tension, sin and the consequences of our spiritual choices. Here is the voice of love drawing us with exquisite charm and beauty, as one of God's choicest gifts. It is in the heart of our human nature, given by God to be used to cherish the meaning of life together.

Consider chapter 4 verse 9, *"you have ravished my heart with one look of your eyes, with one link of your necklace."* . . . Why is this seemingly romantic language in the Bible? Furthermore, it is in a book which has nary a specific reference to God. Try working this one out in a youth discussion group sometime!

238

Though at first it may seem out of place, it is true that the Word of God never flinches at even the most intense and complex challenges that are a part of every person's life. Sexuality and religion are both strong emotional realities that often get intertwined, causing conflicts about right and wrong choices. The Bible, as someone has pointed out, is not just about sweetness and light. It is also about our really tough questions, temptations and struggles as we seek to do and be the persons God created us to be. That is why it can be so powerfully helpful in any situation.

The Bible does not always give specific, literal answers to our questions. What it does give, is the help we need to find our relationship with God. In our human ways, we tend to lock ourselves into thinking there are only two ways to go. Our imaginations can carry us down one trail, and then switch to the other. Back and forth we go, unaware of God's better way.

A typical example of this, as may be seen any day on junky television shows, might be that some single people wish they were married, while some married people wish they were single. This can be a painful and difficult situation, a real test of character, but both are missing the point. **The true and living reality is the Love of God which supersedes any human situation.** Perhaps you recall the great old gospel song:

> *If we with ink the oceans fill*
> *And were the skies of parchment made;*
> *If every stalk on earth a quill*
> *And every man a scribe by trade;*
> *To write the Love of God above*
> *Would drain the oceans dry;*
> *Nor could the scroll contain the whole*
> *Though stretched from sky to sky.*
>
> Frederick Lehman

The toughest questions we face can be discussed openly with God. As we learn to listen carefully to his whispers, we find that he urges us to **not deceive ourselves** about our choices and decisions. There is power in this relationship, a maturing that brings better rewards than we thought possible.

Yes, the strawberries look sweet indeed, but there is a better viewpoint for your consideration. "*. . . Casting down* *imaginations and every high thing that exalteth itself against the knowledge of God, and bringing into captivity every thought to the obedience of Christ.*" II Corinthians 10:5

Is it easy? No, but as a friend once said, "Faith makes everything possible, not easy." And experience has proven over all generations, **Christ did not come to make life easy, but to make people great.**

Thanksgiving – A Habit
Of The Heart

Sermon at Second Congregational Church ~ Nov. 18, 2012

> Text: *"And God is able to make all grace abound to you, so that in all things at all times, having all that you need, you will abound in every good work."* II Corinthians 9:8

Before we read the scripture today, let us realize that there are so many things that could be said about Thanksgiving. It is a great holiday, truly American, with all the trimmings. It is a day of wonderful traditions and memories, but it sometimes gets lost in the commercial rush toward Christmas. Where shall we start today?

Well, the Bible is always a good place to start! So we will read a small part of the letter that Paul wrote to the Christians in the wild city of Corinth so many years ago. It was a place where believing in God was risky and difficult. A place where, at that time, believers were very much in the minority, and therefore needed to stick together to keep their spirits up. They were learning about helping and encouraging each other through tough times.

It is a pure lesson in thankfulness, of really knowing that it is the LORD who supplies our needs:

(Reading of II Corinthians 9:6-15)

What are your plans for Thanksgiving Day? Every year as the day approaches, many rich memories return to build on the feast.

Have you seen the new Bob Evans restaurant ads? Now you can go there and pick up your Thanksgiving meal with all the traditional foods supposedly. "How many will you be having?" the waitress will ask.

Now I like Bob Evans – their biscuits and gravy are very good. But it's a far cry from the childhood roots I remember on this special day.

In our old farmhouse out in the country, not far from the Erie Canal, there was an old cast iron stove. I can see my mother out there splitting the kindling to get the fire going, lifting the round steel lids off the top with that little handle made for that purpose. Then in would go the sticks of firewood from the woodshed, and if there were icicles on the eaves by the door, she would break them off and stick them in the reservoir by the firebox to melt for hot, soft water.

I remember the big white turkey who had been strolling around the back yard, and my dad sending me into the house when he and the axe and the turkey went around back to the chopping block. There the bird made his sacrifice to our festival day. Then he was hung up to bleed out before being plucked and singed and prepared for the big pot.

I can remember the mashed potatoes with chunks of yellow butter and the sweet potatoes with walnuts and toasted marshmallows on top. And the homemade gravy – which I can still taste, and I must say it was better than Bob Evans!

Then how about those homemade rolls – and the pies, two of them, one apple and one pumpkin, all of them out of the oven of that big stove, now hot from mother's fire – her hands flying to keep this entire feast coming together.

I can see it all now – 65 years later.

And maybe there would be maple walnut ice cream. Let me tell you about that! About two miles from our farm was Vaughn's country store. You might call it our "Smallmart". Ben and Minnie Vaughn were the proprietors. Ben and my dad were real horse guys, comparing teams and considering swapping sometimes.

In their little store there were tall shelves and if you wanted something from the top shelf, like a box of Jell-O, Ben or Minnie would get that long stick with the pincers on top and the squeeze handle on the other end and reach up there to get it for you.

Then there was the little side room where the white ice cream freezer was, with 6 black lids that could be lifted off by the round handle on top. 6 lids and 6 flavors, vanilla, chocolate, white house cherry, maybe chocolate revel, strawberry and MAPLE WALNUT.

On special occasions like Thanksgiving, you might get a quart of Maple Walnut in one of those round cardboard containers with the lid that would fit just right on the top. Ben would dig the ice cream out of the big round containers with that wide scoop and pack it in, probably talking horses with dad. "How about a little more" dad might say and so Ben would jam another scoop in there somehow, knifing it in and bulging the sides, but charging no more – because he was GENEROUS.

We had little in those days, no money really, but now I know, we had everything. Why? Because we were grateful for what we did have.

We had the LORD. And we had his WORD. We had our church. We had enough – never too much, but enough. Truly, as the scripture told us this morning, "God is able to make all grace abound to you, so that in all things, at all times having all that you need . . . This will result in Thanksgiving."

And so, just now, as I come back into the present shaking my head, I see that the holiday is a focal point for the world – and a modern commercial success, but we think today, here in God's house which we love, about the attitude of living gratefully, not just one day of the year, but as a 'habit of the heart'. That is a consistent way of seeing life, being realistic about the facts of our lives, but doing so with hope and appreciation of the real blessings of God.

I am speaking of the toughness of our faith, the endurance of our genuine belief in God and his goodness to us. It is our heritage in America, and though I may sound a little hardheaded, it did come through sacrifice and tough time didn't it? It came to us from those travelers on the Mayflower and we all know the danger of losing that core of divine determination, of heartfelt thankfulness bought with sacrifice and very hard work.

What is happening to America anyway?

A few years ago, Bob Halman gave me this piece written in 1857. I don't know where he got it, but it's good.

"When New England was first planted, the settlers met with many difficulties and hardships, as is necessarily the case when civilized people attempt to establish themselves in a wilderness country. Being piously disposed, they sought relief from Heaven, by laying their want before the Lord in frequent set days of fasting and prayer. Constant meditation, and discourses on the subject of their difficulties, kept their minds gloomy and discontented, and like the children of Israel, there were many disposed to return to the land which persecution had determined them to abandon.

"At length, when it was proposed in the assembly to proclaim another fast, a farmer of plain sense, rose and remarked that the inconveniences they had suffered, and concerning which they had often wearied heaven with the complaints, were not so great as might have been expected, and were diminishing every day as the colony strengthened, that the earth began to reward their labors, and to furnish liberally for their sustenance; that the seas and rivers were full of fish, the air sweet, the climate wholesome, above all, they were in full enjoyment of liberty, civil and religious. He therefore, thought that reflecting and conversing on these subjects would be more comfortable, as tending to make them more contented with their situation, and it would better become the gratitude they owed to the Diving Being, if instead of a fast, they should proclaim a thanksgiving. His advice was taken and from that day to this, they have in every year observed circumstances of public happiness sufficient to furnish employment for a thanksgiving day."

When you visit Plymouth Plantation – sure enough you can envision that first feast of gratitude, held within sight of the 50 graves on the hill of those who made the journey but did not survive the bitter winter.

Yes, they faced very big challenges, but they were thankful. Nathaniel Morton, the keeper of the Plymouth Colony record wrote, in 1620: "If they looked behind them, there was a mighty ocean which they had passed, and was now as a main bar or gulp to separate them from all he civil parts of the world." For them, there was no turning back.

I really wonder if modern young people today, with all their conveniences, have any idea of the hard work and sacrifice, any sense of what has been given to us by the price paid by those people. Many of them seem to whine about what they don't have, instead of really appreciating what they do have.

I actually pity the young who never got to go to Vaughn's store and watch that ice cream being packed into that round container. I can taste it now! Will they ever really know the anticipation and longing so simple and just plain good? Will they ever understand what real generosity and helpfulness is?

As for me, they can have their video games and virtual violence and disposable electronics. Will they ever learn that "Less is more?"

I'll take my dad at Ben Vaughn's store where the talk is of horses and the ice cream is a real treat. I'll take that true lesson in friendship and generosity every day of the week thank you!

Of course, sometimes we do have big difficulties. Still, the faith in our God can see us through them. I have met people who have certain buoyancy as they go through life. It seems that their troubles and winds of adversity don't destroy them. Many of you are like that and you amaze me. How do you do that?

Lewis Mumford writes about a person like that, a simple tenant farmer whose life was tough enough to make anyone knuckle under.

He had raised a large family while barely keeping his own head above water. His wife died soon after the birth of a child and he lost a son in the war. A crippling disease struck him and brought with it constant pain. He had reason to be bitter, but he wasn't. He maintained a positive outlook and kept a smile. One day when his illness had about run its course, when he knew he was dying, he said to a visiting friend, "I think my time has come. The feast of life will soon be over."

I want to be like that. I want to be able to see beyond inevitable struggle and the tragedies of life and say the 'life is a feast '.

Have you ever seen that Norman Rockwell painting of the grandmother and little boy sitting in a 'greasy spoon' diner, getting ready to eat some very plain food ? Art critics are not very kind in their assessment of his sentimental approach, but it's a picture that stays with us 'non art critic' sorts. Maybe you remember it too?

The grandmother is wearing a frumpy old hat. The little boy is wearing clothes that certainly didn't come from Dillards. On the table before them is very ordinary food – no banquet for sure. And they're praying. That's the picture – they're praying. The boy has his hands together in the classic pose in which children are taught to pray and they are giving thanks to God.

There are other people in the picture too. Do you remember them? Men sitting at the counter, rough men in baggy overalls, and they're watching with wide eyed wonder the odd couple as an older woman and little boy bow their heads and give thanks for the meager meal they are about to eat. What do they know; those two that I need to know about life?

Like those men, I want to know the secret of gratitude. I want to know that God is active in my life regardless of circumstances.

It is the same truth as we find in the letter to the Christians in Corinth. Paul tells how God really does act in our lives and how Christ touched him even though he didn't deserve it – in fact deserved it least of all because of the way he had lived. But then he says this, and it is true for all of us; "but by the grace of God I am what I am. What I have, I have as a gift from God, none of it deserved but I have it. All that I have, I have as gifts from God. I am where I am, I am what I am, and I am who I am because God is good and generous."

Now that, in Toqueville's phrase, is the 'habit of the heart' that brings you true happiness. It's a habit we can develop and like most habits, we have to work to make it happen. Let us learn it, practice it and develop it, this habit of the heart, and this attitude of gratitude.

When you are thankful, everything goes a lot better doesn't it? Even in the tough times, we can learn that God is always good, kinder to us than we can ever deserve or know. That's a good habit to have, and then we, too, can say "I have learned to be content." Our eyes are then open to the mercies of God every day.

Have you ever seen the Thornton Wilder play "Our Town"? It is famous, for very good reason. It is about Emily Webb, who has died, and is told that she can go back to earth to relive one day and the day she chooses is her twelfth birthday. But the experience is shattering. People are too busy to notice the wonders they enjoy, the passing pleasures, the sudden beauties. She can hear the people talk but they can't hear her, can't hear her when she cries, "Let's look at one another!"

Finally Emily turns to the Stage Manager, "I can't", she tells him. "I can't go on. It goes so fast. We don't have time to look at one another."

Then she breaks down, sobbing, "I didn't realize," she cries. "So all that was going on and we never noticed. Take me back . . . But first; wait! One more looks. Goodbye. Goodbye world. Goodbye Grover's Corners . . . Mama and Papa. Goodbye to clocks ticking . . . and Mom's sunflowers. And food and coffee. And new-ironed dresses and hot baths . . . and sleeping and waking up. Oh, earth, you're too wonderful for anybody to realize you."

Then she looks toward the Stage Manager and asks, through her tears, "Do any human beings ever realize life while they live it? —every,

every minute?" And the Stage Manager answers, "No. The saints and poets, maybe – they do some."

Could it be, I wonder, that that is why we come here to this place, this beloved church? Is it God's heart speaking to our hearts, drawing us here so that in worship we may glimpse, for a moment at least, the goodness of God and the bounty we've been given ? Is God pulling us here to encourage a habit for our hearts of true thankfulness? Does God want us to see what we so rarely take time to see, how great he is and how tender his love, so that the day shall come when we will live in this habit of the hearts, knowing that life is a feast and that in all conditions there is cause for praise and that by the very grace of God you are what you are and I am what I am.

Well, I could go on endlessly, but its best I think to just return to that letter to our brothers and sisters in Corinth all those centuries ago.

They were learning a whole new way of life, about the importance of helping and encouraging each other. I borrow the great words from that letter and which Carolyn Tallbacka wrote on a card for me long ago: "*. . . and yet we live on, beaten and not yet killed, sorrowful yet always rejoicing, poor, yet making many rich; having nothing, yet possessing everything.*"

And, we are all in this together . . . in this church of fellowship.

"Before I was born, MY CHURCH gave to my parent's ideals of life and love that made my home a place of strength and beauty.

In helpless infancy, MY CHURCH joined my parents in dedicating me to Christ leading me to baptism in his name.

MY CHURCH enriched my childhood with the romance and religion and the lessons of life that have been woven into the texture of my soul. Sometimes I seem to have forgotten and then when else I might surrender to foolish and futile decisions in life, the truth MY CHURCH taught become radiant, insistent and inescapable.

In the stress and storm of adolescence MY CHURCH heard the surge of my soul and she guided my footsteps by lifting my eyes toward the stars.

When first my heart knew the strange awakenings of love MY CHURCH taught me to chasten and spiritualize my affections.

When my heart has been seamed with sorrow, and I thought the sun could never shine again, MY CHURCH drew me to the Friend of all the weary and whispered to me the hope of another morning, eternal and tearless.

When my steps have slipped and I have known the bitterness of sin, MY CHURCH has believed in me and wooingly she has called me back to live within the heights of myself.

MY CHURCH calls me to her heart. She asks my service and my loyalty. She has a right to ask it! I will help her to do for others what She has done for me. In this place in which I live, I will learn the new habit of the heart of thanksgiving, and I will lift aloft the torch of encouragement and living faith for all I meet.

Thanks are to God, for his unspeakable gift.
And all God's people said; AMEN.

Speechless

PSALM 19

In high school you may have studied Ralph Waldo Emerson, a great thinker and writer over a century ago. The literary movement of that time was known as Transcendentalism. Simply understood, it was about rising above ourselves through the contemplation of nature. I remember the satisfaction of sitting on the big rock near the creek and reading his essay Self Reliance. He said and wrote many memorable things, such as this quote on a wildlife calendar, "Each moment of the year has its own beauty . . . a picture which was never before and shall never be seen again."

I believe that statement, and he was a brilliant person, but there is Someone much greater whom we can read. He is the WORD who shares the **continuing** process of creation with us. He ". . . *made the earth by his power, he has established the world by his wisdom, and has stretched out the heavens at his discretion.*" Jeremiah 10:12 NLT

Reading the **scripture of nature** brings it all together, and always helps us comprehend God's presence with us today. It often is hard or even impossible, to find words that express it, but God knows our hearts as he reveals himself to us. Consider this modern version of Psalm 19 from The Message Bible:

God's glory is on tour in the skies,
     God-craft on exhibit across the horizon
Madame Day holds classes every morning,
     Professor Night lectures each evening.

Their words aren't heard,
     Their voices aren't recorded,
But their silence fills the earth:
     Unspoken truth is spoken everywhere.

God makes a huge dome
     For the sun—a superdome!
The morning sun's a new husband
     Leaping from his honeymoon bed,
The day breaking sun an athlete
     Racing to the tape.

That's how God's Word vaults across the skies
     From sunrise to sunset,
Melting ice, scorching deserts,
     Warming hearts to faith.

The revelation of God is whole
     And pulls our lives together.
The signposts of God are clear
     And point out the right road.
The life-maps of God are right,
     Showing the way to joy.
The directions of God are plain and easy on the eyes.

God's reputation is twenty-four-carat gold,
     With a lifetime guarantee.
The decisions of God are accurate
     Down to the nth degree.

God's Word is better than a diamond,
  Better than a diamond set between emeralds.
You'll like it better than strawberries in spring,
  Better than red, ripe strawberries.

There's more: God's Word warns us of danger
  And directs us to hidden treasure.
Otherwise how will we find our way?
  Or know when we play the fool?
Clean the slate, God, so we can start the day fresh!
  Keep me from stupid sins,
From thinking I can take over your work;
Then I can start this day sun-washed,
  Scrubbed clean of the grime of win.

These are the words in my mouth;
  These are what I chew on and pray.
Accept them when I place them on the morning altar,
  O God, my Altar-Rock,
    God, Priest-of-My-Altar.

Heavenly Country

"Instead they were longing for a better country – a heavenly one. Therefore God is not ashamed to be called their God, for he has prepared a city for them." Hebrews 11:16

Many farm buildings in Ohio have the significant history of being part of the **Underground Railroad.** Ohio was an abolitionist state and became a safe haven for slaves escaping from bondage in the south. There were secret compartments in barns, houses and even wagons where **conductors** would hide the fugitives on their way north. It is fascinating to see the places where these events actually took place.

The saga of the **passengers,** as the slaves were called, is an outstanding story of faith in action. In their fervent hopes and efforts for a better life, their faith in God may be understood as **"longing for a better country."**

For many of them, the Hubbard home in Ashtabula was the **station destination.** It is unknown how many were helped by the Hubbards, but one record tells of thirty-nine being there at one time. The home still stands as an interesting historical landmark and interesting museum just a few hundred yards from the shore of Lake Erie. The lake, instead of being a barrier to freedom, was a route to liberty in Canada.

For them, the **better country** was both the strong desire to live in a different place, and secondly, this was driven by the **hope** for a new life of freedom. A country can be an internal hope for something better, a sacred place where we may go for encouragement and strength.

This hope for a better country, this better life, is common to all of us. It is a persistent appetite, given to us by God, to find and fulfill our destinies. The journey and the goals are up to us. One danger however, is to be so focused on the destination that we miss the details of the travel.

Several of us were sent to visit a company on the eastern end of the Netherlands. Leaving Amsterdam by train, we traveled for several hours across the countryside. It was fascinating to see the farms, windmills, canals, Dutch belted cattle, little towns, fields of flowers and various field equipment being used.

I had been looking out of the window at all these things when I noticed that others in our group were asleep! How could they miss this experience? They were bored and said, "Wake me when we get there."

Our Christian journey to the better country is one of daily details and of learning fresh interesting ways to complete them. That is how we grow into that future God has for us. All our hopes for the future and even our confidence in life after death are based, always, in the WORD who walks with us all the way.

There is a certain tension in the journey. It is the tension between **what is, and what God wants it to be.** Our challenge is to be so aware of these two things that the tension is kept so taut that it sings.

We and God together, can do great things. What is your vision of the heavenly country ?

"'In the last days,' God says, 'I will pour out my Spirit on all people. Your sons and daughters will prophesy, your young men will see visions, your old men will dream dreams . . . And everyone who calls on the name of the Lord will be saved.'" Acts 2:17, 21

Kingdom Country
MATTHEW 4:1-11

Have you ever heard the expression, **"This is God's Country"?** It is said by people who love certain places such as their home or a favorite part of the earth. It is a sign of affection that comes with a deep sense of pride and a happy smile. There is a certain security and sense of ownership from the comforting knowledge that this is **where I belong**. Old black and white snapshots of my childhood home and family ignite that feeling all over again. I see now how fortunate I was to have lived there.

In Exodus 3:7-10, the LORD told Moses that he would deliver his people from bondage and bring them into *a "good and spacious land, a land flowing with milk and honey."* It was inhabited by others, but God was giving it to Israel saying that he would help them *"take possession of the land."* Exodus 23:30. The scripture includes the geographic borders involved. That issue is still much in the news concerning who has rightful ownership of parts of that Promised Land.

This covenant relationship was and is, based on our faithfulness to God. It is an agreement to do things his way. When we do, we are rewarded and greatly blessed. If we do not, we forgo the greatest wisdom and help that has ever existed in the entire world.

This applies to every area of life, not just to property. **Covenant Country** is wherever you meet God on any concern or decision. He has taken the initiative toward us. This is called **grace**.

An eternally historic example of this is recorded in Joshua 1:3; 6-9. God tells Joshua to go over the Jordan *"unto the land which I do give to them, even to the children of Israel. Every place that the sole of your foot shall tread upon, that I have given unto you . . .".*

Covenant Country is the spiritual life where you and I are privileged to live, regardless of our residential address. It really is **God's Country**, that wonderful citizenship where he is always reaching out to us with the greatest hope and concern for our personal happiness and success. So let us study the Book and do what it says.

"I will never leave you or forsake you. Be strong and courageous because you will lead these people to inherit the land I swore to the forefathers to give them. Be strong and very courageous. Be careful to obey all the law my servant Moses gave you; do not turn from it to the right or to the left that you may be successful wherever you go. Do not let Book of the Law depart from your mouth; meditate on it day and night, so that you may be careful to do everything written in it. Then you will be prosperous and successful. Have I not commanded you? Be strong and courageous. Do not be terrified; do not be discouraged for the LORD your God will be with you wherever you go."

The trusting and loving obedience to the LORD will go before you into whatever **country** he has promised you. Are you where he wants you to be in your life ?

The WORD In The World

Green Flash

I CORINTHIANS 2:6-16

Have you ever watched a sunset or perhaps an early sunrise with someone and heard them ask, **"There! Did you see it? Did you see the green flash?"** A friend of ours often entertains others with a big smile and that quick question, at just the right instant.

The green **flash** is thought by many to be a myth, a nonexistent experience, while a very few others swear they have seen it. It is said to happen on any clear horizon in the country near mountains, deserts or large bodies of water. A medieval legend from Scotland declares that if you can see it, you have especially strong powers of perception about yourself and others, particularly in matters of the heart.

I have yet to see a green flash at sunset but I keep looking. Those who believe in it and have photographs to prove it say that it is caused by **atmospheric refraction** similar to a mirage in the desert. They say the fading sunlight bends and splits as it passes through our atmosphere causing a thin band or splotch of green light at the top edge of the sun, lasting one second, or two at most.

As I was diligently watching for this elusive phenomenon last evening, I thought of something even more exciting; *"No eye has seen, no ear has heard, no mind has conceived what God has prepared for those who love him but God has revealed it to us by his Spirit."* I Corinthians 2:9-10. St. Paul wrote that to the struggling Christians in Corinth, quoting from the Old Testament prophet Isaiah.

There are great things in store for those who believe and who walk by faith, not just by sight. They do not just know the important facts of Jesus' life, death and resurrection, but also what they really mean. It is the deeper level of mature thinking. It is about being seriously Christian in a very secular world. It is about not being a green chameleon that changes color to hide and blend totally into the environment. It is about being willing to live in high anticipation by the promise of what God has prepared for us.

Sometimes we worry too much, unnecessarily. We may be so infused with responsibility that we forget the ultimate power of God to direct our paths.

A small group of us decided to invite major Christian artist *Sandi Patty* to speak and sing at the annual prayer breakfast in our small, rural community. It seemed an unlikely vision of bringing our fragmented population and declining economy into meaningful worship together. In the first blush of enthusiasm, we dreamed of a fourfold increase in the usual attendance of past years. To our delight, she accepted! Unbelievable, but true! She was coming here!

Months of planning began. The invitations went out, the funds were raised; the contracts were signed well in advance. Then, for some of us, anxiety began to replace enthusiasm. **What have we done?!** Ticket reservations were sluggish. Eight weeks to go and we lagged behind previous years. Our planning meetings were fearfully somber. Didn't people understand the importance of this?

We gathered for a special time of prayer for the purpose of refocusing on the real reason for doing this. After all, someone said, "this is a PRAYER breakfast and prayer is what we are about." We began sharing favorite verses from the Bible about prayer. One was so memorable: *"Do not worry about anything, but pray about everything. Tell God what you need, and thank him for all he has done. Then you will experience God's peace, which exceeds anything we can understand."* Philippians 4:6-7 <u>NLT</u>

We turned a corner that morning. We walked out into the clear fresh morning light and burdens were lifted. Hope was resurrected and we knew, after all, this is God's work. We will do that which we are called to do, realizing that we can never fit him into our plans. He just doesn't fit. It is up to us to follow him.

Gradually and steadily the numbers increased beyond our expectations. It was a wonderful morning – so awesome and so beyond our little plans. God's Spirit revealed more than we could ask or think. We are grateful that she contributed to the Forward of this book.

Pray, and then get out of the way!

 "Ask and it will be given to you, seek and you will find; knock and the door will be opened to you. For everyone who asks receives; he who seeks finds, and to him who knocks, the door will be opened." Matthew 7:7-8

For the Beauty of the Earth

For the Beauty of the Earth

Folliott S. Pierpoint

Conrad Koch

1. For the beau - ty of the earth, For the glo - ry
2. For the won - der of each hour Of the day and
3. For the joy of hu - man love, Broth - er, sist - er,
4. For Thy Church that ev - er - more Lift - eth ho - ly
5. For Thy - self, best gift di - vine, To our race so

of the skies, For the love which from our birth
of the night, Hill and vale and tree and flower,
par - ent, child; Friends on earth and friends a - bove;
hands a - bove, Of - fering up on ev - ery shore
free - ly given; For that great, great love of Thine,

O - ver and a - round us lies;
Sun and moon and stars of light:
For all gen - tle thoughts and mild:
Her pure sac - ri - fice of love:
Peace on earth and joy in heaven:

Lord of all, to Thee we raise This our hymn of grate - ful praise.

Prospecting

". . . then the Almighty will be your gold, the choicest silver for you. Surely then you will find delight in the Almighty and will lift up your face to God." Job 22:25-26

My first real ministry job after seminary was extremely interesting. I was a Field Pastor which meant locating people who had shown interest in the church sometime in the past. Some were new contacts and others were former members. This meant driving through California, Oregon and Washington states. This was a **"search and encourage mission,"** with a sense of the Holy Spirit's guidance and companionship. I loved it. Much of ministry usually seems to be repetitive tasks in the routine cycles of life, but that was not the case with this work. Every day was different and some were extremely so.

So it was that I was asked to find a man who had been in church but had not been seen by his family for at least 15 years. He was last known to be living somewhere in a mountain town in northern California. At their local post office I was given his last known address, which a mail truck driver referred to as a "hell hole over the mountain." So off I went over 15 miles of gravel road up the mountain and then down into a canyon, then over a bridge, crossing a small rushing river. It was a wild and scenic place.

Further down there by the rapids was a small cluster of really old buildings – shacks really. I parked off the road, and wearing suit and tie, with Bible in hand, walked down, down to them. Suddenly a watch dog began barking loudly and I heard a female voice yelling, "Hey! Hey!" and some other unintelligible language.

Then an older woman appeared from a shed. Her ragged clothes were pinned together and her physical appearance was dirty and unkempt. Her old tennis shoes were mismatched and holding the dog back she regarded me and asked, "Are you a preacher?" When I replied that I was, she asked, "Are you a Jehovah's Witness?" When I replied "No," she said, "They are the only ones who have ever come here." She was courteous and said, "Please excuse my language. The goat kicked over the milk bucket. Please come in the house. I'm sorry I don't have any coffee to offer you."

The yard was littered with those old fliptop Prince Albert tobacco cans and many other old unused items were lying about, junk in other words. The day was sunny and it was pleasant there by the rapids. We sat on hard wooden chairs in the one room shack. A double barreled shotgun stood in the corner and a twelve- string guitar hung on the wall. There was a wood burning stove but no electricity, phone or plumbing. We talked of faith in the LORD.

You never know where you are going to meet the WORD in the Country.

I explained my mission that the family was wondering where the man was and they were concerned about him. "I'm his wife," she said. "He isn't here because he is working further down the river." We talked a long time, read scripture, which she enjoyed, and we prayed. A peace settled over the hour with a strong sense of God's presence. She knew the LORD, even though she seldom saw other people. She talked at length about their lives and challenges and the help they had from God. It seemed she hadn't spoken to anyone for a long time, not since she had been in the hospital in town because she had fallen out of the apricot tree and broke her hip.

When it was time to go, I rose and looked around that remote cabin so far from our modern world and asked, "How do you get along out here so alone all the time ?" She replied, "Oh, we have everything we need." Then glancing out the door, she went to the corner and lifted a plank from the floor. She withdrew two quart jars filled with gold nuggets. My jaw dropped and I sat down again. She showed me various ones – each with a story. "He gave me this heart shaped one for my birthday. He likes to pan for gold out there in the river."

I was speechless then, as I am now, remembering that day. Later, back in the busy city, I recounted the story, (not revealing the location) to a jeweler who estimated the value of those two quart jars to be at least a half million dollars.(Where did you say it was ?) I guess it is no wonder that the prospector was not interested in pursuing close family ties or church, but they had a faith in God and a way of life that was pleasing to them.

Walking back up that gravel road to my car, I thought; gold or no gold, ***surely the presence of the LORD is in this place.***

I have wanted to revisit them but the years have flown and I doubt they are still there. I will always remember that sunny, peaceful morning by the river and the WORD in the Country, who surprises us every day if our eyes are open.

 "The fear of the LORD is pure, enduring forever. The ordinances of the LORD are sure and altogether righteous. They are more precious than gold, than much pure gold: they are sweeter than honey, than honey from the comb. By them is your servant warned; in keeping them there is great reward." Psalm 19:9-11

Logos

JOHN 1:1-14

This morning there were at least 100 seagulls lined up on the breakwall looking like a white picket fence. As Skye and I approached, a dozen of them lifted up, resembling a gate opening in the fence. They caught the shore breeze and climbing, caught the rising sun on the white underside of their wings. Who could create such effortless beauty, or the entire world and universe? Where did it all come from?

The revealed truth in our faith declares that GOD made all that we see in the natural world. Though our human minds cannot totally grasp it, always there has been God. Always there will be GOD, with no beginning and no ending. What is GOD like? GOD is incomparable; there can be no adequate comparison with anything. But we do know there has always been LOGOS with him. The LOGOS is to God what your word and thought are to you before they are expressed. It is the highest possible, ultimate divine reason, the very thought and creative force of GOD.

 These are deep realities, and the term LOGOS is translated into English as WORD. *"In the beginning was the Word, and the Word was with God, and the Word was God. He was with God in the beginning. Through him all things were made; without him nothing was made that has been made. In him was life,*

and that life was the light of men. The light shines in the darkness, but the darkness has not understood it." John1:1-5

> *"The Word became flesh and made his dwelling among us." "No one has ever actually seen God, but, of course, his only Son has, for he is the companion of the Father and has told us all about him."* John 1:14, 18

Jesus Christ, **the LOGOS now known as the WORD,** was present at the creation of the entire universe. It was created **through him,** so it is more than interesting to consider prayerfully everything he had to say and everything he did when he came here later as a flesh and blood person.

Summarizing the creation account in Genesis, The Life Application Bible charts it this way:

First Day: Light (so there was light and darkness)
Second Day: Sky and water (waters separated)
Third Day: Land and seas (waters gathered); vegetation
Fourth Day: Sun, moon, and stars (to govern the day and the night and to mark seasons, days and years.)
Fifth Day: Fish and Birds (to fill the waters and the sky)
Sixth Day: Animals (to fill the earth) Man and woman (to care for the earth and to commune with God.)
Seventh Day: (God rested and declared all that he had made to be very good)

Let's take a journey through what the WORD has to share today. These meditations are about what was created **through** him in 7 evenings and mornings all those many, many millennia ago and are still being created today.

First Day

LIGHT AND DARKNESS

GENESIS 1:1-3

In the beginning, after God created light through the WORD, he saw that it was good and separated it from the darkness. Light was the first requirement before anything else would be created. We must have light if there is to be new life.

Today, the clear dawn is a beautiful, unfolding experience. The darkness is receding, the stars are fading from sight as sunlight gradually baths our part of planet earth for a new day. Details unknown and unseen in the darkness are now emerging, becoming clear and understood.

God's creation through the WORD of physical light is the first and vital necessity for physical life, and **his spiritual light is vital to understand his love for us.** That is why we read with great joy these words: *"In him (Christ) was life, and that life was the light of men. The light shines in the darkness, but the darkness has not understood it."* John 1:4-5 God created physical light and all that exists in the universe through the WORD, and then sent the same WORD to be the spiritual light so we would know that, *"God is light and in him is no darkness at all."* I John 1:5

Bringing these God-sized facts down to our human grasp of things, we read this statement by Jesus the WORD, *"I am the light of the world. Whoever follows me will never walk in darkness, but will have the light of life."* John 8:12 And then we also read this **shout out,** *"And Jesus cried out, when a man believes in me, he does not believe in me only, but in the*

270

one who sent me. When he looks at me, he sees the one who sent me. I have come into the world as a light, so that no one who believes in me should stay in darkness." John 12:45-46

Reading further in the first chapter of the gospel, we discover facts about Jesus' cousin, John the Baptist, who was preparing the way for the WORD. *"He himself was not the light; he came only as a witness to the light."* John 1:8 The deeper meaning of the original Greek language here means that John shone with the reflected, borrowed light of the WORD.

Are you wondering, "What does all this deep thought have to do with me and how I live my life?"

Do you know what a sconce is? It was a useful home furnishing before electricity. It was a candlestick holder with a polished back plate of pewter or glass that was mounted behind the burning wick. This would reflect and increase the amount of light from the candle. It shone with a borrowed glow.

That is the point of knowing who Jesus Christ is, and what he can do in a life that is sincerely following him. He is the **Light of the world,** and through him we know what our invisible God is like. So let us learn all we can about him, every day. It is our purpose to reflect him, the WORD who existed before all time and creation and who lives with us today.

There are many good prayers (the best being your own from your heart). Here is one credited to a person in Alcoholics Anonymous that expresses what is possible for those who really follow him.

"This is the beginning of a new day. God has given me the light of this day to use as I will. I will reflect the Light of the world and follow Him for good, because I am exchanging a day of my allotted lifetime for it. When tomorrow comes this day will be gone forever, leaving in its place something that I have traded for it. I want it to be increase and not loss; good and not evil; beneficial success and not failure. This is my choice and so I will rejoice in the price of selflessness that I paid for it. Amen."

 "But you aren't in the dark about these things, dear brothers and sisters, and you won't be surprised when the day of the Lord comes like a thief. For you are all children of the light and of the day, we don't belong to darkness and night. So be on your guard, not asleep like the others. Stay alert and be clearheaded." I Thessalonians 5:5-6 <u>NLT</u>

SKY AND WATER

GENESIS 1: 6-8

Scientific facts have not changed over the millennia since creation, but our discovery of them evolves very slowly. As J. Wallace Hamilton humorously noted in <u>Serendipity</u>, they could have had electricity in the Garden of Eden but no one even knew or cared that such a power existed. God must enjoy watching the efforts of his children over the generations of time, trying to figure things out and how best to use the new knowledge.

On the second evening and morning, God, through the WORD created sky and water. It is described as a division between the waters; the expansion was called sky. Isaiah refers to it as a canopy spread out like a tent. Though we may seldom take notice of the sky, it is our constant companion. It may seem round like our earth, but of course it is limitless, eventually changing above our atmosphere, into the blackness of space. Here today, it is a beautiful blue with some white clouds. Have you looked up at it lately ? It is a big part of our life-sustaining atmosphere and the water cycle that keeps us going.

Water is absolutely essential to life. That must be why it was created second only to light in the creation sequence. Modern space researchers are always looking for other planets as fortunate as ours, with water to originate and sustain life. Recently some German astronomers announced the discovery of 50 planets unknown to us before. One of them which is described as a superearth, 3.5 times larger than our earth, is circling an orange star like our sun. It is known as HD85512b.

It is a mere 36 light years away (at six trillion miles per year) far out there on the other side of our sun. That's far, far out there, a long way from looking at all that water of Lake Erie with a glorious blue sky above. They cannot get a picture of it which would show its atmosphere and indicate if there is water on it which is essential for life. A new Extremely Large Telescope is being built which may be able to detect those facts in the ongoing search for extraterrestrial life. The Plain Dealer Newspaper 9/13/11.

In John 4 we read that the WORD and his disciples were making the long walk from Judea north to Galilee. He was tired and thirsty in the middle of the day, which probably was hot. He sat down by Jacob's well at noon, while the disciples went off to buy food. It is interesting to note that he, through whom all water and sky were created, was now a thirsty, hot and tired human being.

Have you ever been hot, thirsty and tired? Have you ever wished you could just miraculously create a nice cold drink ? It is interesting, isn't it, that Jesus did not use miraculous powers, ever, for himself or the disciples? Even at the cross we hear his critics mocking, *"He saved others, himself he cannot save."* Matthew 27:42 KJV They didn't know how true that was! There were no unnecessary miracles, no shortcuts in obedience to God's will. Perhaps this lesson seen over and over was not lost on the very human disciples who saw thousands miraculously fed, but still had to go buy food for themselves.

He was sitting by the well as the woman from Sychar arrived to draw water and they had a most interesting conversation. (John 4:1-38) It changed her life. Moving from his physical thirst for a drink of water from the 100 ft. deep well, he told her: *"Everyone who drinks this water will be thirsty again, but whoever drinks the water I give him will never thirst. Indeed, the water I give him will become in him a spring of water welling up to eternal life."* John 4:1-14

He is the answer to all spiritual thirst with an endless supply of life saving truth.

That is coming down a long, long way from the creation of the universe to our own daily needs for significance in our living, but what Jesus said to her is so very true. No one can express it better than Oswald Chambers:

"The picture our Lord gives is not that of a channel but a fountain . . . We are to be centers through which Jesus can flow as rivers of living water in blessing to everyone. Some of us are like the Dead Sea, always taking but never giving out, because we are not rightly related to the Lord. As surely as we receive from Him, He will pour out through us, and in the measure He is not pouring out, there is a defect in our relationship to Him. Is there anything between you and Jesus Christ ? Is there anything that hinders your belief in Him? If not, Jesus says, **out of you will flow rivers of water.** It is not a blessing passed on, not an experience stated, but a river continually flowing. Keep at the Source, guard well your belief in Jesus Christ and your relationship to Him, and there will be a steady flow for other lives, no dryness and no deadness." <u>My Utmost for His Highest</u>.

The physical miracle of the atmosphere of our earth with its sky and life giving water is truly amazing. And even more amazing is this: the WORD is still creating life giving water for the spiritually thirsty world. For those who believe, we are artesian wells of his **grace and truth.** Stay close to him and let it flow!

"If you are thirsty, come! If you want life-giving water, come and take it. It's free!"
Revelation 22:17 <u>CEV</u>

Third Day

WATER, LAND, VEGETATION

GENESIS 1:9-13

Here in northeast Ohio, it is early spring and the maple trees are being tapped. It's going to be a great maple syrup season, due to the recent freeze and snowfall followed by rollercoaster temperatures. Each spigot will provide 10-12 gallons of sap during the brief, intense collection season. About 40 gallons of sap are needed to produce 1 gallon of syrup, and more if it is the darker type. Can you taste it?

Also within sight of the lake are numerous vineyards. It is said that the tumbling warmer air from the lake's surface moderates the climate and promotes good growing conditions. As a result, many wineries flourish along the southern shore corridor.

Grapes and vineyards are prominently mentioned throughout the Bible and may be considered some of the seed-bearing vegetation that first appeared on the dry ground in the Creation account. The life in the seeds is powerful and continues over all generations, reproducing itself again and again. A scientific study reported today that researchers have recently grown a new champion flower from seeds thought to be 32,000 years old, having been frozen in Arctic permafrost all that time. The Plain Dealer Newspaper 2/21/12)

The WORD often spoke of vineyards and grapes in his teachings. The most significant was in reference to him. As we read about that last evening with his disciples, we may visualize them leaving the Upper Room on their way to Garden of Gethsemane. It was a full moon night of Passover. Passing the temple they would have seen the great carvings, on the outer wall, of the vine and great clusters of grapes. These were the national symbol of Israel, with great patriotic significance for them, much as the Stars and Stripes have for us today. Perhaps seeing that, Jesus may have used it as an opportunity to express to his closest friends who he was and what this was all about.

He said to them, *"I am the vine, you are the branches. No one can bear fruit if they are not connected to the vine. If a man remains in me and me in him, he will bear much fruit; apart from me you can do nothing . . . . You did not choose me, but I chose you and appointed you to go and bear fruit - fruit that will last."* John 15:5, 16

In his perfect teaching, this simple fact is of absolute importance to us. There cannot be ongoing spiritual life and growth unless there is a living union with him. **It is a connected and remaining relationship with the WORD.** Jesus Christ came to do more than to live and teach among us. He also came to instill his spirit in us so that it would live on and on like a living vine of God's redemptive work in the world. If this is to be true, we must stay attached to him because we simply cannot do it in our own strength.

We read in Colossians 2:10, *"In him you have been made complete."* Realistically we know that it is only in Christ that we are able to fulfill the great challenge of living his way. It's a mystery, but we understand it. In the WORD, God has become flesh like us.

Here is a very simple idea. When our new washing machine was delivered, it had big yellow tag on it that read, "No good if detached." If we stay attached to the Vine, he enables us to face the challenges of life and death just as he did.

How does this really work? It is something that we must take on faith. This unwritten story about E. Stanley Jones has been retold many times because it is so true. He was a great preacher a few generations ago. He started out full of enthusiasm and hope. He was invited here and there and on one occasion went to fulfill his obligation to speak.

He was fervent and tried hard. Day after night after day after night his words went out to the crowd, but not a single person responded to the invitation to accept Christ. He grew so discouraged that one afternoon he walked up a hillside behind the church and threw himself down on the ground. He cried out to God: What's wrong? It seems that nothing I say or do results in anything! God! It seems the harder I try, the less people respond.

After he poured all of this discouragement out, he just rested on the ground, there under an apple tree. His emotion spent, he looked up through the branches to the blue sky and sunshine and white clouds floating along. Then, he said, it was as if God was speaking to him: Stanley Jones, do you see this tree? Do you see how hard this tree is working? This tree is just being a tree. It is just doing what it is called to do. I am the One that is giving the increase. I am the One that is providing the fruit that is so wonderful from this tree. It is not by human strength, but by my Spirit that people are converted.

Jones was transformed by that experience. He relaxed in the arms of God and began to allow the Spirit of God to flow through his words. **He became connected again to the living vine.** He went back down that hill and began to preach with new freedom and power, riding on the crest of God's spirit. Listeners then began to recognize that this was the spirit of Christ flowing through him. It was no longer just a person crying his heart out to make things better. It was now the power of the living God.

If we are **attached to the living vine, allowing the abiding presence of Christ to be in us, there will be much fruit, fruit that will last.**

Fourth Day

SUN, MOON AND STARS

GENESIS 1: 14-19

This page could be left blank, I suppose, because there simply is no way to describe our expanding universe adequately. We are awed and simply believe that, *"The heavens declare the Glory of God and the firmament sheweth his handiwork."* Psalm 19:1 KJV

President Abraham Lincoln is credited with saying, "I can see how it is possible for a man to look down upon the earth and be an atheist, but I cannot conceive how he could look up into the heavens and say there is no God."

Compare that statement with E. B. White who, on the pessimistic side said, "I see nothing in space as promising as the view from a Ferris wheel." Now there's a man that needed to go out at night and really look at the stars in the heavens! He would be blown away by God's endless workshop out there and the meteor showers of celestial fireworks in late summer.

The universe is endless and without borders. Our fascination with it is endless too. It is infinite yet we try to measure it in light-years, one light year being the distance light would travel in one year. That is six trillion miles. Astronomers tell us that we are part of the Milky Way Galaxy and that is 100,000 light-years across. (That's 600,000,000,000,000,000,000 miles.) Furthermore, there are about 350,000,000,000 galaxies in the universe. Quick! How much is that?

God, through the WORD, spoke and caused it to form. *"And there was evening and there was morning - the fourth day."* Genesis 1:19

Psalm 8 is a **creation psalm** giving us the important, needed bridge between our awe of God's heavens and our own inner feelings. *"When I consider your heavens, the work of your fingers, the moon and the stars which you have set in place, what is man that you are mindful of him, the son of man that you care for him? You made him a little lower than the heavenly beings and crowned him with glory and honor."* v.3-5

It is our faith that God keeps the planets in their orbits, and also keeps our bodies and minds alive. We are so miniscule in the universe, but the Lord thinks of us and hears our prayers of adoration or supplication. We are part of his creation and he wants to hear from us, about how we are doing and what we need.

Yes, the wonder of intuitively knowing that we are creations of the same hand that created the entire universe brings unexplainable courage and commitment to us. If all those stars are possible, then new hope and strength can be created in my soul too. That's a good definition of faith. Thoughts become clear, confusion slinks away, and we know ourselves in a brand new way.

By the lake on a clear starry night I was looking up and praying with the WORD about my future goals. I am amazed at the scientific fact that we are made of **star stuff**, the same kind of atoms as the stars. Seeing the order and power of it all out there, I remembered Jeremiah 10:12: *"He has made the earth by his power, He has established the world by his wisdom, and has stretched out the heavens at his discretion."*

These three facts somehow changed into three clear thoughts about my life. 1). Have I been too concerned to be the person others want me to be? 2.) Can I just be the person I want to be? 3.) How can I be the person God wants me to be? It was like looking into one of those three sided revealing mirrors in clothing store dressing rooms. Sometimes a well stated question is the answer itself, and needs only to be asked. It is very illuminating.

There are those who think the answers to our destiny questions are to be found out there by studying the stars and their movements. For me, the answers are not found in worship of the created heavens, but rather in the worship of the **WORD** who put it all together and sustains it with such positive and amazing love.

In the fullness of time, that same **WORD** was made flesh and dwelt among us. He was not some cold, remote star umpteen bazillion miles away, but right here, God with us, *"Who, being in very nature God . . . being made in human likeness . . ."* Philippians 2:6-7

He created it all, and if we listen, teaches us how to live in it. *"From his abundance we have all received one gracious blessing after another. For the law was given through Moses, but God's unfailing love and faithfulness came through Jesus Christ. No one has ever seen God. But the unique One, who is himself God, is near to the Father's heart. He has revealed God to us."* John 1:18-18 <u>NLT</u>

FISH AND BIRDS

GENESIS 1:20

This mild winter of 2012 has been a great season for bird watching along the shore. It is a mid-February sunny morning and a flock of 50 or more sea gulls was parked on the break wall looking like a big white starched collar. Then they lifted off, circled and found a rich buffet of small fish in the waves. It was a sight to see, the flock facing the offshore breeze, hanging nearly motionless, then diving to the water and grabbing breakfast.

There have also been less common birds here this winter because this area is said to be the best bird watching place in the whole state of Ohio. Binocular strung visitors have been here from faraway places hoping to spot a black tailed gull that is usually indigenous to Japan. The other big news is the Snowy Owl hanging around the harbor. They nest and live in the Arctic and every few years migrate south in what is called an **irruption**. One local resident had traveled all the way to the Arctic to see a Snowy, but did not. So it is rewarding and ironic that he finally saw one here, in our own back yard.

Also, we have recently seen eagles cruising along the coast, and some are nesting here. What a majestic bird of prey!

It is fascinating to watch birds fly and it is no wonder that mankind has dreamed of flight for many centuries. The Smithsonian Museum of Flight and Space in Washington is full of wonderful things like real space capsules, moon rocks and flying machines of many kinds. Outside the main entrance is the signature sculpture, a tall spire representing our desire to fly. It was amusing to see a large live crow perched on the very top of it cawing at us mere mortals. It was as though he was laughing and saying "What's the big deal? We birds have known how to fly for many millions of years. It's easy!"

Scriptures tell us that God through the WORD, created the creatures in the sea and in the air before any land animals. We may also read about the WORD sitting on a mountainside, teaching great crowds. He spoke in parables with examples of familiar things known to his listeners. I like to think a flock of birds was flying by, just as he said to those who were anxious, *"Look at the birds of the air; they do not sow or reap or store away in barns, and yet your heavenly Father feeds them. Are you not much more valuable than they? Who of you by worrying can add a single hour to his life?"* Matthew 6:26-27 He was saying that since God had given the great gift of life, he would not leave any of his creation without care.

Worry can be destructive to our health, relationships and faith in God, reducing our trust in his perfect provision. Of course we must think responsibly and clearly, but constant worry can immobilize us and leave God out of the many decisions we must make. Dr. Sam Shoemaker once wrote a piece entitled Alcoholics are Charming People. In his work he had found that addictions were often caused by excessive and compulsive worry. He knew many who learned to face their lack of faith by believing in the loving authority they called a **Supreme Being.** They then became very aware of so much more about themselves, gaining a deep sympathy and tough love that could help others find healing. Among his many wise principles of this healing are these:

"Just for today, I will try to live through this day only, and not tackle my whole life problem at once. I can do something for twelve hours that would appall me if I felt that I had to keep it up for a lifetime.

"Just for today, I will be happy. Abraham Lincoln is quoted as saying 'Most folks are as happy as they make up their minds to be.'

"Just for today, I will have a program. I may not follow it exactly, but I will have it. I will save myself from two pests: hurry and indecision.

"Just for today, I will be unafraid. Especially I will not be afraid to enjoy what is beautiful, and to believe that as I give to the world, so the world will give to me.

"Anyone can fight the battle of just one day. It is only when you and I add the burdens of those two awful eternities . . . Yesterday and Tomorrow that we break down. Let us, therefore, live but one day at a time."

Like the birds who live in the present, we too may live in the present with our knowledge of God that gives us hope. **We can fly.** Remember these words ". . . *but those who hope in the LORD will renew their strength. They will soar on wings like eagles; they will run and not grow weary, they will walk and not be faint.*" Isaiah 40:31

Possibly you don't really see yourself as majestic or impressive as an eagle. Well, the WORD has that covered too. *"Are not two sparrows sold for a penny? Yet not one of them will fall to the ground apart from the will of your Father . . . So don't be afraid; you are worth more than many sparrows."* Matthew 10:29-31

FISH AND BIRDS

GENESIS 1:20-23

Every year there are fishing derbies on the lakes. Serious fisher folk travel here from many miles around, hauling in their boats and gear. The Wine and Walleye festival in our harbor offers significant prizes for the largest walleye caught. One year's winner was a 15 year old boy whose biggest catch won the $1,000 prize. He was very proud.

A different tournament was to catch a certain tagged fish. An insurance policy on the fish's life would bring $10,000 if some lucky angler actually caught it. Needless to say, one fish out of many thousands in this large lake was quite safe from being mounted on someone's wall. Many devoted fishermen would say, "Well why not? I was going out fishing anyway."

Read again Genesis 1:20-23 in the contemporary language of <u>The Message Bible.</u> *"God spoke: 'Swarm, Ocean, with fish and all sea life! Birds fly through the sky over Earth!' God created the huge whales, all the swarm of life in the waters."* <u>TM</u>

It reminds me that on the Columbia River near Portland, Oregon. Native Americans can fish for huge Sturgeon which may grow to eight feet in length. Near the Bonneville Dam, the sportsmen stand on a high sloping bluff about 100 feet above the Columbia River. Casting out that distance requires some very inventive skill. One of the most creative I saw was a large homemade slingshot made of square iron tubing about six feet high and three feet wide. It was mounted in the stake hole of a pickup truck and had a long rubber sling. When pulled back to maximum stretch by two strong people and then released, it could launch the bait far out into the river below. It was fun to watch the greater distance they could achieve rather than just normal casting.

The economic value of fish in the waters of the world is in the billions of dollars. The high nutritive quality and digestibility of fish proteins class fish among the more desirable food products. Much of the yield of the fisheries is consumed as human food, while the remainder may be converted into such essential by-products as vitamin oils, livestock and poultry feeds, fertilizers, and industrial oils.

We thank God for these treasures of the waters and are grateful that God said, *"Be fruitful and increase in number and fill the water in the seas . . ."* v.22

Seafood can be very good eating! It has been nourishing the human race for thousands of years. We find many references to it in the Gospels. The fish is also one of the hidden symbols from the first century, signifying that we are followers of Christ. One of his major miracles was the feeding of the 5,000 men (besides women and children) near Bethsaida. Most of his miracles concerned only one person and the immediate family and friends. This one touched thousands and is recounted in all four Gospels with a lot of interesting detail.

Just as he filled the seas with fish at the miracle of creation, he filled thousands of people with fish and bread by the miracle of looking up to heaven and giving thanks.

Mark 6:41-42 tells the story. Everyone was hungry and it was late after a big day of his teaching and healing. The disciples said the people should go and find their own food, but Andrew the fisherman knew something and said, *"Here is a boy with five small barley loaves and two small fish, but how far will they go among so many?"* The disciples, no doubt, had more resources than the boy, but knew they didn't have enough in their pockets for thousands of people so gave nothing. They were all near Philip's home town, who was thinking practically about the probable cost (200 silver pieces) of feeding everyone. Jesus wanted to teach him that financial resources are not always the most important ones. If God truly wants something done, money is but one factor, not the total issue. The real question is this: **Does God want this done ?** If so, are you willing to pray and believe that he will provide all that's needed? It may not come in the ways we would normally expect, but if we truly and faithfully trust him, he will provide what is needed.

"The boy gave what little he had and it made the difference. If we offer nothing to God, he will have nothing to work with. But he can take what little we have and turn it into something great." Life Application Bible notes

So here were these two small fish and five barley loaves. Imagine the WORD looking at those two little fish, perhaps remembering with a smile the creative multiplication process on the fifth day of creation and the millions of fish in all the seas of the world. He gave thanks and the food was distributed. Everyone had all they wanted, and there were twelve baskets of fragments left. There was a basket for each of the disciples, who had seen something **impossible** happen.

I wish I had been there that day, but **impossible** things still can, and do, happen when we are present with Christ today. We may think our time or talents are meager, but if it is God's Plan, something that He wants done, our smallest offering can be multiplied in ways far beyond our dreams. It is his work after all.

It is our privilege to be a part of it, but not to become so caught up in doing God's work, that we forget God. *"For God loves a person who gives cheerfully. And God will generously provide all you need. Then you will always have everything you need and plenty left over to share with others."* II Corinthians 9:7-8

ANIMALS, MAN & WOMAN
GENESIS 1:24-31

The Bible was written over a period of at least 1,000 years when life was sustained by agriculture and hunting. There were towns and villages in the rural countryside but none of the modern conveniences we know today. Its timeless message therefore, is often expressed in simple farming terms. One of the great **I am** passages by Christ is, *"I am the good shepherd. I know my sheep and they know me."* John 10:14

Looking at the sixth day of creation by God through the WORD, there is so much that could be said about populating and sustaining life on the earth. The creation of animals and people takes me back to childhood memories on the dairy farm where our family lived. We had animals, crops, gardens and physical work responsibilities. The traditional Bible language is so close to what we knew and did every day that it remains my core way of understanding and loving it. There are many new, modern translations that make the message more relevant to those in this modern age who never knew about country farming.

God created the animals before man; sheep and lambs became important in Israel's religion, and oxen, horses, donkeys are all mentioned in scripture as are livestock and cows. Cows. Now there's an animal I can relate to. We raised, bred, fed, milked and sometimes had to chase cows. We sometimes wondered if we owned them or they owned us. We knew them by name, sometimes using names of people who seemed to have similar characteristics, flattering or not. But I digress.

If you are not familiar with the farming life, take a moment to read a good nostalgic description by John Parker of the Ohio Agricultural Extension Office:

"A few of you may remember the time, way back, when most dairy cows were out on pasture from spring until winter arrived. Many of these pastures were not very good, just annual grasses and some weeds thrown in. They might be way back in the farm, and the cows had to walk down a long lane to get to them. They were good feed in the spring when there was plenty of rain and they made a lot of growth. When the heat and dry weather of summer came, they weren't much good. Cows didn't have enough to eat and had to be fed extra feed in the barn. Milk production dropped some. Then a few of you might remember what a cow path was. It was a wandering path that the cows would follow to get from place to place. They wanted to wander along the same paths when going from the barn to the pasture; creatures of habit. Early in the morning or at night, when it was milking time, dairy farmers could be heard out back of the barn, calling the cows to come up for milking. Each farmer had his own distinct way and voice to call his cows, usually small herds. So if you were awake early or near a dairy farm at evening, you might hear that distinct 'c-boss. c- boss' calling them to come to the barn. If they could hear, usually they would follow their cow paths and slowly wander up to the barn. If they didn't hear, someone had to go back and get them. That was often the youngest member of the family, maybe barefooted and had to be careful where they walked." The Star Beacon newspaper

However old fashioned this may seem, the world now depends on more high tech farmers. Now cows are in the technology world, wearing collars that signal their owners about various field conditions. But I wouldn't trade that early life for anything, for both reasons; **the farming lifestyle of 60 years ago and the ease of understanding the WORD's way of speaking.**

The sequence of creation on the sixth day ends with, *"God created man in his own image, in the image of God he created him; male and female he created them."* Genesis 1:27 the word **created** is emphasized three times in this verse describing the central act of God on the sixth day. Male and female are created in the image of God. This is not about physical appearance or other distinctions, but about the finer qualities of character, love, patience, forgiveness and kindness which apply to either sex. *"For we are God's handywork, created in Christ Jesus to devote ourselves to the good deeds for which God has designed us."* Ephesians 2:10 <u>NEB</u>

What **good deeds are these? How do we know what they are?** We only need to look at and know his Son, the WORD.

 "He is the image of the invisible God, the firstborn over all creation . . . For God was pleased to have all his fullness dwell in him and through him to reconcile to himself all things on earth or things in heaven, by making peace through his blood shed on the cross." Colossians 1:15-16; 19-20

Seventh Day

SABBATH

GENESIS 2:1-3

"By the seventh day, God had finished the work he had been doing;
so on the seventh day he rested from all his work." Genesis 2:1

It is Friday evening, the beginning of God's Sabbath. Our sunset is spectacular, a real treat that looks like a big tub of triple flavored sherbet - orange, raspberry and lemon. A big scoop has been taken by the setting sun, his rewarding snack as he finishes this day's work and welcomes the Sabbath to our shore. The colorful flavors swirl across the surface of the lake, as they may have when the WORD was with God on the original seventh day Sabbath. It is no wonder that Isaiah called the Sabbath **a delight,** (Isaiah 58:13-14) a special time to find **joy in the LORD.**

When the WORD became flesh known as Jesus Christ, he observed the Sabbath. It was a blessed way to honor and remember his part in God's tremendous work of creating the universe. This remembrance was so important that it had been established as one of the Ten Commandments through Moses in Exodus 20:8 No one, including animals, was to work on that seventh day. All were to rest, as God had rested on the Sabbath.

Over the centuries however, the special day given by God in love, was turned into controlling and rigid rules. **Finding joy in the Lord** became secondary to obeying legalistic religious rules. Extremism had

291

distorted the simple great idea that Sabbath time should be a significant and rewarding practice in our lives.

God had given it to be worship time, enjoying the creative work of the other six days. It became a specific point of attack on Jesus' teachings by certain Pharisees (Matthew 12:1-14), leading to their plot to kill him. When they challenged his doing well on the Sabbath, he replied, *"For the Son of Man is Lord of the Sabbath."* Matthew 12:8

It is sad and strange that anyone could fault the value of doing well on the Sabbath, especially attacking the WORD himself who was there at creation. But of course, there was more to it than that; power struggles, jealousy, self-righteousness, and a threat to religious authority.

A study by Juan Carlos-Leman at the University of Arizona confirms our common sense knowledge, concluding: "Failing to rest after six days of steady work will lead to insomnia or sleepiness, hormonal imbalances, fatigue, irritability, organ stress, and other increasingly serious physical and mental symptoms." <u>True to the Sabbath-True to Our God</u>

What about you and me, here and now? How do we spend the time given to us for this purpose? Do we really observe Sabbath time? Do we delight to spend it with him who is **Lord of the Sabbath?**

The year, 2012 was a leap year with 366 days. A **leap day** was added in order to keep up with the whirling rotations of our solar system. We live in years, months, days, hours, minutes and seconds. And, oh yes, we got an extra **leap second** too, an extra second for you to spend somehow. This is to keep earth time synchronized with atomic time, the human measurement of time worldwide. It was important because of the effect on modern communication networks like GPS satellites and the Internet.

It's a frivolous question, but as a busy human being, what did you do with your extra second?

Wasting or losing time is a modern irritation which can happen when we are focused on doing something of real importance to us but get interrupted. I was amused at the comment by someone who was trying to solve a billing problem on the telephone. He got stuck listening to endless recorded messages, finally only to be told to call back later. His frustrated question was **"Whom do I see about getting the last 30 minutes of my life back?"'**

This is not the case when we spend the Sabbath with the WORD. It **resets our body clock**, so to speak, and we actually will get a lot more done when it is time to go back to work. A friend of ours recounts a true story from her great, great grandfather. He was in a wagon train enroute from St. Louis to Oregon. The travelers were devout Christians so the whole group observed the habit of stopping for the Sabbath day. The trip got tedious and long, however, and some grew impatient, wanting to travel on without stopping. This became contentious and so they split into two groups, one going on non-stop, the others maintaining their Sabbath rest. Who got to Oregon first? The ones who rested, of course. Their equipment and horses were in much better shape, not to mention the people themselves.

The WORD is with us **every** day of course, to help us in our work and responsibilities, and then the Sabbath eve comes, like this one with the **sherbet sky**. It sends us to bed, not with anxiety or the concerns that drive us through the rest of the week. It is restful with soul-refreshing peace in the presence of God. We contemplate his goodness to us and provision for our health.

As we sleep naturally, something good takes place in our minds and souls. Our subconscious levels of faith restore our poise and give us power. The Sabbath morning dawns differently from all other days. So let us *"Remember the Sabbath day to keep it holy."* Exodus 20

"Then Jesus said, 'Come to me, all of you who are weary and carry heavy burdens, and I will give you rest. Take my yoke upon you. Let me teach you because I am humble and gentle at heart, and you will find rest for your souls. For my yoke is easy to bear, and the burden I give you is light.'" Matthew 11:28-30 <u>NLT</u>

Knothole Faith

ACTS 1

Among the many pieces of driftwood along the shore after a big storm was a stout beam about six feet long. It had been used for something somewhere, for a short length of rope was still knotted through a 2 inch hole on one end. Looking through the hole at a freighter out on the lake, I could isolate the ship but of course that was all I could see. It reminded me of the story of the kid who couldn't afford to go to the circus, so he looked through the knothole of a board fence as the circus parade passed by. He went home and told his parents that he had seen the circus, but had he really?

Sometimes when looking at the lake, I wonder how much of it can really be seen? A few miles to the west and a few to the east is the limit. Some people say they can see Canada which is 40 plus miles to the north. They claim that **inversions** occur when the right temperature and humidity form a sort of lens that bends the light. You couldn't prove it by me as I have never seen it.

I am beginning to understand how miniscule our view is of this lake, just one of all the **H O M E S** Great Lakes. Erie is the smallest of Huron, Ontario, Michigan, Erie and Superior. Geologists tell us that over 10,000 years ago, the 5 stream valley soft landscapes were carved out by the Lauren Tide Ice Sheet Glacier, creating this largest freshwater body in the world. Then as the glacier lobes receded, their meltwater filled the 5 cavities which cover 94,560 square miles, stretching 690 miles north to south and 860 miles west to east. They are huge. So my **knothole view** is hardly worth mentioning.

Spiritually speaking, sometimes we have a **knothole faith,** peering through a small hole in some church fence at the rest of the big world passing by. That's alright when we are young because we do have to start somewhere in our awareness of the rest of the world. When I first became a Christian just out of high school, I was sure that God's total truth was revealed only in certain language and music. Our mission in life then, was to help people learn the real truth! Many human debates resulted in lots more heat than light! Few people in my experience ever really changed their minds about their religion. My grandfather used to say, **the man convinced against his will, is of the same opinion still.**

We read in Luke 10:1, 2, 17, *"After this the Lord appointed seventy-two others, and sent them two by two ahead of him to every town and place where he was about to go. He told them, 'The harvest is plentiful but the workers are few. Ask the Lord of the harvest, therefore, to send out workers into his harvest field.'" He gave further instructions and they went out. When they returned with joy, they said, "Lord, even the demons submit to us in your name.'"*

In human terms this task given to a handful of people would be impossible. In their own strength and **knothole vision** it could not happen in a world of many millions of people with no money or mass communication systems. However God is always a majority and we are not restricted to just our own limited vision and resources . . . The promise is sure that the LORD surely is with his people, offering his resurrection power to change the world, no matter how big it is.

Introducing the book of Acts about evangelizing the world, Dr. Lloyd Ogilvie uses a wonderful phrase, **between the lightning (of the Resurrection) and the thunder (of Pentecost).** It refers to the period of prayerfully waiting for the arrival of the Holy Spirit and the opportunity to share the good news to the *"uttermost parts of the earth."* Reading Acts 1:8 and bringing it close to home, we each have our Jerusalem, Judea,

Samaria and beyond, and our work for the LORD, like theirs, must be motivated and empowered by his Spirit.

Are you just looking through a limited knothole of personal witness today? Are you always talking to the same people? Have you met anyone new lately? There is a big world out there full of people with a demanding ache to know the peace and power of God in their lives. The LORD will always do what he said to those disciples who wondered what the future held, *"I am with you always, to the very end of the age."*

I still remember that hefty weatherworn driftwood beam that resembled the cross, and all the thoughts that came from it that day. What possible meaning could it have for the kind of life and witness you or I can have in the world? **In our calling from Christ, let us be smart enough to follow the grain of our own wood, becoming the real selves God created us to be.**

If you are interested in Bible study and the way God works, take a good look at the book of Acts. Learn how the resurrection power of Jesus Christ carried out the world-wide mission through the disciples. It was the only way that it could happen.

 There are 6 sections showing the expansion of the gospel across their known world. If you want to know the sequence of how it happened, check out and mark these summary verses: chapter 6:7; chapter 9:31; chapter12:24; chapter16:5; chapter19:20 and chapter 28:31.

By the Spirit's power, where can your world expand today?

Supply and Demand

MATTHEW 28:16-20

One of the most genuine experiences of the WORD in the world happened to a man named Bob Pierce. He was one of the original founders of World Vision, the mission outreach organization that has helped multitudes of people around the world to know and accept the love of God.

It is a documented event that he was deep in the South American jungles to bring the good news of the gospel to remote villages and tribes. The approach that often worked best was to share the facts of Jesus Christ with the chief of a tribe. If he became a Christian, it was a natural opening to share the news with all others in the village.

This was the approach when Bob was offering the gospel to a chief of an isolated village. Imagine the surroundings. It is in the jungle with deep undergrowth, wild animals, colorful birds and no outside communication. When he explained the facts of Jesus' crucifixion by being nailed to the cross, the chief could not understand the meaning of the word **nail. "What is nail?"** he asked over and over.

Pierce thought and thought how to describe this. He looked through all the baggage but couldn't find a nail or way to illustrate it. He laid two branches on the ground as a cross. He lay down on them, stretching out his arms to show the means of Christ's sacrificial death for our sins. Still the meaning of nail eluded the chief, who finally walked away. It seemed the message was lost.

Pierce was discouraged and decided to rest while eating his lunch. Prayerfully he considered the situation further. His lunch included a small can of oranges which he opened and poured out into his metal dish. As he did so, he heard a **clink**. What was that? He looked and to his amazement saw a small nail in the dish. "A nail!" he shouted. "I found a nail!"

Once again he talked with the chief, showing him the nail and pressing it into his own hand to demonstrate its brutal purpose in God's plan for our salvation. This made the message clear. The chief accepted Christ and the message of God's love for him and his people. The WORD had come to this remote part of the world.

Often it may seem that others are not interested or open to the message of God's love. I recently read the phrase, **"No one who really understands the gospel of salvation from our sins will refuse it."** It is just too good to reject, and truly you will not miss the old life.

Do we have what we need to share the gospel? The whole world is waiting for it. When we seem to hit brick walls in our efforts to live and share it, let us remember Bob Pierce in the remote jungle that day and the proven promise of God.

"And God is able to make all grace abound to you, so that in all things at all times, having all that you need, you will abound in every good work." II Corinthians 9:8

Pacific Pines

*"How can a young person stay pure ? By obeying your word.
I have tried hard to find you – don't let me wander from your
commands. I have hidden your word in my heart, that I might
not sin against you."* Psalm 119:9-11 <u>NLT</u>

The very name, Pacific Pines, recalls some great weeks spent in the San
Bernadino Mountains of Southern California. Driving up to summer
camp on winding roads and going past the Rim of the World highway
filled us with high expectations of the new things God had in store for us.

It was a simple place, including a couple of rustic bunkhouses,
lodge, and craft hall and volleyball court among towering Ponderosa
Pines. Each summer the churches ran a few camps there for young
people. It was a different world, as we escaped the busy, smoggy Los
Angeles metropolis for clean, pine scented air. One kid, a real comedian,
said he wasn't sure about this. He said he "liked to be able to see what
he was breathing."

The campers were from mixed backgrounds, including a few
Hollywood movie stars' kids, as well as many underprivileged ones.
No distinctions were ever discussed. They were all just kids. This was
the pre-cell phone era and emergency calls only were accepted on the
one pay phone in the kitchen.

Up on the slope behind the lodge, hidden from view by the trees,
was a quiet, outdoor chapel. It was very plain. A tall stump served as an
altar with a homemade wooden cross and an open Bible. Benches were

flat boards nailed onto short stumps. The sun filtering through the tall pines provided the stained glass effect. It was a place where **"Be still and know that I am God"** was easy to understand.

A typical day's activities included meals, learning to work together with camp chores (such as raking pine needles away from buildings to prevent fire hazard), recreation, Bible class and crafts. Nothing in those wonderful camping days with those young people was more important than the vesper hour in the chapel, listening for God's voice within.

The pastor/teacher was popular with the campers. He would rise from his bench, all eyes upon him. He often illustrated his remarks, with a hand drawn poster. One showed a wide highway full of activity, but with a smaller road, really just a trail, leading away from the busy traffic. As we considered it there in the stillness, he would read: *"You can enter God's Kingdom only through the narrow gate. The highway to hell is broad and its gate is wide for the many that choose that way. But the gateway to life is very narrow and the way is difficult, and only a few ever find it."* Matthew 7:13

These words from the WORD in this quiet, beautiful country would capture our attention. They were spoken kindly, and with the authority of truth. It meant that your thoughts and actions matter a lot. There are consequences, large and small, to everything you do.

The opportunity for meaningful discipleship was offered with this gentle approach and understanding smile. The choice was clear. The Pastor had chosen the **narrow way,** and if he had, so could we. It was our choice. The sense of the divine purpose of life was being born within us. It was a mystical and practical moment of decision. **When you gave your heart to the LORD, everything was good and OK in your life. He would always help you through the years ahead.**

Now when I consider the huge religious denominations, the megachurches, the multiple years of education required for professional ministry and millions of books written about God, I remember that simple, quiet vesper hour with the WORD in the mountains. I remember the gentle nudging of the Spirit and how we sang that old camp chorus with full hearts:

> *Only to be what he wants me to be, every moment of every day,*
> *Just to be clay in the potter's hand, only to do what his will*
> *commands,*
> *Only to be what he wants me to be, every moment of every day.*

What a privilege to have been there. To be sure, some camp experiences are not the best, but this one introduced **the WORD in the right way, at the right time and in the right place.**

 "For I am persuaded, that height, nor death, nor life, nor angels, nor principalities, nor powers, nor things present, nor things to come, nor height, nor depth, nor any other creature, shall be able to separate us from the love of God, which is in Christ Jesus our Lord." Romans 8:37-39

Thy Kingdom Come

PSALM 90: 10 -11

The weather forecast for this March day today is for a big wind and rain storm soon, so Skye and I hustle down to the beach in the gray dawn. Cinnamon the cat trails along, as usual, always up for a new adventure. It is very still and the lake has a few small waves quietly rippling in. We crunch along the stony margin of the water, watching the sky.

It is a **half and half** zenith today, as the dawn strengthens and first light wins over the night. A flotilla of mallards is bobbing along; two of them launch away, quacking their protest loudly and flying surveillance over the Redbrook Boat Club. Two loons are diving in the lake seeking the early hatch of minnows in the shallows. The water is very clear today, revealing the ancient floor of stones and sand. The riparian has many birds singing, "calling for rain," my mother would say.

The distant western horizon is crowded with dark clouds. Forks, knives and spoons of lightning slash continuously. To the northwest, spider lighting flashes from cloud to cloud for miles. Distant thunder rumbles deep and quietly. Will the storm come along the shore or veer inland as it sometimes does? It is a dramatic prelude to the day.

The eastern half of the sky is full of light. The sun is not yet visible but legions of radiant rays are advancing across the light blue firmament. One brilliantly white cloud, very high and directly overhead, is a forward scout preceding this army of the sun. In this vast sky of anticipation, early morning thoughts bring memories galore of loved friends, many now gone but not forgotten. I see their names and faces in the clouds and thank God for his goodness seen in their brave lives. I whisper their names in gratitude that I could know them. *"LORD, make me to know mine end, and the measure of my days, what it is; that I may know how fleeting my life is."* Psalm 39:4

Seven miles up over all of this, a jetliner is soundlessly flying toward the rising sun. They seem to be above it all. Who is up there? Where are they going? What are they thinking about? Do they have any sense of the miracle of our lives and destinies? Do they know the LORD? Is anyone up there reading the Bible right now?

This is a morning like no other but in fact, **every morning is like no other** . . . Today has arrived, a true original waiting to be lived. It is a fresh, new start. Let us always understand the value of each **new** day with its golden opportunities. Sometimes they are surprising or disguised as work! Good things can happen, though sometimes that seems quite unlikely.

Luke 19:1-10 recounts the surprising and interesting story of that short tax guy, Zacchaeus. He was not regarded as a good candidate for the Kingdom of God. He didn't fit the image but Jesus saw something very different in him and invited himself into Zach's home. People muttered about this but the LORD said, *Today salvation has come to this house.*

What surprise does the LORD have in store for you this unique and brand new day? And furthermore, what surprise might you have for him? Are you really alive, using all the life he has given you?

 TODAY

Look well to this day,
For it is life –
The very best of life.
In its brief course lie all
The realities and truths of existence.

The joy of growth,
The splendor of action
The glory of power.

For yesterday is but a memory,
And tomorrow is only a vision,
But today, if well lived, makes
Every yesterday a memory of happiness,
And every tomorrow a vision of hope.

Look well therefore, to this day.

<u>The Sanskrit</u>

The WORD in the Far Country

LUKE 15

Perhaps the most famous story told by Jesus in the New Testament is about the prodigal son. It has all the elements of personal rebellion and divine forgiveness.

The younger son asked for his inheritance and *"he took his journey into a far country and there he squandered his property in loose living."*

Then he ran into a lot of trouble, actually having to eat pig's food and *"no one gave him anything."*

Having hit the bottom, *"he came to himself,"* and returned home, a very humbled son. The far country wasn't as wonderful as he had believed it to be. In rebellion he had rejected and traded off his father's love for waste and disappointment. He realized through bitter experience that he had made a big mistake and needed to go home.

Just how far away was the far country? Sometimes it is a very long way. It may not be a physical place, but a mental and emotional one. The separation is just as real or perhaps even more so. Some compulsion causes the break, something selfish takes control somewhere and the split happens.

The story is very interesting because it is so true. We may think it's amazing the younger son did something so foolish. The real point is that he *"came to himself"* and it's most amazing of all that the Father gladly received him home. These are all great realities. We may make foolish mistakes but we can come to ourselves and humbly return to the waiting Father.

I love the way Sister Mary Flannery of Jesuit House in Cleveland has said it: "God waits patiently for our acceptance of his love . . . we can find the peace that may have been submerged by destructive behavior or doubt or simply lack of motivation – any of which provided the grip of chaos in your life."

What happens when a person comes to himself? It means really admitting that he has left God's love behind in the dust and gone his own way. No doubt the compulsions were strong with a response to demands which turned out to be false and deceptive. This admission may not come easily as he may dance around the facts and put on a brave front.

Eventually something quiet and strong, representing God's love, allows the realization that he wants to come **home.** It may be the sound of a loved one's voice, a comment that recalls those who love him, a kind word spoken in the right moment, or an old photograph - anything that speaks to him in the moment of repentance. This stops the **out of control mistake** and the return journey begins.

 "Let the wicked forsake his way, and the unrighteous man his thoughts; and let him return unto the Lord, and he will have mercy upon him; and to our God, for he will abundantly pardon." Isaiah 55:7

GOD, or whatever . . .

ACTS 8:26–40

At sunset time on summer evenings, several of the neighbors gather on the grassy Common on the bluff overlooking the lake. Some have field glasses while others have wine glasses, and all enjoy watching the western skies. Usually there are a number of friendly dogs as well. It is an easy, pleasant social time. Recently, one of the sunset watchers made this observation, "Nice sunset. Created by God I guess, or whatever."

"**Whatever**" is a catch-all word that has found its way into our modern language and seems to imply the "I don't care about it anyway" thought. It is said often in that dismissive tone of voice, as though there are more important things to think about.

His comment really caught my attention. I like the person who said that, a pleasant soul who lives a good life and tries to help lots of other people with their problems. I debated with myself if I should ask just what **whatever** meant to him. I let it go as just another viewpoint that passes for faith these days, this doubtful secular religion in the world where God is seen as just another option.

It was just a passing social comment perhaps oiled by some good wine. We all have these **surface**, lives, like the surface of the lake where we see only a very small portion of deep realities. It's considered an OK way to live these days, not going deeper into the meaning of life. Many are content to know and discuss only the casual.

There are exceptional moments however, when ordinary casual times and places become **sacred spaces in the world.** Flying home from a business trip last year, I was sitting in seat 6-D next to a man who built new strip malls and was also under contract to Starbucks. I was quietly reading <u>Chronicles of Wasted Time</u> by Malcolm Muggeridge, the late, great British TV personality.

Suddenly Mr. 6-E spoke up, "That looks like a good book." Over the next two hours, our conversation deepened more and more. I simply repeated what Muggeridge had written, about being a cynical atheist who began to sense there was a lot more to life than he had ever imagined. The turning point came for him while filming a documentary of sheep shearing in Australia. The pressing question of his own reason for living was much on his mind. Then he saw the shears accidentally nick the skin of the sheep. Some red blood trickled through the white wool and his mind was eternally changed. He learned in his own experience the **Agnus Dei**, he said, **"Behold the Lamb of God who takes away the sin of the world."**

The man in 6 E spoke freely, more and more openly about his life. "You should see some of the Bozos I have to work with," he said. He was highly successful and extremely well organized. He knew people everywhere and his profitable work schedule stretched out many months. The surface of his life was a model of business success and the <u>Wasted Time</u> title caught his attention. How could a successful person like Muggeridge think he had wasted his life? What was more important than chalking up all those worldwide victories and awards? Mr. 6-E wanted to know what was below the surface of his life, but had always been a bit afraid to start looking. Some people call this "poking the bear."

Seats 6 D & E became sacred space, "a time and place where we discover God who is seeking a relationship with us and waits patiently for our acceptance of his love." 6-E began to realize that it is simply seeing the importance of a new, living relationship with God. It is feeling the deep and sincere desire to know more and more about him. It is not a scary thing after all and became a very easy transition. He sat in thoughtful silence for a while and then said, "I never really thought about these things."

Actually I said very little, as it was God at work in him. As I silently prayed for him, I could almost see the new discovery taking hold of him. He was thinking about his life in a whole new way and finding a new strength he had never known. It was marvelous to see. I thought about what happens when a new source of stream water flows into the lake. It sinks below the surface, causing a current. Likewise 6-E was receiving new knowledge and thought below the surface of his life, stirring things deep in his soul. He was moving from **Whatever, to a deeper life.**

The flight landed. As we rose to leave he simply said, "Thank you." I watched him walk away and thought how good and important it is to have good, ethical business success when we include the LORD in major decisions.

Perhaps you have heard these comparisons. A basketball in my hands is worth about $19. In an NBA superstar's hands, it's worth many millions. It depends whose hands it's in. A slingshot in my hands is a kid's toy, but in David's hands, it can defeat a giant adversary. It depends whose hands it's in. Two fish and five loaves of bread in my hands are a couple of fish sandwiches, but in the WORD's hands, they will feed thousands. It depends whose hands things are in.

There is always so much more than we see on the surface. In Luke 5:4, Jesus tells Simon to *"Launch out into the deep,"* resulting in a greater discovery and catch than could be imagined. The same opportunity is out there for everyone.

Are you on the surface or **in the deep** with the LORD?

". . . being confident of this, that he who began a good work in you *will carry it on to completion until the day of Christ Jesus."*
Philippians 1:6

Shadow Man

ROMANS 7: 21-25

On this early May morning, I watched as the earth slowly rotated in its orbit around the sun bringing yet another crimson, golden and copper sunrise. Its expanding light gradually rose into the illimitable space above. It painted the smooth lake surface before me, as the Master Artist transformed the blank canvas from gray vacancy into a spectacular morning scene of new life.

As I was responding in my mind to these natural wonders, I suddenly noticed another person. Actually, it was just my shadow there on the sand. It obediently duplicated my every movement, a raised hand, or a turning profile.

It spoke not, expressing nothing of itself. It was only a lifeless, dark mirror of my body, a puppet having no vitality of its own except the movements that I gave it. It saw not the sunrise nor felt the stirring of life and vitality. I laughed at myself, having thought at first it was another person on the beach, perhaps sneaking up on me. Yes, I was briefly scared of my own shadow.

Shadow is a word of many meanings, some of them about the unknown or undesirable aspects of us. Hebrews 12:1 tells us to: "... *lay aside every weight and the sin which doth so easily beset us, and let us run with patience the race that is set before us . . .*" Some personal problems that we may have can stick to us like a shadow wherever we go, no matter how hard and fast we run.

The truth of the Good News from God is that his grace can overcome any problem we have, if we will simply allow him to really do so. *"This then is the message which we have heard of him, and declare unto you, that God is light, and in him is no darkness at all. If we say we have fellowship with him, and walk in darkness, we lie, and do not the truth; But if we walk in the light, as he is in the light, we have fellowship one with another, and the blood of Jesus Christ his Son cleanseth us from all sin."* I John 1:5-7 <u>KJV</u>

> *Were it not for grace, I can tell you where I'd be,*
> *Wandering down some pointless road to nowhere*
> *with my salvation up to me. (see page vii)*

 "Yet I still belong to you: you hold my right hand. You guide me with your counsel, leading me to a glorious destiny." Psalm 73:23-24

Joy

"Never be lacking in zeal, but keep your spiritual fervor, serving the Lord. Be joyful in hope, patient in affliction, and faithful in prayer. Share with God's people who are in need. Practice hospitality." Romans 12:11-13

There's an interesting lighthearted question going around the internet: "If Jesus drove a car, what kind, year and condition would it be?" Would it be a van, SUV, Hybrid? It has a serious side to it, of course, and might get some interesting conversation going, such as, "Why would he choose **that** one?"

Country roads near the 490 miles of the Blue Ridge Parkway are very interesting for sightseeing or adventurous drivers. A listing of "Best Mountain Roads" calls them fun **rides** of many curves, elevation changes, steep sided gorges, cascading waterfalls and beautiful views of the mountains. One 300 mile loop is an 8 hour drive including the famous "Tail of the Dragon" with over 300 curves in 11 miles. If that seems too much, try the "Diamondback" with only 190 curves with steep grades, covering 12 miles. The "Moonshiner Trail" of 107 miles has even more than that.

The joy of driving these in a sports car is a real adrenaline rush for many enthusiasts. Experienced drivers of these roads say that you can't take your eyes off the road ahead and should not stare into the rear view mirror to check out where you have been. Each year, those coming to rallies at the BMW plant near Greenville, S.C., may include these roads in their travel plans. I wonder if BMW chose this manufacturing site partly because of the resemblance to European mountain roads. Their automobiles are exciting vehicles, built with a passion for excellence. Consider this mission statement from their Zentrum visitor's center:

"JOY – On the back of this three-letter word, we built a company. Independent of everyone, accountable to no one but the driver. We do not build cars. We are the creators of emotions. We are the guardians of ecstasy, the thrills and chills, the laughs and smiles and all the words that can't be found in a dictionary. We are the Joy of Driving. No car company can rival our history, replicate our passion, and see your vision. Innovation is our backbone but joy is our heart. We will not stray from our three-letter purpose. We will nurture it, we will make Joy smarter. We will push it, test it, break it – then build it again – more efficient, more dynamic. We will give the world the keys to Joy, and they will take it for a ride. And while others try to promise everything, we promise one – the personal, cherished and human of all emotions. This is the story of BMW. **This is the story of Joy.**"

What automobiles! After reading this **over the top** statement, is it any wonder that so many people are drawn to driving their vehicles?

The exhilaration of driving a great car through such beauty on challenging roads stirs awareness of an even greater joy. We may find great happiness just in our daily blessed existence if it points beyond us to the very Source of our lives. We are talking real JOY here, the quiet, confident assurance of God's love for us that does not depend on circumstances.

The exhilaration of the WORD in this part of the world, these wondrous Carolina Mountains, is found throughout scripture. We can have profound contentment, inward strength and peace, no matter what happens, if Christ is in our hearts and we know him.

St. Paul writing a letter of Joy to his friends in Philippi said it so well. *"Yes, everything else is worthless when compared with the infinite value of knowing Christ Jesus my Lord."* Philippians 3:8 He really wanted to know Christ and the more he knew him, the more joy was in his life, regardless of the extreme troubles, losses and curves in the road he experienced.

Knowing more and more ABOUT Christ is good scholarship, of course, but **knowing Christ is more important and personally rewarding**. It is a huge difference when you know a person, rather than just knowing ABOUT him. That's what this letter of joy is really saying. If you read it prayerfully, the joy of KNOWING Christ comes through loud and clear. It details the reality of joy beyond circumstances: joy in suffering; joy in serving; joy in believing; joy in giving. It means being more involved, aware and engaged in this relationship with the WORD, even more than driving a high powered automobile on a challenging Blue Ridge mountain road.

Isn't this what our Lord meant when he said, *"I have told you these things so that you will be filled with my joy. Yes, your joy will overflow!"* John 15:11 My joy, your joy. It is a mutual experience of two parties, so it is OUR joy.

How does this happen? **How can we have this experience of the joy of the LORD?** The good news is that it is not entirely up to us. We do not have to grit it out on our own. Do you KNOW the Lord? Yes? Then read another great truth expressed in Philippians 2:12:

". . . continue to work out your salvation with fear and trembling. for it is God who works in you to will and to act according to his good purpose."

God is at work within us, giving us the desire and acting in our lives. It is up to us, not to just allow it, but to want it, really want it, if we expect the fullness of his joy. Fear and trembling are not a childish worry about punishment. They are positives here, the hopeful desire to seek and to find God, since we know that without his help, we cannot live our lives in the best and happiest way possible.

He is waiting, always waiting for us to accept his love. What an opportunity!

Perspective

PSALM 22:1-2

Lake Erie from 5,000 feet up is a turbulent seascape washing and embracing our bit of the north coast known as Ashtabula, Lake and Cuyahoga counties. I have flown in and out of the Cleveland, Ohio, airport hundreds of times. Today is the first time I remember passing over the town of Chardon before circling out over the lake for the southerly approach to the field.

Three days ago, a troubled student entered Chardon High School and shot five students, three of whom died. The news media is full of the tragedy, including one of the most devastating interviews ever seen of grieving parents, shattered, speechless and helpless in the hell of losing their son to a maddened peer. Our entire region is shaken, and talking of very little else. Other schools are on alert and parents are checking up on their children. The usual questions are heard: "How can God allow this to happen?" "Why didn't someone see this coming?" "Why did this have to happen here?"

Shock and rage may rise up in the mind, seeking revenge. But seeing Chardon with its town square and courthouse down there, far below, and then nearby the majesty of the lake brings to mind the words of the Master to Peter: "*Get away from me, Satan! You are a dangerous trap to me. You are seeing things merely from a human point of view, not from God's.*" Matthew 16:23 <u>NLT</u> *His* words are very firm, spoken not in anger, but in gentle reprimand to one of his most trusted friends. Satan is a Hebrew word for **Adversary**. Sometimes, like Peter, even words spoken in concern for others serve only to distract from the real issue. William Barclay wrote that Jesus was saying to Peter: "Your place is behind me, not in front of me. It is your place to follow me in the way I choose, not in the way you would like me to go." Commentary on Matthew

That is a big part of growing up in Christ, regardless of our age. It happens over and over again throughout our lifetimes. It is humbling, and it takes some of the sting out of the correction, and is good for us. It is the process of learning to see things from 5,000 feet up, trying to see things, as it were, from God's perspective.

It is a real challenge for us to **see things from God's point of view** rather than from our own. While no reasonable excuse can be made for the teenage shooter at Chardon High School, there are reasons, however unacceptable, why he did this. Many people, young and older, are confused. Not long ago I saw a young person wearing a message T-shirt that said, "I am lost. I've gone to look for myself. If I should return before I get back, please ask me to wait."

It can be a rough time for young people, made rougher by neglect and various pressures. Many live with very unrealistic expectations. If they see a complicated situation on television or in a film, it is resolved within 20 or 30 minutes, often by violence. If they encounter that same kind of problem in real life, they may think it can be solved quickly the same way. Factually however, it may take years of diligent effort to grow into the real maturity of adult thinking. As Bill Cosby once said, "If you pull the trigger, you cannot wish that bullet back into the gun."

Someone recently noted that real spiritual maturity is the ability to **live successfully without all the answers.** This is not an easy concept to grasp, but thinking about it further it seems so very true. The reaction of many people to the shootings is one of deep caring for the devastated families. They can give comfort even by being silent because they simply do not know what to say.

We do not believe that violence is God's will, or that he enabled it to happen. A story out of World War II concentration camps described a prisoner who was tied to a stake and shot. "Where was God?" a horrified observer asked. A person of faith replied, "He was tied to the stake with the dying one." Our faith believes that God's Son, the WORD made flesh, died and suffered for us and has ultimate victory over death.

We also note, that many young people in Chardon are responding positively to the crisis. It was a scare they will never forget. Yet they are pulling together in growing strength. They are helping each other and learning some of the most important lessons they will ever know in all their lifetimes. It is inspiring to see them rising up, unified in community strength over the irreparable loss of some of their own. The opposite reaction of giving in to desperate fear would lead to a very different end of hopelessness and fear.

They are finding a ray of hope, a tiny glimpse of our God who cares and saves, even in the darkest hours we can know. We offer this excellent prayer to all young people today. It is found in Romans 15:13:

"May the God of hope fill you with all joy and peace as you trust in him, so that you may overflow with hope by the power of the Holy Spirit."

Space Station

"He has made the earth by His power, He has established the world by His isdom, and has stretched out the heavens at His discretion." Jeremiah 10: 12 <u>NKJV</u>

Coming up from the shore one evening, I met a small group of our neighbors on the Common, all looking up into the evening sky. They were watching a steady white pinpoint of light moving slowly from the northwest to the southeast. The International Space Station was speeding by at 17,000 mph on its 90-minute orbit around our earth. I had read that the astronauts can see the Great Lakes from their ride up there, 220 miles above us. I wondered if they were looking at us at the same time we were looking at them! I doubt that, but waved anyway!

The NASA website has fascinating pictures and information about the ISS, such as its size which is larger than a football field, weighing over a million pounds. Over 200 astronauts working in relays have traveled 1.5 billion miles over the past 10 years. You can even find its itinerary and when it might be visible from your back yard. Good binoculars can actually pick out a few details of the station, such as the huge solar panels.

So here we were, a few earthbound humans watching a technological miracle of our modern age, with one of those **Deep calls to deep moments** as though God speaks to us from his deep space and we hear him down deep in our souls. Then the solid, hopeful words of John, the beloved disciple, came to mind: *"Dear friends, now we are children of God, and what we will be has not yet been made known. But we know that when he appears, we shall be like him, for we shall see him as he is."* I John 3:2 A good friend, Pastor Elmo Randolph, once wrote about that verse and the inspiration of space travel: "This evening, new and different ideas grip our minds. Dreams have become reality . . . what was once believed impossible is now achieved. With God all things are possible - we can become spiritually new."

It is awesome when you first think about space travel and the discipline it has taken to build and sustain those living quarters up there. They are high above our atmosphere and gravitational pull. When that amazing reality sinks into your mind, it gives a boost to your own life and challenges. People have really accomplished great things, and so can you. It may not be about you flying into space, but about fulfilling your own dreams. It is about finding the confidence that is born of your faith in Christ, and his great faith in you. The WORD who created all that we see in the universe, will also create in you strength, vision and abilities that are far, far beyond your own limitations. He will make you greater than anything you could ever be just by yourself. Are you ready and open for that today? Yes ( ) No ( )

 "This is what the LORD says; Heaven is my throne, and the earth is my footstool. Could you build me a temple as good as that? Could you build me such a resting place? My hands have made both heaven and earth; they and everything in them are mine. I, the LORD, have spoken!" Isaiah 66:1-2 <u>NLT</u>

Down to Earth

PHILIPPIANS 2:1-18

Some brave little blue flowers along the riparian are trembling in the chilly breeze today. They remind me that **flowers are the world's laughter**, and of the LORD's words, *"Be of good cheer. I have overcome the world."* John 16:33

A solitary walk on a nature trail by the river provides good soul **time** to think through many things and remember past wonderful experiences. The WORD has provided good practical answers to tough personal questions, very often through good friends. So much of life has to be taken seriously that it is good to remember the fellowship times among friends who care. Through them, the WORD often provides saving grace, and the balm of human kindness.

The book of Philippians is a book of joy. The love among real friends in the faith shines through. We are fortunate when we know someone who automatically brings a smile to our face. Such good friends make a huge difference in our living so let us seek to be that to others as well. It is a priceless and redeeming quality. It is also important to be a friend to ourselves and this often means being able to laugh at ourselves. **Truly we are called to live above the circumstances, not under them.**

One morning I needed a couple of big cardboard packing boxes and stopped by a service station that advertised them. I asked the attendant about them, since he was the only one there. He was a burly guy with grease on his arms, coveralls and baseball cap which he wore backwards. "Sure," he said. "Hang on. I'll get some down."

They were stored on a high shelf over the cluttered workbench. Standing on a small step stool he reached up for one which happened to be holding a lot of others up there, and they all came crashing down! I expected some frustrated, loud language as he ducked away from the avalanche. Instead, I heard his laughter. I was amazed and said, "You handled that well!" He laughed again and said, "It's early in the morning. If I get mad now, it will ruin the whole day."

His wisdom and self-knowledge have stayed with me like a favorite song. He knew how to make the right choice when things go wrong.

That is a powerful secret to happy living. Don't get bent out of shape through an angry attitude. Of course we can't always do this entirely alone. The WORD in your heart can train and give you the strength to overcome the twinge, (or surge) of anger. When we ask him, he empowers the right and personal choice. When we learn to walk and talk in prayer with him, the patient wisdom of the ages can flow into our thoughts and emotions. We know this ". . . *is God who works in you to will and to act according to his good purpose."* Philippians 2:13

When the WORD helps you learn that skill, a new maturity strengthens your life. It is proven to you that salvation is real and when taken seriously makes life much more enjoyable. As Christ dwells in your heart by faith, a new appreciation for the comical side of life develops. We take him seriously, but ourselves – not so much.

Can you laugh at yourself? If you want to improve that important skill, ask the WORD and he will gladly teach you how. It's one of his good gifts to us.

 "Our mouths were filled with laughter, our tongues with songs of joy. The LORD has done great things for us." Psalm 126:2-3

Memories

ISAIAH 42:9

It's a peach/pink morning with light dawning out of the eastern horizon, sending fingers of glory westward into the receding darkness. A million sparkles like glitter confetti on the water are celebrating yet another day of life. We walk along, our collie Skye and I, checking out beach conditions and prospecting for new discoveries. Some mallards are rocking gently fifty feet off shore. Skye steps in for a closer look and they decide it's time to go. They launch themselves north with beating wing tips tattooing the surface with trails of ripples as they quack their farwell. What a morning! It's good to be alive!

Light and grateful thoughts occupy my mind. Years ago we knew a lady who couldn't walk and lived in a wheelchair. She had a great sense of humor. She read and memorized poetry and could recite entertaining programs to different groups. One day she delighted us with this:

> *I walked along the sandy beach*
> *And with a fragile reed I wrote upon the sand,*
> *Charles! I love thee!*
> *A mad wave rolled up*
> *And blotted out the fair impression.*
> *Fragile reed – Cruel wave!*
> *I'll trust thee no more,*
> *But with a giant's hand I'll pluck from*
> *Norway's shore her tallest pine,*

Dip it in the crater of Vesuvius
And write upon the high and burnished heavens
Charles! I love thee!
And see if that darned old wave
*Will wash **that** out!*

She was one who knew how to really gain by sharing blessings when other privileges, like walking, were lost.

And on the subject of losing something, I have been noticing lately some memory lapses. What good can come of this? I laugh at this item, **Partsheimers,** that my brother Dick sent to me:

"I have been diagnosed with AAADD - Age Activated Attention Deficit Disorder. Yesterday I decided to water my plants. As I turn on the hose in the driveway, I look over at my car and decide it needs washing. As I head towards the garage, I notice on the deck table some mail which I had picked up earlier. I decide I had better go through it now in case there is something important in there, before I wash the car.

I put my car keys on the table, put the junk mail in the recycling box under the table and notice the box is full. So I decide to put the mail down and take out the recycling first. But then, I think, since I'm going to be near the mailbox while I am taking the recycling out, I might as well pay the bills first. I take my check book off the table but notice there is only one check left.

My extra checks are in the desk in my study, so I go into the house and to my desk where I find the cup of coffee I had been drinking. It is getting cold so I decide to make another cup. As I head toward the kitchen with the cold coffee, a vase of flowers on the counter catches my eye - they need water.

I put the coffee on the counter and discover my reading glasses are there. I had been looking for them all morning. I decide I better put them back on my desk, but first I'm going to water the flowers. I put the glasses back on the counter, fill a container with water and notice that the TV remote is on the kitchen table. We will need that tonight when we want to watch TV and we will be looking for it and not remember it is on the table, so I decide to put it back where it belongs, but first I am going to water the flowers.

I pour some water in the flowers, but quite a bit of it spills on the floor. So, I put the remote back on the table, get some paper towels and wipe up the spill. Then, I head down the hall trying to remember what I was going to do.

> At the end of the day;
> The garden isn't watered,
> The car isn't washed,
> The bills aren't paid,
> There is a cold cup of coffee sitting on the kitchen counter,
> The flowers don't have enough water,
> There is still only one check in my check book,
> I can't find the TV remote,
> I can't find my glasses,
> And, where are the car keys?

And when I try to figure out why nothing got done today, I am really baffled because I know I was busy all day and am really tired!"

So, the sunrise is beautiful this morning. These dawning moments are real keepers. Like many other wonderful experiences over the years that enriched my life, I will remember them.

 *"This is what the LORD says, he who appoints the sun to shine by day, who decrees the moon and stars to shine by night, who stirs up the sea so that its waves roar - the LORD Almighty is his name . . . For everyone, both great and small, shall really know me then, says the LORD, and I will forgive and **forget** their sins."* Jeremiah 31:35

How good it is to know that when the WORD is really in our hearts, our God *"will remember our sins no more."*

Déjà vu

JOHN 1:44-51

Have you ever had a **déjà vu experience?** (Deja vu is French for **already seen.**) It is a strange yet normal thing. Most people have sensed it at some time in their lives. It is the eerie sense of having experienced or seen something before, even when we know that it's just not possible. Some people think it is proof of reincarnation, the return of experiences or interests from a previous life.

A fascinating study recently reported new theories that this is a brilliant function of your brain. Sometimes its lively neurotransmitters send new, first time information into the long-term memory area instead of the short-term center. Then when your brain **recalls** the image from the long term memory area, it tells you falsely that it is information from the past. **Déjà vu!**

Another fascinating theory is that **been there done that before** feelings are a result of one eye sending information to the brain faster than the other. Almost everyone has a dominant eye. If that stronger eye sends information to the subconscious before both eyes focus and register the input as a conscious experience, your brain will tell you, "I've seen that before." And you have - but it was just a nanosecond ago. "The Plain Dealer Newspaper 3/20/12)

Fascinating!

Anyone, including you, can have déjà vu experiences with the WORD . . . They bring a sense of familiar knowledge and certainty to your thoughts. It is like that when we feel close to him. Like close friends, they are mystical and comforting feelings as we find peace in his presence.

The truth of this is found in John 1:44-47, when Philip told Nathanael to just **come and see the Messiah for himself.** No one is ever argued into faith in Christ. So Nathanael did and met Jesus for the first time near Galilee. When Jesus saw him coming, he said, *"Here is a true Israelite in whom there is nothing false." "How do you know me?" Nathanael asked. Jesus answered, "I saw you while you were still under the fig tree before Philip called you."*

Open your mind to this meeting. When one really connects with the WORD made flesh, that deep sense of familiarity and comfort flows freely into your life. It is true recognition and he **looks very familiar. I must have met him somewhere before**. Then it is the realization that you have **always been known by God.** It is the deep, healing knowledge that God loves you, always has, always will.

It is a discovery of the obvious, and you can step out in welcoming faith to accept it. Nathanael had been seeking God, studying and praying in sacred space - there under the fig tree. Into his seeking and prepared heart, came the One who knew his thoughts, hopes and dreams.

For a person like that who is honest and open, it is very liberating and comforting to realize that God knows the **real you** inside and out. He knew us before we were born or ever met him so we really have nothing to hide. Psalm 139 is about God's Plan in Scripture for you. Give yourself a 10 minute vacation by reading it, and then write it in your own words.

"Search me, O God, and know my heart; test me and know my anxious thoughts. See if there is any offensive way in me, and lead me in the way everlasting." Psalm 139:23-24

Tyre

MATTHEW 15:21-28

Today is an extraordinary, uncommon day. It is January 31 in northeast Ohio on the shore of Lake Erie. The sun is shining, the sky is clear; the temperature is 49 degrees, making a day of **false spring**. Unbelievable! There is no wind and there are large, gentle waves washing our shore. Wading along there in my high boots I wondered if the WORD ever saw any waters and big waves other than Galilee? It seems we usually just read about that but in Mark 7, we discover that he visited Tyre on the coast of The Great Sea, which we now call the Mediterranean. Watching these picturesque waves today I thought of what a visit to Tyre would be like to those disciples. Like this unusual day, it must have been a rare and life changing experience.

Those provincial fishermen who owned small boats and sailed on a lake bordered with a few small villages, walked with the LORD to the major harbor of Tyre in neighboring Phoenicia. It was an ancient city on a peninsula with long sandy beaches that jutted out into The Great Sea.

The Phoenicians sailed throughout the Mediterranean and perhaps even out into the ocean all the way to Britain. They are thought to have developed celestial navigation by the stars, allowing them to leave visible coastlines far behind for longer journeys. Therefore Tyre became a great trading center and was immensely wealthy and powerful from its export of purple dye that was known around the known world. It was sophisticated Gentile territory, probably not much interested in

327

their neighbor, Israel. Tyre was no Cana of Galilee with its small fishing operations.

So the Galilean group headed into a very different culture, a big city/harbor of big ships on a big sea, with big businesses, and big differences. I like to think they had never seen anything like this and were awestruck by the busy industry of this bustling seaport. What an adjustment to leave a life and trade that you knew very well, to become **fishers of men** venturing into new territory. The book of Acts reports that in fact a church was founded there.

They were there incognito, as Mark explains, *"He entered a house and did not want anyone to know it, yet he could not keep his presence secret."* Mark 7:24 This section of the gospel tells us that they were skirting Galilee for a while, because there was opposition to Jesus by his own race. Their travels took them into new, unknown territories, an extraordinary and perhaps dangerous thing because the ancient ethnic barriers between regions were high and strong.

It must have called for a lot of new thinking and courage for the disciples to follow his call, just as it does for us today. As interesting as it must have been for them to see this huge cosmopolitan harbor, it also required a lot of trust in him. I can imagine them sticking very close together, right on his heels every step of the way looking around at all these new circumstances

Then this adventure gets even more bizarre and profoundly moving. *"Yet he could not be hid but immediately a woman, whose little daughter was possessed by an unclean spirit, heard of him, and came and fell down at his feet."* Mark 7:26-27

Word got around that he was there, and it is still true, that when the LORD is really present, he will be discovered. He is the surprise of the ages and is often found in the most unlikely times and places. The conversation between the woman and the LORD is fascinating and endearing, inviting thoughtful study. Dogs are mentioned as are table scraps. What is this?

We must get beyond that to the real exchange between them - the heart of the encounter. I have often thought how it would be so wonderful to actually hear Jesus speaking, to catch his tone of voice. It seems to me that this event is light and even humorous. I think Jesus speaks to her with a smile and gentle wit. She responds in kind, with a cheerful grin and perhaps he loves it. It is a unique and genuine connection between them. He understands fully what she asks and that she will not take no for an answer. She has a very sick child at home but still a lighthearted faith in this man called Christ. They are instant friends even though he is a Jew from remote Galilee and she is Syrian-Phoenician living in one of the great cities of the world. **The real point is her daughter's great need and his power to heal.** Her faith was tested and it was real. The WORD spoke the word and the daughter was healed.

So on this beautiful unwinter January day I consider those Galilean disciples having such a totally new experience in Tyre. I think about the unlikely exchange between a person with a real tragedy at home and her most enjoyable meeting with the WORD. How true it is that we have much to learn, and that the unexpected, new experiences of our lives can be the exciting, growing edge of our faith when we follow the WORD.

Where is your Tyre today? Who needs healing that you are praying for?

 "We give thanks to God always for you all, constantly mentioning you in our prayers, remembering before our God and Father your work of faith and labor of love and steadfastness of hope in our Lord Jesus Christ." I Thessalonians 1:2-3

Brugge

LUKE 15:8-10

One of the most rewarding experiences of my work life was representing our manufacturing company at an international trade show in Paris. Preparing for it and then attending our stand there was a challenging learning experience. I enjoyed it tremendously. I had also hoped to see some European culture but time was too short for that on this trip.

Many new business contacts were made and when the show closed, I hand wrote 14 pages of new opportunities with addresses and phone numbers. This was before modern, amazing e-mail technology, so I asked the business office at my hotel to fax it all to my office in Ohio.

I had a train to catch, traveling on to Brugge, Belgium, where another important business meeting was scheduled. I packed up and left for the next business adventure. The next day, speaking with the Ohio office, the secretary asked why 14 blank pages had been fax'd to her! **OH NO!** I called the previous hotel and learned that the trainee had put the report in the machine the wrong way, and then, since I had left, discarded the papers.

This was very bad news, to put it mildly. Devastated, I went for a walk in the ancient streets of Brugge to calm my thoughts. I wandered into the medieval, soaring cathedral there. I sat there, listening to magnificent organ music, and prayed. I knew I would never be able to recover all of the information, but would just have to research it somehow.

As I started to leave, I noticed a small sign, **MICHAELANGELO,** with an arrow pointing into a small side chapel. At least I might get to see some European culture after all. Walking in there I saw one of his works, a large marble carving of the Christ child. It had been intended for installation high up in a cathedral, where it would appear normal size. It was just a few feet away and I considered its beauty for a long time. **"No one would ever throw HIS work away,"** I thought, laughing to myself. Seeing such beauty in my present frame of mind was relaxing and healing.

As I was leaving, I passed the prayer candles table, where an invitation card offered anyone the opportunity to light a candle for a special need. In the spirit of the moment I did so, asking God to help me recover the lost work.

How can I describe the moment? All the emotion and thinking of the entire trip came to the surface. I sensed just a whisper that the WORD was passing by right then. **Thrill** is not a word that I use often, but it fits that moment as I felt a prickling of my neck and scalp. All would be well, somehow.

Returning to my hotel, a message was waiting for me. The Paris hotel had found the report and resent it, as requested, to Ohio. This time, the pages were right side up.

That evening I read Luke 18:37 about a blind man in desperate need. He sensed excitement in the crowd around him and asked what it meant. *"And they told him, Jesus of Nazareth is passing by."* He called out loudly twice, in his great need. He would not be denied even though others were telling him to be quiet.

The WORD stopped and asked him what he wanted. Hearing the man's request for sight, Jesus healed him right then and there. Jesus of Nazareth is always passing by when we are in need.

 "And they told him, Jesus of Nazareth is passing by." Luke 18:37

Wonder Lake

"Don't be deceived my dear brothers. Every good and perfect gift is from above, coming down from the Father of the heavenly lights, who does not change like shifting shadows. He chose to give us birth through the word of truth, that we might be a kind of first fruits of all he created." James 1:17-18

The Alaska Railroad passenger train takes eight hours to travel from Anchorage to the entrance of Denali National Park. There you can catch a kind of school bus and ride another six hours over a gravel road into the Park, arriving at the Lodge. Not far from the Lodge is Wonder Lake – some say it is so named because you wonder if you will ever get there! During the ride in, you may see moose, caribou, grizzly bears or Dall sheep. There are also wolves but they are seldom seen by tourists.

The Alaskan scenery in the land of the midnight sun is a magnificent gift from God. There are braided rivers, massive peaks, tundra and glaciers. The handcrafted Lodge near Mt. McKinley (or Denali, meaning **The High One)** is called one of top ten lodges in the National Park system. It is truly a place apart, being fully self- contained in the heart of the wilderness. Mt. McKinley at 20,000 feet is the highest peak in North America and is only visible about 30 percent of the time.

Wonder Lake is so named because on a perfectly clear day, The High One may be reflected there in all its majesty, causing awe and wonder in the soul. Visitors are advised in advance that, due to weather, it may not be visible at all – so enjoy the journey getting there. Good advice. My experience there was doubly blessed. The mountain was clearly visible. It truly was an indescribable sight. Random clouds, however, obscured the reflection but the surface of Wonder Lake was shining like polished chrome with gently swirling patterns. It was so worth the effort to get there.

The indescribable beauty of this experience peeled back the layers of appreciation we can have toward our very lives. It is to be pierced to the heart by the miracle of our everyday existence. It is great worship when we really forget ourselves and realize the immeasurable greatness of God, who is available to us. Unbidden, the words of the Psalmist rose from memory, *"I say to the LORD; I have no good apart from you."* Psalm 16:2

A certain man underwent knee-replacement surgery and immediately made amazing progress. He could walk the next day, amazing other patients. Believing that it was due to his own physical strength, he quit taking the pain medication. He quickly learned that without that help, his **recovery and pride** deserted him. He felt like he had been trampled in a stampede of wild horses.

Looking at the Alaskan **scripture of nature**, the certainty of God's goodness was enormous, wild and strong. Anything we do that is worthwhile is sourced from God's Holy Spirit. We can't take the credit for good living; it is due to the same WORD that creates our highest mountains of achievement and the deepest lakes of accomplishments.

"And I will pray the Father, and he shall give you another Comforter, that he may abide with you forever." John 14:16

Moonset/Sunrise

PSALM 8

"The best remedy for those who are afraid, lonely or unhappy is to go outside, somewhere where they can be quiet, alone with the heavens, nature and God. Because only then does one feel that all is as it should be, and that God wishes to see people happy, amidst the simple beauty of nature." <u>Anne Frank, the Diary of a Young Girl.</u> Her words are eternally true and proven over and over again in our own experiences.

An unusual event is visible in January each year when the full moon **sets** on the western horizon simultaneously with the sun **rising** in the east. The ending of the night and the beginning of the new day are termed **moonset/sunrise.** These are only our human terms, of course, as our earth rotates at the angle to make this possible. It is so rich in symbolism yet passing by so quickly that many people never witness it. It is a most moving experience.

Were there such mornings of a moonset/sunrise on Galilee? I like to think so, and we know the LORD spent a lot of time there with a 24/7 schedule. I like thinking that he saw the same moon then as we do now.

We are all on a journey which this year will take 366 days as our earth revolves at 1000 mph around our sun. Our moon is our traveling companion, providing celestial reckoning of the journey with its 29 day revolution around our earth, marking the time with changing phases. Its gravity affects our oceans and its visual phases are used by sportsmen, farmers and scientists for many reasons. Our moon is important to us.

This same old moon also held important significance for Israel throughout the Bible, for the ancients knew and watched its reliable schedule and changes in appearance. It was important agriculturally and religiously. The "New Moon" is mentioned several times, and of course God was always acknowledged as Creator of all the heavens and the earth. The scriptures do warn us, however that, "*bowing down to the sun or the moon or the stars in the sky*" was a form of idolatry punishable by stoning! Deuteronomy 17:3

Today it is fascinating to read that in 2013 Israel will send a small scientific space craft to the moon. It will be about the size of a coke bottle to study and report back its findings. "A small nation sends a small spaceship," says their Prime Minister. It is intended to create greater interest in science among high school students. Remember Jeremiah 10:12? It tells us that, "*God has stretched out the heavens at his discretion.*" *NKJV* This new Israeli moon lander will be reading the fine print and wonder of our Creator's handiwork.

The moon has an eternal mystical quality about it and is sometimes blamed for evil things that people think or do. Our 'interesting neighbor' also has a romantic quality but it is such a normal part of our routine lives that we don't even think about it very often. Seeing the **moonset** over the lake brought the rush of faith and praise once again to our Creator, "*When I consider thy heavens, the work of thy fingers, the moon and the stars which thou hast ordained: What is man that thou art mindful of him? And the son of man, that thou visits him.*" Psalm 8: 3-4

How small we feel in the vastness and majesty of the universe! This healthy humility brings us back to reality, and it is good, very good. It grounds us and we realize that we, too, are creations of the same God. Yes, as Anne Frank wrote, "only then does one feel that all is as it should be."

Some years ago there was a global mini-movement referred to as the Harmonic Convergence. It was about the rare alignment of the planets which some believed meant the birth of a new age. Advocates actually traveled to other places in the world to spend that night, imagining that they were supposed to be in that certain place to get the maximum enlightenment from the occasion. An interesting scientific fact captured the imagination of people with certain spiritual needs and a manmade religion resulted.

Conversely, the moon is mentioned in Paul's letter to the Colossian church as he corrected their mistaken ideas which were veering away from the WORD who is the way, the truth and the life. *"Therefore do not let anyone judge you by what you eat or drink, or with regard to a religious festival, a New Moon celebration or a Sabbath day. Theirs are a shadow of the things to come, the reality however is found in Christ."* Colossians 2:26

Because of Christ, the old cult ideas of being in total, obedient harmony with nature were now seen to be empty spiritual wanderings. Nature will not save us. Even today, we can become hypnotized when our emotions are engulfed by the endless wonder of the heavenly bodies circling relentlessly above the moving platform of our earth. It truly is awesome, but do we trust in them for salvation from our fears, false hopes and the errors of our human ways? Do they really do anything to meet our personal challenges?

It is true that **nature is beyond comprehension and never makes mistakes**, but it is not the final reality for our human destiny. There is no salvation for us in the stars.

I don't know if I will ever see another moonset/sunrise like the one January 3, 2012, but I do know this: "In *the beginning was the Word, and the Word was with God and the Word was God. The same was in the beginning with God. All things were made by him; and without him was not anything made that was made. In him was life; and the life was the light of men . . . . And the Word was made flesh and dwelt among us, (and we beheld his glory, the glory as of the only begotten of the Father), full of grace and truth."* John 1:1-4; 14 KJV

I believe that the WORD saw his created moon and the sunrise as he walked in Galilee. When I see the same moon and all the heavenly bodies, I want to walk with the **Light of the world** who made them all.

 "He is the image of the invisible God, the firstborn over all creation. For by him all things were created; things in heaven and on earth, visible and invisible, whether thrones or powers or rulers or authorities; all things were created by him and for him. He is before all things, and in him all things hold together." Colossians 1:15-20

Epilogue – A Sermon

WHAT TO SAY WHEN TALKING TO YOURSELF

Text: *"Not by might nor by power, but by my Spirit' says the LORD Almighty."* Zechariah 4:6

Do you talk to yourself? I have noticed lately that I seem to be doing that more than usual. I guess it means that I am trying to make sense of something, trying to organize myself and gain control over some matter or other.

I am reminded of the two little boys discussing their fathers one day. One said, "My father talks to himself sometimes." The other little boy said, "'That's nothing. My father hit his thumb with a hammer and he talked to the hammer all afternoon!"

We are living in the age of **multitasking**, the old problem of trying to do many things at once, too many things on our minds, too many deadlines too soon. I believe this overloading of pressing matters makes it difficult to process them clearly, so we talk to ourselves, attempting to get our life back in order and under control.

Have you read the story of Elijah in the 19th chapter of I Kings in the Old Testament? He was stressed out. He had seen great success against the prophets of Baal in their big showdown on Mt. Carmel. God had sent fire down from the heavens to accept and burn the sacrifice, and even the altar itself, to prove that he was God. It was a great day of triumph and victory for the one true God and his people.

The aftermath of this victory, however, was brutal. Queen Jezebel immediately swore that she would have his head within 24 hours. This caught him off guard and all his courage vanished. He ran until he couldn't run anymore and crawled under a scrawny broom tree.

He was out there in the boundless creation of God, surrounded by the **scripture of nature** but his spirit was crushed. He just couldn't go on. He asked God to just let him die and take him home.

That didn't happen. God let him sleep and then sent an angel with bread and water for him. Then he met him in a lonely place and listened while Elijah poured out his heart. Then God spoke very softly to him.

We all face these times when it seems that "life is doing us instead of us doing life." Life has its highs and lows. The death of beloved friends, family or even favored projects may be co-incidental with high points of achievement.

Traveling through airports recently, I saw many people who appeared to be talking to themselves as they rushed for their connections. They have these little microphones dangling down their chins so they can do other things at the same time, eating a sandwich, for example. I wondered, with all this talking going on, who is listening?

I was amused to hear one man say that he spent eight hours conversing in business meetings, but he did spend twelve hours with his wife. "Of course," he said, "eight of those were time sleeping, but I was there!"

With whom do you spend all your time? Yourself, of course, regardless of your appointments with others. It's no wonder you should learn more about yourself and what you need.

We know how to talk to the spouse, to the boss, to the dentist, to the garage man, but do we know how to talk to ourselves in the highs and lows of life, the victories and the defeats? More importantly, do we know how to listen to God?

In her classic book <u>Search for Silence,</u> Elizabeth O'Conner writes, "The one journey that ultimately matters is the journey into the place of stillness deep within one's self. To reach that place is to be at home, but to fail to reach it is to be forever restless. For it is **there** that our life and spirit are united with the life and the spirit of God."

Big discouragements in life can leave us feeling quite alone and spiritually homeless.

So what about Elijah? He had everything to be thankful for after the Mt. Carmel victory. He was sturdy, desert born, daring and brave enough to stand against those heathens that ruled the nation, including the royal family that had promoted him. But here he is whining, whimpering, running, fleeing to the mountains and wanting to die. What is the matter with him?

Well, there was a powerful enemy who happened to be the Queen, threatening him. Jezebel had no use for preachers in general and Elijah in particular. Her heathen background in Phonecia was rooted in Baal worship. She ruled her palace in pagan grandeur and scorned the Hebrew people . . . She bossed around her Hebrew husband, Ahab, saying "You go" and he went, or "Come here" and he came.

You can't always tell about size. Sometimes a woman's thumb has a man under it. Jezebel's thumb had a King under it. She wore the pants and ran the kingdom, and so it is written that Ahab did more to provoke the wrath of God than all of his fathers in his choice of a Queen.

But then there was Elijah who was the only one in the kingdom she could not manipulate. He alone stood in her way of completely paganizing Israel. This was a tough situation, one against many. His faith in the One True God was more powerful than all the idols and priests of Baal, and so she decided he must die.

Elijah was a human being, so he was vulnerable to a paralyzing discouragement. We might say that half of the human heart is an "Elijah heart." Death tomorrow, ordered by a very powerful figure, is a sobering fact. As many have noted, "Nothing clears your head faster than the prospect of your own hanging."

It is the fact of our faith that God is greater than our fears. First he provided Elijah with rest and food. "Arise and eat," the angel said.

It helps us to remember that some discouragement is chemical and physical in nature. The mind and the body are so closely linked that the health or sickness of one affects the other. Elijah was emotionally exhausted and physically spent. His nerves were stretched tight and he was stressed to the point of strong reaction.

Even the great saints of God have had their bad days. When you read their letters, Bunyan, Wesley, Luther, John James and many others had days when they could hardly believe that God existed. One anecdote tells us that Luther's wife came to dinner all dressed in black. "Why are you dressed that way?" he asked. She replied, "The way you are behaving, I guess that God is dead."

We read further that, after eating, God took Elijah to the mouth of his hiding place, a cave of discouragement. In the awesome grandeur of those mountains God told this disheartened man to put his trust in silent forces. So Elijah sat there while the LORD passed by. First there was a mighty wind, but the LORD was not in the wind.

After that, an earthquake rumbled through the rocks, filling the mountains with strange and fearful sounds. But the LORD was not in the earthquake. Then there was fire that was crackling up through the undergrowth, blazing up the dry fir trees and filling the skies with smoke, but the LORD was not in the fire.

Then, after all these things, there was a still small voice. The Moffat translation calls it the "breath of life," just a whisper, a quiet sound of gentle silence.

These amazing events indicate the extreme power that is in all of God's creation. But when all of those things have passed and there is a stillness, we may hear the voice of God. When every little sound was audible and every gentle breeze was clearly heard, this prophet, who was brooding in his discouragement and fear, found a clear insight about what he should do. That is **sacred space.** The LORD sent his still, small voice, incredible in its power.

Then came the question from the LORD, ***"What are you doing here, Elijah?"***

I like to think that Elijah sat there and thought about that. Of course he did! We can be thinking about it too. Loud things try to capture our attention, loud headlines, loud music, and loud cars, loud, loud, and louder! It seems that the entertainment world is obsessed with explosions and violence, appealing to the 'unholy' fascinations of the modern age.

The hurricanes get the headlines, but gravity is a far more powerful force, even though it is invisible. Sunshine draws millions of gallons of water every second in total silence, but storms make the news. Spring arrives in a stealthy manner as creative, irresistible power pushes up the grass and flowers to new life.

How quietly God works in his world! He told Elijah to put his trust in those silent forces. Even those preachers who fight paganism with loud, warlike noise, can listen to the stillness. They can realize that even the loudest things on the surface are not the decisive things. God's way is ***"Not by might or by power, but by my Spirit."*** says the LORD. Zechariah 4:6

If we went to Ahab and Jezebel's palace today we would find there a threshing floor, because the foundation of that civilization is buried under centuries of debris. On that threshing floor we might see a farmer tossing his grain in the air so the silent wind could separate the good from the useless. ***"The ungodly are not so; but are like the chaff which the wind driveth away."*** Psalm 1:4

In times of discouragement, it is good to reflect on times of victory in the past. Those moments of greatness happened because we listened to God. In those times when we may think we are all alone in our faith, that the world is going to pieces and there are no other Christians, let us remember the still small voice of God; "you see, you are not alone." I have many people *"who have not bowed a knee to Baal and every mouth that has not kissed him."*

It does come as a surprise to realize how much goodness there is in the world that never makes noise or headlines. And it would probably surprise us to see how many allies we have, people in unsuspected places whose hearts beat with our hearts, whose hopes are one with our hopes.

Elijah is not the last person to come through that experience and discover that he was stronger than he thought. Most of us, who believe in the LORD, need to be with other believers to make us brave and strong. That is an excellent reason for being involved in good Christian fellowship. *"And let us consider one another to provoke unto love and good works: Not forsaking the assembling of ourselves together, as the manner of some is; but exhorting one another: and so much the more as ye see the day approaching."* Hebrews 10:24 – 25

It is better to listen to God than to mutter to ourselves. Get a good night's sleep and don't be upset by the noise around you. Put your trust in God's silent forces. Get up and tackle your work with fresh energy and renewed faith. Your faith makes you stronger than you think. Not all the good people in the world are dead! God's cause is stronger and greater in all the earth than we think.

There is **sacred space** waiting for you. We hear the whisper of these eight great words in scripture, *"Be still and know that I am God."* Psalm 46:10

And with Elijah, we hear the LORD's question, "**What are you doing here?**"

> *Prayer*
>
> *LORD God, lift up our hearts, strengthen us and help us to strengthen others by our faith in you rather than depressing them with our doubts. The world really is not 'too much with us' even though at times it seems to be shouting and is too much after us. Let your mind be in us like a seed in the soil, quietly*

growing up into full maturity. Subdue every noise in our world or in our hearts that prevents us from listening to the quiet word and way of Christ.

"Breathe through the heats of our desires thy coolness and thy balm. Let sense be dumb, let flesh retire, speak through the earthquake, wind and fire, O still small voice of calm."

And all God's people said, AMEN

345

The Works of the LORD
Are Created

The Works of the Lord Are Created 354

. . . who by his understanding made the heavens. Ps. 136:5

1. The works of the Lord are cre - a - ted in wis - dom!
2. Not e - ven the an - gels have ev - er been grant - ed
3. The sun ev - ery morn - ing lights up all cre - a - tion,
4. The wind is his breath and the clouds are his sig - nal,
5. The song is un - fin - ished; how shall we com - plete it,

We view the earth's won - ders and call him to mind;
to tell the full sto - ry of na - ture and grace;
the moon marks the rhy - thm of months in their turn;
the rain and the snow are the robes of his choice;
and where find the skill to per - fect all God's praise?

we hear what he says in the world we dis - cov - er,
but o - pen to God is all hu - man per - cep - tion,
the glit - ter - ing stars are ar - rayed in his hon - or,
the storm and the light - ning, his watch - men and her - alds,
At work in all plac - es, he cares for all peo - ples—

and God shows his glo - ry in all that we find.
the mys - ter - ies of time and the se - crets of space.
a - dorn - ing the years as they cease - less - ly burn.
the crash of the thun - der, the sound of his voice.
how great is the Lord to the end of all days!

The Works of the Lord

Dedication

Writing is a gift apparently known only to human beings. From the earliest primitive drawings to today's amazing electronic technology, it has been the human desire to somehow describe in words the deepest realities of our existence.

If the theory is right that 100,000 thoughts pass through our minds every day, (approximately equal to the number of heartbeats), how are we to clearly choose and express the best of them? We must try, even though our efforts will be partial.

My parents and four older brothers Alva, Garth, Maurice and Dick will always be the family cradle and first teachers of my whole life. Through them has come to me, the love of God and the eyes to see The WORD in the world.

Front row: Maurice Wayne, Dad-Stanley Newey holding Glen Wallace, Mother-Elmina Myrtilla, Richard Stanley. Back row: William Garth, Alva Camenga.

Christian faith was central and practical to our farm family. Our lives centered on farm work and attendance at our country church. Worship and youth groups were the strong spiritual core of our farming life. The country settings in the Bible made a lot of sense to us in our rural living with all its challenges and rewards. Our way of life left little time for leisurely recreation or school sports. I especially remember that the book of Psalms helps us worship God, and the book of Proverbs teaches us about living with people.

As I think about these other 6 people who comprised our family, I especially honor our parents who believed *"The fear of the Lord is the beginning of knowledge, but fools despise wisdom and discipline."* Proverbs 1:7 They took it seriously and lovingly and we were all taught not **to get the big head.**

As I continue to desire the kind of genuine faith and humility our folks had, I turn to the third chapter of Proverbs, verses 1-12, as a guiding scripture for this dedication. Each member of the family represents to me, in some ways, the wisdom of God's word.

DAD -*"My son, do not forget my teaching, but keep my commands in your heart, for they will prolong your life many years and bring you prosperity."*

MOTHER - *"Let love and faithfulness never leave you; bind them around your neck, write them on the tablet of your heart."*

ALVA -*"My son, do not despise the LORD's discipline and do not resent his rebuke, because the LORD disciplines those he loves, as a father the son he delights in."*

GARTH -*"Trust in the LORD with all your heart and lean not on your own understanding; in all your ways acknowledge him, and he will make your paths straight."*

MAURICE -*"Then you will win favor and a good name in the sight of God and man."*

DICK - *"Blessed is the man who finds wisdom, the man who gains understanding."*

Seeing these ideas as scaffolding around our daily lives has a profound effect on our relationships. George Eliot wrote it so well: "Oh, the comfort, the inexpressible comfort of feeling safe with a person, having neither to weigh thoughts nor measure words. But pouring them all out, just as they are, chaff and grain together, certain that a faithful hand will take and sift them, keep what is worth keeping. And with a breath of kindness blow the rest away."

Dad had that kind of understanding. It is not surprising that our first knowledge of God's love comes from observing our parents, for theirs are the first faces that we see over our cradles. In his way of living he was proof of *"My son, do not forget my teaching, but keep my commands in your heart, for they will prolong your life many years and bring you prosperity."*

One early impression I have of the Fatherhood of God was on a hot summer's afternoon. My mother sent me with a pint jar of cold well water, sealed with a lid and wax paper, to dad who was planting oats across the creek. He was driving the team while sitting on the wooden lids of the hoppers of the single disk grain drill which planted twelve rows at a time. He stopped the team while I climbed up next to him and watched as he drank the whole jar of water. For the first time I noticed how handsome he was, and how sweaty his gray work shirt was. The team shook their heads rattling their harnesses, mouthing their bits and stamping a big hoof now and then. "Thanks" he said with a smile. "I was pretty dry."

Then with a gentle word, we started up again, riding to the end of the row where he pulled back the lever with the spring handle to stop the flow of seed. Turning the team then, we began another pass over the field. The team patiently plodded along, their heads bobbing up and down, and I could hear the grain and fertilizer rattling down the metal flexible tubes into the waiting soil. The discs turned with a whisper covering the seed with a light cover of our farm's earth.

What a system! It was one of those moments when several related things come together for you, for the first time. Man, horses, seed drill, earth – everything working and all was right with the world. All working in partnership with God. I remember thinking **God is good and so is dad.**

Mother - Next I turn to Proverbs 3:3; *"Let love and faithfulness never leave you, bind them around your neck, write them on the tablet of your hearts."*

It should be easy to write about your mother but it is a real challenge for she still defies description.

She was born in 1902 in the quaint village of Brookfield, New York, which was nestled away in beautiful hill country of Madison County . . . She grew up loving those hills with their woods, flowers and lots of big rocks. She was a bright student, nurtured by her mother who was a practical nurse, and her father who was a dairy farmer. Their home had been known as Locust Lodge, which was a country retreat for Governor Dix before the Camenga family owned it.

Elmina (Miney) was valedictorian of her class at Brookfield High. Her valedictory speech was "Build for character – not for fame." She was excellent in music, writing and reading, interests that she maintained throughout her long life. A favorite book was <u>Girl of the Limberlost,</u> a novel about a young girl with high aspirations, funding her college education by finding various mountain floras which she sold to a research lab.

Miney earned her teaching certificate at Alfred University and began teaching in a one room school near Brookfield. She harnessed, hitched and drove her horse and buggy, or sleigh in the winter, to her tasks.

Growing up, she had four brothers, and after marriage to Stanley, five sons. Her mother was her best friend in this male dominated world. She appreciated beauty, fair discipline, hard work, music, friendships, learning, teaching and always learning more. She once told us about the day in her childhood that the luxury of a new piano arrived at their home and her overwhelming excitement about it. She had a strong determined side, often saying, "Let's make a plan," when facing a new day of challenges. She always wanted to get things done, and would say "Things will work out."

"Let love and faithfulness never leave you . . ." It is no wonder our father fell in love with her. The life they lived together of fifty years of marriage was a lot of hard farm work, but they believed in God and knew his help in their challenges.

So much could be said about her. One memory, when I was 9 or 10, is sharp and clear. It was a cold winter's day and I was sitting by the dining room floor register which was right over the big wood burning furnace in the dark cellar, down there by the cistern. I thought I could hear crackling flames and had heard the phrase about how hot H____ was. I began to think about something I had done that I knew was wrong. Finally, I confessed to her that I had been saying bad words that I learned from older boys at school. She put down her sewing and told me quite seriously, that Dad had the same problem when he was a boy, learning bad language from the crews who were digging the Barge canal with horses and slip scoops on the northern border of our farm. He had told his mother, just as I had told mine. Comforting me, she got out the big family Bible, opened it to Psalm 141:3 and taught me then and there (and I still remember it 65 years later), *"Set a watch LORD, before my mouth, keep the door of my lips."*

Yes, she is indescribable. *"A wife of noble character who can find? She is worth far more than rubies . . . Many women do noble things but you surpass them all."* Proverbs 31:10;29

Much can be said about my four older brothers and their positive influence on me over the years. They always were and always will be great resources as I still ask myself what each of them would do in certain challenges that come along in my life. **I thank my God upon every remembrance of them.**

Moving on to the boys, as mother called us, **Alva** recalls to my mind Proverbs 3:11; *"do not despise the LORD's discipline, because the LORD disciplines those he loves."*

When Alva was born, of course our parents didn't know there would be four more boys coming along over the next 18 years. His middle initial is C for Camenga, but I have often thought it stood for Challenge; others thought it stood for Charm. After high school he went out into the world and so I never knew him very well in those early years.

I did learn, however, that he was very ambitious and quite charming with a good sense of humor. He became the morning voice of the farm show at WFBL, 1390 AM on your dial, in Syracuse. We would listen to him, of course, starting at 5 am and I remember going to his studio once with him when I was quite young. It was a dark winter morning when we got up at 4. It was a very exciting, new experience for me to think of the thousands of people out there listening to his voice.

He was one of the first people I ever knew personally, who had high hopes and big plans. He was also a strict older brother, an influence I have never forgotten. Now as I reflect on Al's charisma and energy, I take seriously the phrase about not despising the LORD's discipline.

He had several personal disappointments, but his heart always was committed to his family and to his ideals. His charm and humor remained intact, despite the fact that his hopes for big success never came his way.

Now, six decades later, I remember my oldest brother with affection and humor. Success in life and good character traits are not automatic, but the WORD wants to teach us all about them, so that we may live and have the best lives possible.

> *"Do not despise the LORD's discipline and do not resent his rebuke, because the LORD disciplines those he loves."* Proverbs 3:11

Then there is **Garth** whose initial G calls to mind the word Guidance. What you see with him is what you get. Look up the word 'cool' in the dictionary and there would be his picture.

"Trust in the LORD with all your heart and lean not on your own understanding: in all your ways acknowledge him, and he will make your paths straight." Proverbs 3:5-6

I remember the very sad day at our house when Garth's 1-A draft notice arrived and he had to go into the Army. Fortunately I also remember the night we drove in the '39 Plymouth to the Rome train station to pick him up. I can still see him in his army green uniform and Eisenhower jacket, and I can feel the cool brass button he gave me that said U.S. We were so glad when he finally came home for good.

He was stationed in Biloxi and he wrote letters home. How old fashioned is that? One said, "Every night before sleep I go outside, look at the stars and have a talk with God and I know that everythng is going to be all right." He still has that faith and is committed to right choices and right pathways even when they are hard choices. He is a rock for me, and for many others

Garth advised me and many other young people on many occasions. He listens very well to concerns, prays simply, and gently suggests possible solutions. He has never let me down and is a treasure beyond counting. He was the one who made accepting the LORD a real life changing experience for me.

Yes, he is the coolest Christian I know. And he sometimes asks exactly the right question, **what would you do if you knew you couldn't fail?**

Next is **Maurice**, the solid middle guy, who reminds me of Proverbs 3: 4, *"Then you will win favor and a good name in the sight of God and man."*

There are scholarly works on **birth order** and its possible effect on each child in the family group. A recent study of family sizes considered the loss of the middle child, due to modern smaller families of 1 or 1.5 children.

Farm families in our era tended to be large. In our group of five children, Maurice might be thought of as the middle child. This one sees and usually considers the expectations of the older ones and the sometimes special treatment of the ones younger than he. This is thought to develop strong leadership and social skills because he thinks he has to do it largely by himself. There may be a heightened sense of responsibility and interest in group associations that are rich in new ideas. This is sometimes described as **deeply woven life fabric.**

Maurice was valedictorian of his high school class and was active in church and young people's groups. He married the love of his life at nineteen and they produced four children. His life was one of early, strong family commitment. All this impressed me profoundly as a young teenager, as I watched this new family develop and grow. It was the way things were and supposed to be.

I was learning a lot from him as he was willing to spend time talking as we worked around the farm. He was honest and always there with many duties teaching me farming skills and saw to it that I had appropriate work to do. We hit it off well and now I realize that he saved me from several mistakes.

To this day Maurice wears the coat of many colors, those of approachability, ease of communication, interest in others, and the ability to reflect good options in discussion about important decisions. He has helped me many times at crossroads in my life. I often hoped my life would turn out like his.

When I read *". . . then you will win favor and a good name in the sight of God and man,"* I think of the intuitive knowledge of my brother Maurice. He is still the Valedictorian in the school of life.

Finally there was the one I spent the most time with and knew the best, my brother **Dick**. He was always inventing things. I really have never known anyone more creative with mechanical projects. I also recall what mother often said about him, "That grin has gotten him out of a lot of trouble!" He was born with a great sense of humor and a cheerful outlook on life which was matched by excellent study skills.

He was a tough act to follow in school, as I sometimes heard, "why don't you get good grades like your brother?' He was just a few years ahead of me in school and I learned a lot from him about making high school work out right. He was a protector, always helpful to me, taking me along in activities and friendships. I was proud of him as Student Council President (Vote for Warner for More and Better), and wanted to follow in his footsteps. He was a good guy with many friends.

He was good in Math and has always had a strong sense of self, showing confident leadership in the organizations he joined. He was elected to Statewide Office in the Future Farmers of America – another achievement that mentored me into doing the same a few years later. He was my much needed bridge in those years. I have never forgotten his defense of me when I was bullied at school one day.

He was physically strong and husky; a condition maintained in part, I am sure, by his love of our mother's excellent cooking. Dick was smart, liked to work hard and figure things out, sometimes with that tuneless, breathy whistle. He grasped ideas quickly and sought to excel in every task undertaken.

We were the last two kids left at home, so I watched what he did and still marvel at his patience with my immaturity. I picked up many ideas from his life and I think my interest in fundraising really started when watching his creative business ideas.

He is a person of deep affections, responsibility and constant loyalties. He is incredibly proud of his children and grandchildren and protective to a fault of the family,

Perfect? Well none of us are. I want to be like Dick when it comes to accomplishing things through a strong faith in Christ. Did it come easily to him? Great things are not easy to achieve. He has had some hard challenges to deal with and with God's grace and love they heal over time.

Which wisdom Proverb fits him like a tailor made coat? *"Blessed is the man who finds wisdom, the man who gains understanding."*

To these 6 family members I sincerely dedicate this written effort about the pure joy of **Meeting the WORD in the World.**

Glen W. Warner
Ashtabula, Ohio.
Spring planting time - 2013

Afterword

SCIENCE, FAITH, NATURE AND PSALM 19

It has been said that the longest journey a person can take is only about twelve inches long, meaning the distance from our brains to our hearts. I would add that it is a two- way street, for sometimes we must travel from our hearts to our brains.

This is in reference to our thoughts and our emotions. Both of them must be included and interact in a full and satisfying existence. All of one or the other would be an incomplete life.

Picture a beautiful coastline between the physically stable (mostly) earth and the sea which is dynamically in motion and full of life. As we live and move, we are often at this border between the known stability and the unknown adventure yet to be.

What stirs your thoughts? What stirs your emotions? Where do the two meet? That is the search behind most of this book of meditations. The beauty and living power of nature, and how it came to be, are fascinating facts. Likewise, in our spiritual need for meaning, our Judeo-Christian scriptures reveal the truth of God, the Creator of all that exists.

As followers of Jesus Christ, we may look upon both thoughts and emotions with enriching results. When they intersect, it is **sacred space where order replaces the chaos of any conflict in our lives.** When that happens, we want to somehow capture the joy of it. This is when God is speaking to us, and we are listening.

I have wanted to be able to write such experiences in a unique way that others may enjoy and find helpful. It is very enjoyable as I walk along this shoreline, to search for the right words to express the ideas of science and religion. Just as many others look for beach glass or shells along that shore, I look for words and ideas. Psalm 19 is a perfect beach guide about the two- fold revelation of God – created nature, and his moral law. The two facts call for a third response from us – *"Let the words of my mouth and the meditations of my heart, be acceptable in thy sight, O LORD, my strength and my redeemer."*

To that, I add. "and may the words from my pen be acceptable too." There are those of us who continue to write the old fashioned way before computers arrived, even though schools are dropping the requirement to learn cursive writing. Spelling and vocabulary are becoming a lesser discipline, than the immediate technology of sending constant messages electronically.

A TV commentator recently noted that we are losing the simple pleasure of receiving a hand written note from a friend. "Have we forgotten," he asked," that we really do learn new things as we write by hand – as the words pour out of our pens ?" Another writer, Eleanor Erikson, wrote," I can go back and read my Twitter timeline, but I'm never going to be able to pick it up and hold it in my hands and see how my handwriting has changed over the years, or see the tear stains on the pages. You'll never get that from your computer." <u>American Profile.</u> <u>com</u> 1/2012

We are losing the distinctive style of penmanship that reveals the real personalities of our family and friends. It shows part of the personal truth about who they are in their core. How long has it been since you wrote, and sent, a significant note, or received one from a friend? I remember the fun of having a pen pal in Holland when I was in Junior High School. Does such an experience exist anymore?

Then consider the importance of scripture, hand-written with limited tools in many past centuries. We wish that more had been written and survived. It is a miracle that any have. Consider Paul's request to Timothy: *"When you come, bring . . . my scrolls and parchments."* II Timothy 4:17

The written word has always been essential to our faith. Paul, again to his young protégé Timothy ; *"All scripture is God breathed and is useful for teaching, rebuking, correcting and training in righteousness so that the man of God may be thoroughly equipped for every good work."* II Timothy 3:16-17

There are only four biographies of Jesus, one historical record of the early church known as Acts, and 22 letters written to churches and individuals about being new Christians in a pagan world. The last verse of John's gospel says, *"Jesus did many other things as well. If every one of them were written down, I suppose that even the whole world would not have room for the books that would be written."* John 21:25 How we wish there were more!

But that's all we have in writing and it is enough even though our curiosity is aroused by John 20:30; *"Jesus did many other miraculous signs in the presence of his disciples, which are not recorded in this book. But these are written that you may believe that Jesus is the Christ, the Son of God, and that by believing, you may have life in his name."*

There is also, however, the creative hand of God in nature. Creation doesn't need words because its actions speak louder than words. *"There is no speech or language where their voice is not heard. Their voice goes out into all the earth, their words to the ends of the world."* Psalm 19:3-4 The **scripture of nature** is silent. It is we who try to describe it.

Finding my own writing voice about the WORD through whom it is all being created, is challenging and learning from greatly talented writers is helpful. Quoting them can be overdone, but these words from Annie Dillard, author of <u>Pilgrim at Tinker Creek,</u> are just the way I feel today about writing this book about the **scripture of nature** and appreciating the life given to us by our Creator.

> "One of the few things I know about writing is this; spend it all, shoot it, play it, lose it all, right away, every time. Do not hoard what seems good for a later place in the book, or for another book; give it, give it all, give it now. The impulse to save something good for a better place later is the signal to spend it now. Something more will arise for later, something better. These things fill in from behind, from beneath, like well water. Similarly, the impulse to keep to yourself what you have learned is not only shameful, it is destructive. Anything you do not give fully and abundantly becomes lost to you. You open your safe and find ashes."
>
> <u>New York Times Book Review</u> (5/28/89)

That is how I have attempted to write as I enjoy nature while reading the Bible, and as I am <u>Meeting the WORD in the World.</u>

Bibliography with reference pages in this edition

A Century of Sanctuary by Lyman Hafen
Zion Natural History Association 2008

A Diary of Private Prayer by Dr. John Baillie
Copyright Charles Scribner's Sons 1949 (p.173)

Black Beauty by Anna Sewell
Saalfield Publishing Company 1905 (p.185)

Breakfast with Billy Graham edited by Bill Deckard
Servant Publications 1996 (p.179)

Elizabeth Elliot Publications by Elizabeth Elliot
www.elizabethelliot.org 2003 (p.128-130)

Giants in the Earth by Ole Edvart Rolvaag
Harper Perennial Modern classics 1999 (p.222)

Memoirs of Childhood and Youth by Albert Schweitzer
The Macmillan Company 1949 (p.19, 138)

My Utmost for His Highest by Oswald Chambers
Dodd, Mead and Company 1935 (p. 275)

Practical Lessons in Agriculture by Ivins and Merrill
American Book Company 1915 (p.186)

Prayers by Fr. Michel Quoist
Avon Books 1963 (p.124-125)

Search for Silence by Elizabeth O'Conner
Innisfree Pr.1986 (p.341)

The Communicator's Commentary by Dr. Lloyd J. Ogilvie
Word Books, Publisher 1983 (p.295)

The Diary of a Young Girl by Anne Frank
Contact Publishing 1947 (p.334-335)

The Heavens Proclaim His Glory Compiled by Lisa Stilwell
Thomas Nelson 2010 (p.21)

The Quest of the Historical Jesus by Albert Schweitzer
The Macmillan Company 1964 (p.84, 180)

The Daily Study Bible Series by Dr. William Barclay
Westminster John Knox Press 1975 (p.157, 166, 198, 316)

The Great Partnership by Chief Rabbi Jonathon Sacks
Hodder & Stoughton 2011 (p.4)

The INTERPRETER'S BIBLE in Twelve Volumes
Abingdon Press 1957 (p.109)

The Meaning of Persons by Dr. Paul Tournier
Harper and Row 1956 (p.235)

The National Parks: America's Best Idea by Ken Burns
Documentary film for PBS 2009 (p.15, 61, 62)

Then SINGS My Soul by Robert J. Morgan
Thomas Nelson Inc. 2003 (p.79)

True to the Sabbath-True to our God by Larry Graffius
American Sabbath Tract and Communication Council 1998 (p.292)

Views beyond the Beauty by Gary Ladd
Grand Canyon Association 2008 (p.9)

Abbreviations Of Reference Bibles

CEV	Contemporary English Version
KJV	King James Version of the Holy Bible
LB	Living Bible – Paraphrased
NEB	New English Bible
NIV	New International Version
NKJV	New King James Version
NLT	The Bible: New Living Translation
RSV	Revised Standard Version
TM	The Message: the Bible in Contemporary Language

It Is Written

In Zion National Park, you can walk for an hour over unmarked, slick rock to Petroglyph Canyon and study 150 examples of rock art, dating back thousands of years. It is not idle doodling, because carving in rock is not easy. Some of the pictures appear to have been etched into 'desert varnish', the dark red/black colored mineral deposits on the surface of rock. It is an early form of writing, telling stories, unclear in their meaning. Figures of humans and animals like big horn sheep express themes of great importance to those first inhabitants. Concentric circles are common, often connected somehow to other scenes. What were those artists saying, without words?

Our modern ability to handwrite words of significance is a great gift, one that some say is dying due to modern electronic technology, such as texting on cell phones. Cursive writing classes are being dropped from schools. Spelling and vocabulary are becoming less important, it seems, to the immediacy of sending constant messages. A TV commentator recently bemoaned the loss of the simple pleasure of hand writing a note or letter to someone. "Have we forgotten", he asked, "that you really do learn new things as you write – as the words pour out of your pen?"

There are those, of course, who continue to write every day, the 'old fashioned way'. Daily diaries, journals or personal letters still work for them.

And who can deny the pleasure they have when recognizing the handwriting of a friend or loved one? You just don't get that from a typewritten message. The distinctive style of penmanship reveals the 'real' personality, the truth about who they are in their core. It is so, well, personal.

The Holy Bible is known as the written word of God. Some call it "God's personal love letter to the human race" and it is a wise saying that "No one's education is really complete without reading and knowing the Holy Bible." The apostle Paul wrote most of what is known as the New Testament. Two letters were written to his young protégé Timothy with this instruction: *"But as for you, continue in what you have learned and have become convinced of, because you know those from whom you learned it, and how from infancy you have known the Holy Scriptures, which are able to make you wise for salvation through faith in Christ Jesus. All Scripture is God-breathed and is useful for teaching, rebuking, correcting and training in righteousness so that the man of God may be thoroughly equipped for every good work."* II Timothy 3:14-17

Timothy is also named as co-writer with Paul of 6 other letters.

As I consider the petroglyphs and the very partial knowledge they convey of another time and culture, I remember how partial our knowledge is from written records of Jesus Christ. Only 4 biographies, 1 historical record of the early church known as Acts; and only 13 letters written to persons and churches about being Christian in a pagan world. The last verse of John's gospel reads: *"Jesus did many other things as well. If every one of them were written down, I suppose that even the whole world would not have room for the books that would be written."* John 21:25

This is also expressed in John 20:30: "Jesus did many other miraculous signs in the presence of his disciples who are not recorded in this book. But these are written that you may believe that Jesus is the Christ, the Son of God, and that by believing you may have life in his name."

We might wish that more was written, but it seems that eyewitnesses selected from the many experiences they had seen and these are now known to us who believe. Our historical knowledge of the LORD is, at best, partial, but we have been given all we need to know.

Yes, we have enough. St. Paul, writing to the Church at Corinth may have been thinking about mirrors in those days. Usually they were polished metal resulting in a dim reflection, but in faith, we know the day is coming when we shall see the LORD as he is.

"Now we see but a poor reflection as in a mirror; then we shall see face to face. Now I know in part; then I shall know fully, even as I am fully known." I Corinthians 13:12

Study Guide

Glen Warner's books make an excellent discussion format for Sunday School classes or Bible Studies. I have had the privilege of facilitating a Sunday School class in which we used the separate chapters – one a Sunday over several months. We found this to be a wonderful method for enhancing our joy and understanding of Glen's work and for bringing us to focus on the glory and wonder of our Lord, Jesus Christ. The brevity of the lessons gave us time to prepare and time to have good conversation about each week's study. This practice was very comfortable, peaceful, and purposeful.

Here are some suggested discussion questions that might help as you use his works.

1. How did the suggested referenced scriptures help you in understanding the section?
2. Did those scriptures take you to a **memory** that brought about more memories? Please share if you can.
3. What are your **thoughts** as you think over each section? Did this week's study take you to a particular story in your life? Please tell us!
4. As you studied, what descriptive sentences really drew your mind and heart to think deeper about God ? Please read one of those sentences aloud.

5. What was your favorite thought concerning the lesson and how will this affect you this next week, month, year?

6. ENJOY! And PRAY!

Thank you Mr. Warner . . . and Blessings to all who will peruse his works.

Patricia Inman, Retired High School Guidance Counselor, Jefferson, Ohio

Endnote

Stay awake and hang in there!

"Now unto him that is able to keep you from falling,

and to present you faultless before the presence
of his glory with exceeding joy,

To the only wise God our Savior, be glory and majesty,
dominion and power, both now and ever. Amen."

Jude 1:24 -25 <u>KJV</u>

CPSIA information can be obtained at www.ICGtesting.com
Printed in the USA
BVOW03*0536250314

348628BV00001B/3/P